Almanach

ALMANACH

A NATURAL HISTORY OF TIME AND FICTION

Helen Solterer

STANFORD UNIVERSITY PRESS
Stanford, California

Stanford University Press
Stanford, California

Library of Congress Cataloging-in-Publication Data
Names: Solterer, Helen author
Title: Almanach : a natural history of time and fiction / Helen Solterer.
Description: Stanford, California : Stanford University Press, 2026. | Includes bibliographical references and index.
Identifiers: LCCN 2026024944 (print) | LCCN 2026024945 (ebook) | ISBN 9781503647565 cloth | ISBN 9781503648371 paperback | ISBN 9781503648388 epub
Subjects: LCSH: Fiction—Technique—History | French fiction—To 1500—History and criticism | Literature, Modern—Medieval influences | Comparative literature | LCGFT: Literary criticism
Classification: LCC PN3355 .S578 2026 (print) | LCC PN3355 (ebook)
LC record available at https://lccn.loc.gov/2026024944
LC ebook record available at https://lccn.loc.gov/2026024945

Cover design: Susan Zucker
Cover art: *Dialogue de creatures*, detail. Colard Mansion. c. 1482. Manuscript Painting. 12.4 × 8.8 in. (314 × 225 mm) Vienna, ÖNB, Cod. 2572, fol. 9. Photo © Österreichische Nationalbibliothek. *The Moon*, detail. Tarot Cards of Charles VI. c. 1460. Manuscript Painting. 7–7.2 × 3.5–3.7 in. (180/185 × 90/95 mm) Paris, BnF, rés. Kh-24-boîte Écu. Photo © Bibliothèque nationale de France.

The authorized representative in the EU for product safety and compliance is: Mare Nostrum Group B.V. | Doelen 72 | 4831 GR Breda | The Netherlands | Email address: gpsr@mare-nostrum.co.uk | KVK chamber of commerce number: 96249943

Printed and bound by CPI Group (UK) Ltd, Croydon, CR0 4YY

For Jonathan & Jim
and librarians/archivists who support all those thinking ahead

Want to live? . . .
Lots of reading—What kind?—Read for knowledge. . . .
Now act before things go from bad to worse
The Debate between Villon and His Heart

Veux tu vivre ? . . .
Lire sans fin.—Et quoy lire ?—En science, . . .
N'attens pas tant que tourne a desplaisance
Le Debat de Villon et Son Cuer
text and trans. Galway Kinnell

Table of Forms

Almanach

Prologue

Calendar

ARTS AND SCIENCES FOR LIVING WELL

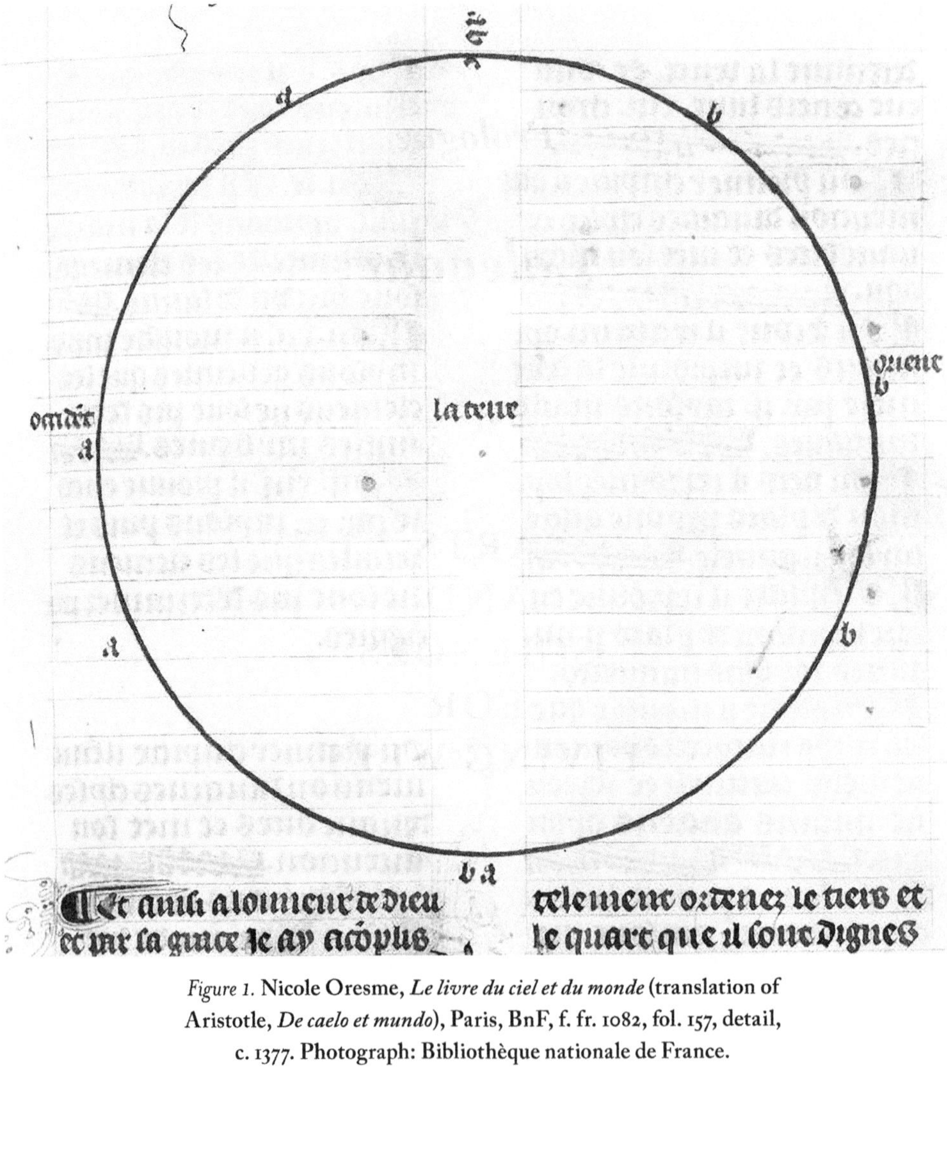

Figure 1. Nicole Oresme, *Le livre du ciel et du monde* (translation of Aristotle, *De caelo et mundo*), Paris, BnF, f. fr. 1082, fol. 157, detail, c. 1377. Photograph: Bibliothèque nationale de France.

Around 1370, in Rouen, the capital of Normandy, Nicole Oresme began imagining the Earth, round and spinning in a starry cosmos.[1] This inquisitive thinker was considering how to calculate time's passing around this sphere (Figure 1). He posed a problem that historians today call the traveler's dilemma: two people going in opposite directions toward the east and the west take an unequal number of days to circumnavigate the Earth.[2] When the pair, named "a" and "b," return to their point of departure, where a third person, "c," has remained, we start to perceive a time difference.[3] Oresme hit upon the need to account for the Earth's rotation, and our experience of it: how is it that "a," going west, passing through a town—say, Angers—is simultaneously in another time than "b" who is going eastward—say, toward Baghdad?[4]

Oresme pursues his thinking through what he calls "a marvelous consideration or circuit around the earth." He tells the story of Pierre (a), Jehan (b), and Robert (c) and their round-about travels, with Pierre returning to his base on Saturday, and Jehan on Monday. Oresme's experiment, which takes the form of a short travel tale in his *Treatise on the Sphere*, becomes a poem in his *Book of the Sky and the World*. Through two micro-fictions he articulates this scientific question of the time lag familiar to anyone traveling the world today.

Oresme conducted his thought experiment through an imaginative form, exploiting the two chief fictional modes of his culture. To probe an idea that astronomers had been wrestling with for some hundred years, he was not only inventing a story, drawing on the work of his contemporary, Muhammed ibn Muhammed Nasir al-Din al-Ṭūsī, who had charted the moon's movement at the Persian observatory in Maragha.[5] He also counted on images that artists create. The simple design of Pierre (a) and Jehan (b), located in eastern and western places, with Robert (c) in Rouen, enables us to see them moving around the sphere, and passing through what are distinct and simultaneous time zones.[6] A poetic tale with such a diagram constitutes his way of making sense of the effects of the rotating Earth on all who inhabit it.

Oresme's micro-fiction, pictured here, draws our attention, first, to the ways the verbal-visual arts of such fictions are dedicated to creating knowledge—what writers in this culture based in Latin called science. The idea-generating force of literary work, its so-called scientific significance, is a principle Michel Foucault brought back into debate a generation ago, with writers from around 1660 providing his chief example.[7] I look to writers from Oresme's era because they too were mobilizing all the resources and techniques of art to make "science." They do so in a primordial sense of knowledge, one that is practiced in a humane way for others and yields wisdom.

What deserves equal attention is a model that Oresme provides for conceiving of fiction in time. It recognizes how such work is subject to its ongoing passing. Fiction exists in several time periods simultaneously because it continues to move. The happy dilemma Oresme imagines for Pierre and Jehan is equally true for writing and images: any work of any person acquires multiple temporal circumstances. Individual fictions are composed through their many different eras, the particular knowledge they make, mutating in reaction to the circumstances their creators are experiencing. At any given moment, then, they encompass the full variety of inventive work—and ingenious ideas—of numerous writers and artists in all their different times. You have here the gist of the argument I'll put forth in this book.

Oresme's "marvelous consideration" appears again some hundred years later in the first almanach in French.[8] Let's call his "consideration" what the expression first signified: thinking with the stars. Accompanied by figures, just as Oresme's tale was from the start, it was incorporated into a compendium of "science salutaire": what people need to know to live well. The authors of the almanach (1493) composed a mixum gatherum of ideas, forms, and techniques. For a public that extended beyond the learned and literate, it was a rare and challenging one to get to know ("plusieurs choses exquises et difficiles a congnoistre").

The almanach is itself a potent, ubiquitous form, one that is taken for granted. I take it up because it confirms my argument about fiction in its many times—in several major ways. The almanach constructs, first, an effective time-planner. The inventive writers, artists, and printer who composed the 1493 almanach—including Oresme—created a form that imprints the way many of us organize our days. It lays out a calendar; this one is structured according to a religious order of time that will be secularized, too.[9] Like a Book of Hours, it accounts for the past by commemorating the events of Christian history, and the lives of saints. In this manner, its users, coming from a wide swath of people, ritualize their days.

The almanach is best known for the natural order of time that structures its calendar. It measures the rhythms of the seasons according to the sun and the moon more thoroughly than any liturgical calendar (Figure 2). Day by day, its

Figure 2. Le Kalendrier des bergiers. A shepherd, surrounded by his tools and sheep, keeps an eye on the sun, moon, and stars to ensure his work. Angers, Bibliothèque municipale, impr. Rés. SA 3390, fol. 57v, detail, c. 1493. Author photograph.

calendar outlines a plan for the present. Down to earth, it guides us through the cycles of germination, fruitfulness, harvest, and hibernation in specific climates, in this case in Anjou, a county in northwestern France. Almanachs in the line of this *Calendar of the Shepherds* are designed fundamentally around our relations with the Earth spinning in the cosmos that regulate our experience of time. They are grounded in the needs of people who work the land. They adapt the astronomical theorems of Oresme's tale for those who depend on sunlight and the moon's phases, and who live according to these temporal cycles.

By foregrounding this natural order of time, the almanach also envisages something of the future. It syncopates the religious and cultural memory in its calendar with predictions about a particular climate for several years to come. In this way, it incorporates the various, multiple times that condition human lives.

Writers in French took to the almanach's potent form.[10] For Jean Molinet, already around 1460, it is a fundamental, artful one that articulates knowledge about various times, including inventions for the future. His poems called *Pronostications* prove satisfying ways to imagine in stories and images what can happen next for a wider community. François Rabelais, another inveterate experimentalist, enjoyed inventing his own for the public around 1530.

Their fictions of the almanach confirm why I am making this one. It is writers and artists who respond to the demands of the world with their inventiveness. "When the hours will unwind," Molinet quips in verse, "writers will give them luster again" ("Quand les heures se desloiront / Les escripvains les reluiront").[11] Molinet's rhyming wordplay sets the time that makes and breaks links (*lier/loier*); writers will polish the hours to make them lustrous once more (*luire/reluire*). The days and years, too. The work of writers, then, anticipates the energy of their ideas dissipating; it responds to the inevitable fading out, compensating for this by reversing it in the future through their artistry. Take Molinet's couplet as a maxim for what this almanach demonstrates: the historical process of making fiction in time.

The interpretive challenge for us involves, then, discovering again how fictions from around 1400 become potent in various eras, some registering, and others not at all. It is, of course, only in retrospect that we can ascertain whether a fiction, its particular artfulness and ideas, will be taken up by other creators and their publics. When we consider a work in its first situation, we have to ask the question in the future conditional tense. Will it have catalyzed new thinking and fiction in only one era, or in subsequent eras, for further publics as well? This retrospective view is also accompanied by a prospective one. Not only is our conception of any imaginative creation from the past subject to change, our understanding of its place in the future is also adjusted. How we recognize its art and its knowledge or science in our own epoch will be reconfigured again. We have here the fundamental question: the timely or untimely character of fiction.

Prochrony: One Young Traveler Meets an Old Vagabond

It's a writer from an age and place closer to us, yet still far away, who shows us how a work can become timely. I turn to this episode of poetry from around 1460 engaging a writer centuries later because writers and artists tell us as much about this historical process as critics can. They do so with the insight of those who unleash again the creative force of long-ago fiction.

Around 1905 in Saint Petersburg, Russia, Blaise Cendrars, a globetrotter of sorts, encounters the poet François Villon, in a place outside their French-speaking countries.[12] He discovers Villon's ballads in an era far removed from the first circumstances of the poetry in Paris, its schools, courts, and a tavern or two. Thanks to a francophile Russian bookman, he meets a fellow writer whose personal poetry would come to shape his understanding of the world and pattern his own writing life. The discovery of poems such as "The Ballad of the Hanged Men" and "The Debate between Villon and His Heart," was so engaging that Cendrars made Villon's fiction in verse his companion from the time of this first trip to Russia; he took it with him as he traversed Siberia on his way to China, and as he voyaged on to America in 1912. There and then, in Shanghai and New York, as in Saint Petersburg, Cendrars discovered a middle ages that he would not have been able to understand without traveling the modern world. "For changing countries and cities, taking the railroad, the boat, the plane, surpassing longitudes, jumping latitudes, moving from place to place, this is not so much displacing oneself in space as it is going back in time and diving into . . . the life of yesterday . . . of [the] centuries we thought defunct, and which are reigning still, not only in one or another lost corner of the planet, but often, above all, in the most lofty accomplishments of the contemporary world."[13]

Cendrars's travelogue introduces Villon's fictions in several different time zones, as well as places. We find this personal poetry with him not only in Saint Petersburg in 1905, where people are struggling in the wake of the first, failed Russian revolution. It happens too in a burgeoning Chinese city whose energy Cendrars felt as distinct from that of his Swiss hometown. We travel with them all the way to the center of New York when the first skyscrapers were going up. Cendrars's Villon conjoins "the life of yesterday" and "the contemporary world." This poetry from around 1460 in the work of this Swiss poet concords *avant la lettre* with Zrinka Stahuljak's view of the "contemporary medieval."[14] It is neither fixed in a place that appears backward in time, as many might expect, nor in one still not yet modern. It inhabits what many creative people sense: a tantalizing coincidence of so-called medieval times with a freshly current one. Writers composing in English, John Mandeville or Margery Kempe, for example, capture this understanding, as Carolyn Dinshaw explores.[15] For Cendrars, Villon's poetry is equally present in his own imaginative writing, in what counts as a most up-to-date place on earth. His headlong prose propels Villon forward—toward a New York looking ahead.

Cendrars charts the ongoing existence of Villon's ballads. Russia 1905 to Paris 1460 to New York 1912: the poetry is never contained in any one place, or limited to its own "first" time. For writers and their publics, its movement is reversible and multidirectional. These ballads are true to their name for anyone with an ear like Cendrars's for the vibrant verse of Villon—an ear attuned to French. These imaginative *ballades*, with a fixed verse form, are mobile; they are also *balades*, "strolls," as French speakers would come to say.[16]

Villon emerges for Cendrars as a set of poems engaging him with down-and-out people in Russia on the brink of revolution; or with New Yorkers—their eye on the future just as powerfully as with Parisians caught in an interminable Hundred Years' War. The ballads accompany him yet again, following the bomb blasts of World War I that destroyed his writing hand, and almost killed him. When Cendrars takes them up in the aftershocks of 1914–18, he envisages a people's Villon, a pocket edition of the poetry that fits in a bag for anyone traveling. He continues to write with the ballads in his own fiction. His writing breaks them free of conventional chronological order; it directs them ahead, toward wider audiences in many different places, as he had experienced himself.

Cendrars coins a word to name this oscillating temporal movement of Villon's ballads. "Prochrony" relays this indefinite time-releasing quality of the poetry. "One young traveler of a poet," he says, "loving an old vagabond poet."[17] For many other writers sensitive to this quality of the fiction during other ages, the same holds true. All of them are primed to move the poetry in time through their own inventiveness. Any writer who recognizes a *prochronic* Villon or the work of any other writer or artist does something similar; they create the poetry *for* another public, *for* their times.

This notion of prochrony, devised by one poet engaging with another, gives a name to the first part of my argument: fictions, such as Villon's ballads, become timely when creators activate them for their own personal and social reasons, innovating them in any number of time zones and later eras—with unprecedented effects. Through such inventions, they happen again as part of a historical process that does not correspond to any chronological progression dictated by standardized timekeeping and laid out in calendars. This is the potential of any work to register in multiple times. Even if it is impossible to gauge at the outset whether a fiction will prove timely and engage further publics, or not, its promise is indefinite.

"Prochrony" resonates again when philosopher Jacques Rancière, decades later, conceives of events and notions as impossible to fix absolutely in one era alone.[18] His poetic notion of "anachrony" challenges anachronism, the charge that bedevils historians for entertaining any element that does not 'fit' in the period at stake. Rancière devises a model of events and notions moving back and forth in time. In so doing, he too breaks with any preordained logic and discourse on time that deem an event or notion inconceivable because out of order with its own age.

Anachrony, for him, "takes time at counter-current—*à rebours*." Rancière's metaphor captures how events and ideas can disrupt the usual sequential course of time. It goes against imposed temporal orders that have been fixed, historicized: units of centuries, ideological measures of a middle ages, a renaissance, or any of the post-eras proliferating around us. It exposes the fallacy of assigning anything only to its own time. Rancière accentuates instead the promise of any work to "make meaning circulate in a way that escapes any contemporaneity, any identity of time with 'itself.' "[19] Or, to use another of Rancière's telling metaphors, works and their ideas can make leaps. Their movement is reset in time—much like the leap year Oresme helped to devise that synchronizes standard calendars periodically to the Earth's movement around the sun. A body of work like Villon's poetry, then, is not coterminous with the so-called Middle Ages. Nor can it even be identified with or limited to those years reconceived ideologically as premodern. Such fiction can move out of its initial era, carried forward via the inventions of other writers and artists, as Cendrars discovered and made happen; it becomes present for numerous people in other epochs, too. This uneven, repeated temporal pattern that defines anachrony shows how works can intervene decisively in times beyond those in which creators first made them.

Rancière's anachrony, which has inspired a generation of critics, confronts the limits of chronological logic; it focuses attention on the repercussions for works deemed historical, as well as writing about them.[20] The revolutionary political thinking that anachrony elicits links liberating time from any fixed order to episodes of freer, more egalitarian social relations; the Paris Commune of 1870 offers one stellar case. For critics working with Euro-Mediterranean cultures around 1300, the concept multitasks; it is proving useful for thinking the material conditions as well as the temporal existence of works. This notion of anachrony intensifies the longstanding and vital debate over modernity's order vis-à-vis the Middle Ages, over the various intellectual and artistic genealogies that Bruce Holsinger and Roland Betancourt do much to elucidate.[21]

By bringing Cendrars's prochrony together with Rancière's anachrony, I concentrate on the poetic quality of the historical process involved. First and foremost are the works being made in time—in many eras. Cendrars's invented word exemplifies this process. The ingenious forms and ideas of Villon's poetry or of any other imaginative work are open-ended. We have here a sense of their indefinite time-release.

Imaginative works that become timely depend, as a result, on an unpredictable convergence of circumstances. No matter how enshrined by tradition or promoted by value systems, national, world, or universal, and no matter what political program claims to establish their significance, these works are contingent. Their ingenuity cannot engage creators and publics unless it helps them make sense of particular situations. This is especially striking when it comes to works of Oresme's era, as well as those of writers and other creators around 1200, since they are often deemed timeless by later generations, as if the increasing number of years that separate them from us lifts us out of time and sets these stories in amber. We have only to turn to Cendrars discovering Villon's ballads in Saint Petersburg to see how accidental the connection with an imaginative work can be. In making this almanach, I also find this to be true.

Because chance enters in, the presence of imaginative works is also intermittent. They take hold when and only if writers and artists activate them through their inimitable inventions to speak to their individual situations. For many years, in French-speaking countries, Villon's ballads were no longer engaging, nor did they spur others to create poetry on their own terms. When they entered another language, after long stretches of inactive existence, when poets Rossetti and Swinburne translated some of them into English, the poetry was resituated in another time.[22] In this way, it makes history—off and on—as Rancière points out.

It is the potential of imaginative works for future creators to exploit—as Cendrars's prochrony underscores—that proves distinctive. They carry a recipe for their own later transformations. Far from endowed with a predestined quality that invests them with a quasi-sacred, untouchable significance, they simply exist. They transmit a promise of as-yet-unforeseen creativity to other writers and artists. They will be made anew, in the *beau mot* of Ezra Pound that Nathalie Koble and Amandine Mussou launch again with their collective work on visual and musical poetry.[23]

For this reason, timely imaginative works amount to more than the afterlives of a work. This term, swirling around us these days, designates everything from the latest versions of an artwork to what a contemporary public makes of any object from the past. When art critic Aby Warburg first coined the term *Nachleben*, he often referred to it as "survival."[24] It was key to another model he was building, this one specifically for the visual arts, for manuscript painting, tapestries, sculpture, and their image languages transforming in time. His celebrated *Memory Atlas* (1924–29) assembles, for example, photographs of images from an astrological and astronomical treatise, the *Book of Wonders* [*Kitāb al-Bulhān*], with marvels of other Arabo-Muslim books of science and illuminations from the works of Castilian and Provençal writers who consider the Earth and other planets.[25] Warburg was juxtaposing these pictures of eye-popping ingenuity to trace how this art of astronomy survived. Or how the ancient idea of Fortune survived around 1400, with Christine de Pizan and her mythographic work, *Othea's Epistle*.

Warburg designed this brilliant model with a clear sense of the anachronous times of artworks, as Georges Didi-Huberman establishes and Elizabeth Sears is demonstrating.[26] Warburg uses it to track the aesthetic legacies of works, beginning often with works around 1400, called already in the last century "ancient." His term, "afterlives," still privileges what comes before and casts what follows thereafter as secondary.

By tracking an imaginative work becoming timely or not, I prioritize instead each version of a work in situ. The focus shifts to various creators transforming a work through its ongoing existence. I investigate the specific ways writers and artists take up a work from around 1400 in their verbal and visual forms, to make something unprecedented with their own purpose. No one form and no first circumstance of a work commands priority, because writers and artists exercise imagination to create new works from it for their age and place.

Such fictions are made ultimately through multiple renditions. The various actions of writers and artists making and using them accumulate in time; they become just as much a part of any one work's on-again-off-again presence as its initial creation. Timely fictions are composed of them all. This is the ultimate point in my argument. It bears emphasizing because it is also the most far-reaching. To take the full measure of any fiction in time requires accounting for its myriad components shaped by many, in multifarious circumstances. Whether creative people and their publics are aware of this poesis preceding their fiction or not, they participate in the historical process. Those who set works into prochronous movement are free agents. Their timely fictions are the subject of this book.

Fiction's Universe

What is the sense of fiction here? I take up what writers and artists in Oresme's society are testing out with this name: work that links art with science—or knowledge. Jacques Legrand, an encyclopedic thinker serving in the French court of Charles V, gives a working definition with a variety of elements.[27] Fiction, first, is founded in reason. Legrand comes to this understanding, tradition dictates, through Aristotle. So does Rancière in his own bracing argument for the revolutionary potential of fiction.[28] This is a mode of thinking, and one, according to Roman philosophers on rhetoric, that comes with rules for configuring its languages. In a micro-dialogue with his near contemporary, Boccaccio, he points to an ethical element. Fiction risks representing what is ugly or bad. Equally important for Legrand is considering its logic; in his debate on this aspect with al-Fārābi, the Muslim philosopher working in Baghdad around 900, he gives pride of place to his work, *The Division of Sciences*.[29] Even if he disputes poetry as a logical affair, he shares the view of its imaginative work as knowledge. Legrand was synthesizing the categories of all the philosophies he knew. This ancient idea is transformed culturally once more to convey to those operating in French a notion of poetry as the elementary knowledge or science of making fiction. It is tantamount to what we think about fellow humans and other creatures, functioning, as Foucault reminds us, as an influential mode and medium of knowledge for centuries.

Christine de Pizan, Legrand's contemporary and a prolific writer from the republic of Venice, specifies a second aspect of fiction: its narrative quality.[30] It tells of meaningful things. In her book on general knowledge, composed for Charles V, she aims to define how it creates good sense by what it recounts. As the range of her many works lays out, it narrates love and the conflicts at the center of households of women and men. It tells of warfare, and the urgent task of making peace. It takes storytelling to the heights of the cosmos—the stars. Christine de Pizan was especially familiar and curious about this science, through her father, an astronomer who came to work at the French court; it was fundamental to her imagination and fiction-making.

A writer working with fiction is primed, then, to take on any question. There is no single necessary subject; the sky poses no limit. Both Christine de Pizan and Legrand, like Oresme, understood fiction in this third and powerful sense, as the hyphen connecting a matter of knowledge with a creator's chosen artistic form and expression. Heirs to the wealth of ideas formulated by Muslim, Jewish, and Christian intellectuals working in various idioms, of ancient and newfangled thinking, they each committed to popularizing this idea of fiction. They translated it—in all senses. Starting with Charles's entourage, they opened up its social situations to make it accessible to more people from various walks of life.

The fictions they were constructing stand clear of any charge of falsehood or deceit. These writers did not focus on Aesop's talking animals.[31] Nor do they deal in fables suspected of fraud, characterized often by a wily fox. When they turn to Ovid, it's the shape-changing of characters that catches their interest, humans metamorphosing into plants or, as with Christine de Pizan's persona, a woman becoming, through fiction, a man.[32] They concentrate on what their distinctive artful forms can create, all to express experimental ideas in their most humane guise called, by some, wisdom. They offer fiction to various social groups as a set both of useful lessons and of attractive storylines that respond to people's desire to learn more about the world they share with others.

These writers, and others around 1400, cultivate making such fiction as a way of leading a fulfilling life. It generates a sense of fruition—no matter how sorrowful the subject. So does putting its forms to use in the give-and-take of daily life. Legrand and Christine de Pizan, as well as many anonymous creators, approach fiction as a meaningful and pleasurable activity that they undertake, in part, for their communities. The knowledge they seek and configure in their work is committed to a common public life.

This search also operates through writers creating fictional personae for themselves. Their names prove ingenious instruments of invention: "Christine" who climbs up to the heavens to talk with a Sibyl who imagines the future (while her mother gets supper for the children); "François Villon" who confronts a death sentence, hanging by a thread of a hangman's rope; and more recently, "Blaise Cendrars" whose pen name evokes lighting a candle that blazes briefly before turning to ash.

Georges Chastelain, a prodigious writer in the generation following Christine and Villon, gives us a model of a persona who embodies the ambitious scope of knowledge that fiction-making entails.[33] "I'm the smallest household, a whole one made of sky, air, sea and earth, plump as a drop of lead, and fragile as a glass." ["Je suis un tout de la moindre maisnie du ciel, de l'aer, de la mer, de la terre, Gros comme un plomb et fraile comme un verre."][34] Chastelain makes this fictional persona out of the chief natural elements, like an artist cum scientist working matter to fuse precious materials together. The result is a remarkable whole that consolidates the vastness of the universe into this one persona. This microcosm central to Renaissance ideology is less human-centric than its promoters claim. What appears the "smallest household" is a composite of all materials the universe lends to creative people. For the poet-historian working for the Burgundian court, this fiction is an attempt to condense all that is possible to know. It's a civic creation, too, animated with writers' desires to make their work useful for a community such as Valenciennes around 1460.

Arts and Sciences for Living Well

To recognize the full potency of fiction means investigating its forms together with various types of knowledge. At issue are the ways writers, painters, and other makers choose to articulate their ideas.

Chastelain gives us a sense of the scope of what he and other intellectuals and writers in his culture call science by creating a figure in a letter-dialogue with fellow writers and artists (Figure 3).[35] Dressed in sumptuous red and gold brocade, "Science" sits inside a study, contemplating books that contain the knowledge she embodies. On her desk, a finger reaches out to address her about the book before her. She holds another book close to her heart that bears the word "conclusion," her body language showing us the arc of composition and transmission from one book to the other that her ideas involve. Outside her window, the fields stretch out in a landscape shaped through her knowledge. Science will help cultivate the natural world as well as construct a human one, the city's spires visible on the horizon.

This portrait sets out the first quality of fiction at stake: the curtains are drawn back, and we're invited to behold its diverse, far-ranging materials of knowledge. It's no surprise that Chastelain's figure of Science speaks with a powerful voice that resonates with the fictional persona the writer creates for himself. "I ascend in the sky, go down into hell,' she tells us, "dive into the sea, and fly through the air."[36]

Chastelain and artists depict another figure who embodies a second quality of fiction crucial to my thinking. "Clear Invention" draws attention to the vision and the labor necessary to making any artful object. "I have a sharp eye and well-mustered strength," this figure tells us, "to put out things of great strength, hard to direct and difficult to work."[37] ["Pour mettre avant chose de grant emprise. Dure en conduire et difficile en euvre Jay de vif oeil ma vertu si esprise."] (Figure 4) This very different figure is a laborer. Clear Invention is using her tools to pry loose raw materials, to mine jewels, and to make the books laid out behind her. Outdoors, in a quarry of sorts, she too, like Science, creates things that are illuminating; the lanterns beside her signal an ingenious spirit that guides her physical exertion. This two-fisted worker in her orange tunic looks as indefatigable and single-minded as invention requires. Surrounded by her country landscape, this figure is linked to the land. Chastelain and the artists characterize the clear invention necessary to art as a commoner's work, one that also yields the line of flowering trees leading to the town, and a tree, in bloom, espaliered on the wall. They attribute such artistry to the status of persons associated with the almanach being made during the same period.

Figure 3. Georges Chastelain, Jean Robertet, and Jean de Montferrant, *Les Douze Dames de Rhétorique*, "Astitit regina a dextris in vestitu de aurato circumdata varietate." ["On the right side a queen in golden cloth stands by, surrounded by variety."] Cambridge, Cambridge University Library, ms. Nn. 3. 2, fol. 26v, detail, c. 1467–68. Reproduced by kind permission of the Syndics of Cambridge University Library.

Figure 4. Georges Chastelain, Jean Robertet, and Jean de Montferrant, *Les Douze Dames de Rhétorique*, "Qui petit accipit et qui querit invenit; petenti dabitur et pulsanty aperietur. ["Who asks, receives and who seeks, finds. In asking, it will be given; and in knocking, (the door) will be opened."] Cambridge, Cambridge University Library, ms. Nn. 3. 2, fol. 34v, detail. Reproduced by kind permission of the Syndics of Cambridge University Library.

Both these figures exemplify something of the arts and knowledge or science that fictions around 1400 substantiate. In their forms and materials, these works are poised—perennially—to be objects of experimentation. By conjoining this sense of fiction with their multiple times, I am giving my argument its full shape. Imaginative works with such potential for future creators can be transformed again and again. Investigating these two notions together will make clear this historical process that informs the works gathered here. We have only to look to a recent multilingual collective of writers to see this view of the indefinite promise of fictional works confirmed in time. OuLiPo, in French, *Ouvroir de Littérature Potentielle*, or "Worksite of Potential Literature," deems its avant-garde formal inventiveness already virtually present in the works of writers and artists around 1400 or earlier: several Oulipiens relish calling ballads or troubadour songs, with characteristic playfulness, plagiarism by anticipation.[38]

Fictions that become timely anticipate in such a way. Or they are the fruit of this process. Understood in this manner, they have a future. Their inventions are *adventures*, experiments that can project what is still to come [*advenire*]. This is as true for the ideas that fictions generate as for their forms. It is the ongoing promise of fictions that I examine here.

Such a potential hinges on their creators, in their particular social and cultural situations. Any fiction becomes timely when its ideas and construction speak to people and elicit their desire to know more, for themselves and their communities. This pragmatic understanding of fiction corresponds to the ways we encounter these works in time. Our experience with them is situated and finite. Yet some few of us can envisage further generations creating something new with them during later eras.

Table of Forms

This almanach is organized around several major forms of fiction that Euro-Mediterranean cultures made distinctive around 1400. They span a variety of cultures, in various languages, beginning in French. One of these forms is visual. It proves just as generative and mobile as the word-based forms, inscribed or printed. I devote an entry, or chapter, of the almanach to each artful form of fiction, and a significant idea it configures. I track how knowledge made in this way can metamorphose in the hands of other creators in several ages. It's a process involving a plethora of works. Some are well known; others are little known, including some that I came across in my research—like Cendrars—by chance. The almanach as a whole brings them all together to demonstrate the prochronous movement of fiction.

POLITICAL DREAM VISION

The almanach begins with a form, revered by societies in many parts of the world, that casts up ideals for community-building. The experimental work of a pair of writers represents it here. Honorat Bovet imagined a black Muslim emissary in the *Apparition of Jean de Meun*, and Christine de Pizan, in the *Book of Three Virtues*, pictured a woman laborer. Their fictions launched such figures and their political importance, which were more or less unrecognizable to their initial French-speaking audiences.[39]

Bovet's fictional emissary is the first to voice, in a French idiom, the idea of safe passage of so-called foreigners during wartime. It was an intrepid invention to advance at a time when news reached Paris of soldiers from the French and Burgundian kingdoms having been enslaved by the Turkish Ottomans. Christine de Pizan, an admirer of Bovet who was writing in the wake of his work, imagined an equally unfamiliar idea in her political vision. Through her fictional character, she foresaw women working in a society that valued their labor on equitable terms.

Were these fictions timely in these writers' day? In other eras? To find out, in one entry, I track Bovet's dream vision, and its components that the savant Jean Boivin took up in Paris around 1700, in the Quarrel of the Ancients and the Moderns. In the subsequent entry, I investigate Christine's vision that writer-activist Édith Thomas took up, then composing her own to advance the cause of women's political and economic parity during the 1940s.[40] Bovet's unfamiliar *Apparition*, together with Christine's now celebrated dream vision, provides a clear way to consider what makes for untimely fiction alongside the timely. My own discovery of Boivin's and Thomas's works is part of this consideration, too.

PERSONAL POETRY

Fiction in verse that creates a life-and-death story offers the next form. The ballads of François Villon, with their endearing, cantankerous first-person voice compose a person with a name, an address, and a pack of friends.[41] The set of poems zigzag across the messy, seductive past of this individual, to present a reckoning that takes us all the way to François's last breath, and beyond.

This fiction imagines the equalizing predicament of dying. It's an arresting idea that gains many advocates beyond the globe-trotter Cendrars. These are writers protesting the death penalty, such as Victor Hugo in 1820s Paris, or those who are themselves threatened with execution across many cultures: Langston Hughes wrote ballads against lynching in 1910–1930s New York, George Faludy against hanging in 1930s Budapest, and Édouard Glissant against all such dehumanizing murders in Louisiana and Martinique during those years.[42] Equality in dying—rather than in living—engages so many creative writers and artists that it makes Villon's poetry with his persona a perennial fiction that many recognize today. This outstanding case establishes a paradigm for timely fiction.

THEATER

This form of fiction is a collective one. Large numbers of participants mounted what was called the mystery play in towns during Christian holy seasons. This matrix of theatrical invention engaged them all in bodying forth scenarios from the Bible, mixed with others that are rarely associated now with the play. I concentrate on two, "The Trial in Paradise" and "The Blind and the Lame," in a set of seven different scripts that Eustache Marcadé, Arnoul Gréban, Jean Molinet, André de la Vigne, and unknown writers compose.[43] Their scenarios represent the moral and amoral force of theatrical fictions just as strongly as the Passion that is often deemed the only mystery play. Their dramatis personae, co-created by largely unidentifiable people working in local parishes and guilds, enacted the struggle people face in their daily lives.

The hundreds and thousands of such players and spectators who make these theatrical acts came to embody ideas of dependence. What the religious scenes test through figures of virtue, the amoral ones show through personae who are all too human. Actors who mounted the Trial of Justice and Mercy were also performing two invalids who face off against one another in their efforts to get by. Their struggle gets to the core of what it means to be dependent and to serve others—in all its conflicted meanings.

During the 1930s, '40s, and '50s, an era of war and violent social oppression, theater people responded to this dialectic of dependence, service, and servitude. Simone Jollivet, the first "Simone" in Jean-Paul Sartre's milieu, who initiated him into theater, and Simone de Beauvoir both created work that gave it new impetus in their country under Nazi occupation and Vichy's totalitarian rule; Samuel Beckett pursued it during the postwar years of reckoning with their murderous consequences.[44] In those same years, militant psychiatrist and writer Frantz Fanon began his anticolonial work by composing for the theater. His dramatis personae transformed an amoral one from the mystery play and articulated his pioneering thinking on the struggle to break out of servile behavior engrained by life under French rule.[45] In more recent times, too, actor-writer Dario Fo invented his own mystery play to engage workers in their revolt against disenfranchising conditions that he saw across Europe and the Americas.[46] More surprising is the work of playwright Bernard-Marie Koltès. The inimitable version of these amoral characters that he creates critiques French social life and the power plays it inculcates oppressing, in particular, gay people. To what degree all their theatrical fictions humanize the idea of our *inter*dependence and the interminable struggle against servile behavior—across several generations—is the subject of this entry.

GRAPHIC NARRATIVE IN IVORY

The final form in the almanach introduces another type of narrative, and another matter. Ivory was used by creative people over millennia in French-speaking realms of Norman Ireland, Scotland, and in Scandinavia, Siberia, and America. Merchants brought it to the European continent from cultures in Africa and Asia, too.[47] Around 1150, one of the first terms for ivory in French vernaculars identifies its animal source: *olifant* (elephant) from southern areas. It refers to particular objects from Islamic traditions of remarkable graphic intricacy.[48] The horn is one renowned example that appears in the epic fiction, *The Song of Roland*.[49] Ivory became a prized material that artists in ateliers across Europe used to create these horns, and many other objects: boxes, plaques, utensils, as well as figures of Christian devotion.[50]

This final entry on graphic narrative in ivory changes the context of both the forms and matter in the almanach. It extends beyond the Euro-Mediterranean area, its French-speaking domains, and its climes of *dar-es Islam*. I widen the cultural geography for this era to consider the work of peoples inhabiting what geographers designate the true north, what mapmakers in Oresme's milieu had called *Septentriones* and labeled *terra incognita*, unknown lands. My aim is to turn the perspective around, to turn the historical process I am examining inside out, to add to investigations about these northernmost cultures.

This entry studies graphic narrative of the Inuit.[51] Their creative work is contemporaneous with theatrical scenes and ballads in other entries, as well as with the more recognized Islamic ivory pieces in circulation. It places their ivory forms on a map as Inuit would draw it, one that transforms what is even conceived in the guise of world cultures around 1400. Their traditional knowledge, tested during many hundreds of seasons, across the territories they inhabit, Inuit Nunangat, provides the ground for this inquiry.[52] Their thinking informs how to consider their works.

The Inuit incised graphic stories on tusks of walrus, the animals of their northern circumpolar climate. These nomadic peoples were making their artifacts over terrain they traversed from the Bering Strait of the Chukchi and Iñupiaq to Kalaallit Nunaat/Greenland, across lands that stretched as far as they could tell. Oral traditions of many generations demonstrate that the Inuit were using these storytelling pieces for hundreds of years in the period of contact with

Norse or Irish seafarers.[53] The practice of incising such ivory artifacts belonged to them long before 1600, when the Inuit traded with French and English voyagers, before they entered into further commerce with other non-Inuit peoples, including the Danes, who made territorial claims on Inuit lands around 1720. Today, Inuit communities across Nunavut, the sovereign land north of Canada, their anthropologists and archaeologists, together with others, are at work with Inuit knowledge; their ongoing efforts are elucidating more and more about these artifacts.[54]

Inuit graphic narrative brings to the almanach ideas that cohere with their matter. Hewn from walrus ivory, these artifacts recount hunting the chief animals of their northern circumpolar region: whale, seal, walrus. Their form and function converge to show utmost respect for the animals that these peoples hunt because they ensure their survival in their climate. Indigenous knowledge of living together with their fellow animals that Inuit people incise is created out of their daily practices in synchrony with the longest seasons of light and darkness on Earth.

How would Inuit around 1200 have considered the graphic forms they developed for such an idea? How do their works in ivory change what is conceived as artful fiction by creators in other contemporaneous cultures? I study them, finally, to field these questions. The more artifacts are examined, the more precise the responses can become. All this in an era energized by Indigenous activists and scholars who are leading the way in research and creation, as well as in collective international projects. Inuit graphic narrative in ivory challenges us to account for a fuller range of knowledge and techniques of peoples during these eras when fiction-makers were active in Oresme's societies on another side of the Earth.

Almanach

At the head of each entry you will find a series of dates. The earliest almanachs around the Mediterranean all began with a calendar to give readers bearings in time and place.[55] The Arabic *al-manâkh* and what were called in Ottoman Turkish *takvîm* lay out the year in words and diagrams used to calculate the movement and relative positions of the Earth, the moon in its various phases, the sun, and their eclipses (Figure 5).[56]

In Latin-based cultures, the almanach took shape at the crossroads of Muslim, Jewish, and Christian learning. Complete with calendar and tables, it had appeared in Occitan- and French-speaking domains, already around 1300. Jacob ben Machir ibn Tibbon, the astronomer known as Don Profiat Tibbon

Figure 5. ***Takvîm*, in Ottoman Turkish, or "Almanach." A prized work of Muslim astronomical science in gold. Chester Beatty Library, manuscript T 402, fol. 7v, detail, c. 1430. Chester Beatty, Dublin, CC BY 4.0.**

in Montpellier, and a compiler north of the Loire, had named their calendars *almenack*.[57] For Oresme and later generations, as for their contemporaries, this *takvîm* maker's calculations setting time were integral to making the universe intelligible.[58]

When the almanach first went into print on the European continent, it took a sharp geopolitical turn.[59] The Turkish Calendar that came out of Gutenberg's workshop politicized the longstanding interface of Latin and Arabo-Persian astronomical knowledge. It warned German-speaking communities in the Burgundian realms about the Ottoman Turks, threatening their allies in Slavic kingdoms. Strasbourg printer Heinrich Eggestein typeset the 1454 calendar with a call to Christian monarchs to unite in the face of this formidable rival. This was the latest confrontation with Bāyazīd I, a little-known player who rode into the Balkans with his warriors and defeated a coalition of French, Burgundian, German, and Hungarian warriors in Nicopolis on the Danube in 1396.[60] This calendar was mobilized in this intensifying conflict, its form highlighting a new dividing line between Christians and Muslims, its matter informed by the changing power dynamics that no longer aligned with the east-west fault lines long established by Crusaders. The irony is strong. No matter the renewed political battle, it could not dismantle the wealth of knowledge that intellectuals working in Latin and vernaculars had gained from the milieu of the Ottoman sultan and their peers in Persia and Arabia.

The almanach I am making maintains the traditional opening of the calendar, the sought-after setting of time, according to place, that Muslim astronomical science had done much to develop. Most of the works gathered here were first invented in Christian realms confronted by Ottoman power. Yet I also innovate in several significant ways. To start with, this almanach is not imprinted with the ideological face-off of the earliest ones made in Strasbourg. What polarized the orient/occident coordinates found on Oresme's sphere in absolute adversarial terms does not condition the works considered here. On the contrary, my analysis underscores the interaction between Turkish, Persian, and Arabic writers and those working in French that proves fundamental to their inventions.

This almanach innovates the calendar in another major way. It transforms the conventional chronological sequence. Each entry, with its calendar of dates, represents the prochrony of the works involved; it specifies their multiple eras that entail an irregular and reversible pattern. The diagrams help us to conceive of these works as open-ended—hardly fixed in time—in a way that no progression of dates or lunar chart can represent.

The particular diagram also addresses the challenge that periodization poses. Since I approach works in their prochrony, another temporal structure is needed, one that no single period accommodates, especially one called, by tradition, the Middle Ages.[61] This sense of time provides for the movement or—to use a common metaphor—the leaps these works make, or those "odd wandering days" that English poet Edmund Spenser accounts for in his own *Shepheard's Calendar* some hundred years after those printed in French.[62] It is capacious enough to incorporate designs that other cultures use to order and measure time; Muslim and Inuit systems of times are also in play.

To end the almanach, I design a particular entry. This one is shaped by the earliest almanachs in French that continued to be innovated for communities in the Americas, in Québec, and in New Orleans into the 1800s.[63] This final entry has everything to do with accounting for time. It does so through an idea that surprises us. Compost refers to a particular formula for determining dates in a Christian calendar before it also comes to mean that fertile material cultivated by gardeners and valued by today's environmentalists.

I work with this notion to qualify the historical process of making fictions timely and untimely, as a natural one. Nature constitutes the largest scale of knowledge that people seek about "the disposition of their world."

As a whole, the almanach offers its calendar, its mixum gatherum of ideas for living well, and compost to publics that become larger and wider. The one handwritten and printed in 1493 pictures those laboring at ground level (Figure 6). Its compendium of knowledge is made for them, in their time and place. In addition to intellectuals, it is designed for those whose work on the land ensures the well-being of the entire social system. The almanach helped to launch a social model

Figure 6. ***Le Kalendrier des bergiers.*** **One shepherd shares his ideas with others on living according to nature's course. Angers, Bibliothèque municipale, impr. Rés. SA 3390, prologue, detail. Author photograph.**

that would take hundreds of years to take effect: a powerful one that the *People's Almanach* would reconfigure in year II of the French Revolutionary Calendar.[64] It was made for many more peoples who sought ideas for building their lives more freely, in a time considered a fresh start—something Benjamin Franklin grasped when he began composing his *Poor Richard's Almanack* anonymously for homesteaders in 1732.[65]

I tap into this social history of the form made by inventors working in French, and in many other languages, too, for readers in Isphahan and Ireland. It gathers ideas for those beyond a noble elite and bourgeois readership that, starting around 1490, are articulated through fiction.

⁂

One proviso for reading and consulting this almanach: the decades in which it was composed leave their stamp on the ensemble. I put it together when archivists and writers were digitizing their holdings. Year by year, the numbers of handwritten, handmade books available online grew exponentially, and with them, the screen time that appears the norm for reading now. Still I traveled to places, and sought out materials that opened my eyes to what is not yet a click away—the books of Christina of Sweden laid out by librarians in a Stockholm library, for example, or the dozens of Inuit ivory artifacts on exhibit in Nuuk, at the Greenland National Museum, or brought out of storage by anthropologists in a Washington museum, or the historical marker around the corner from my home in North Carolina that presents poet Pauli Murray. I draw on objects and hand-cut pages that groups of people work with in public settings—as well as on high-resolution digital files. This uneven digital condition is very much the sign of its times.

The almanach was completed in December 2025 / January 2026, at a time when the politicization of what critics do and how we think is intensifying. This criminatory atmosphere in the United States and Europe fed sectarian visions of a middle ages at complete odds with the sense of time in this almanach. It also sets my purpose into sharper relief: to recognize how fictions are composed through their various historical situations; to consider some that take root in one age, and others yet to make their mark; to think through their effects and imagine a future with them.

1400

1700

Entry 1

Free and Safe Passage

HONORAT BOVET AND UNTIMELY FICTION

Figure 7. Honorat Bovet, *L'Apparition de Jean de Meun*, Paris, BnF, f. fr. 810, fol. 6v, detail, c. 1400. Photograph: Bibliothèque nationale de France.

This first entry takes up a forgotten work, and a little-known writer who creates a fictional Muslim intellectual of color around 1400. Honorat Bovet imagines this figure in dialogue with a medical doctor wearing the cap of his profession, a Jewish merchant wearing the required identity badge, and a Catholic cleric, tonsured and hooded (Figure 7).[1] All four characters come together outside the walls of Paris to discuss political questions that mark them as suspect, and lead to banishing them from the French kingdom. Bovet sets them in a dream where master Jean de Meun, the most authoritative writer in French at the time, listens to their discussion. With one writer asking the other, Bovet's own persona, to transcribe what the four characters say, their controversial views are legitimated.

At the heart of this debate, the writer gives the Muslim character the dominant voice; the artist puts him at the center in a rich fur-lined robe. Bovet created his "Saracen" in a political vision composed shortly after the Muslim Ottomans first defeated Christian crusaders at Nicopolis, Bulgaria 1396.[2] His approach to the Ottomans differed starkly from that of the French and Burgundian courts, which were receiving reports of their nobles slain, and stripped to their chemises, humiliated before the sultan (Figure 8). In one of the earliest critiques of the Christian world, Bovet represents an authoritative Muslim advocating and modeling a more open, productive relation between the two vying powers.

This almanach begins with Bovet and *The Apparition of Jean de Meun* because it disappears for centuries: an untimely fiction. Its absence reveals much. What seems forgotten, fixed in its first era long ago, has presence, philosopher Judith Schlanger reminds us.[3] While writers become unrecognizable, their work remains protean and can become generative again. It can gain new publics at an unpredictable tempo. How and why fictions in French of this era have been coming and going in time to engage further readers is a detective story that this almanach composes. An untimely work such as the *Apparition* begins to tell it as well as any work dubbed a classic. Its particular prochrony has no time limit.

Bovet's Muslim character of color holding pride of place among this group catches our eye. Here is a figure who is both Ottoman Turk and black. In contrast

Figure 8. Jean Froissart, *Chroniques de France et d'Angleterre*. The aftermath of the Battle of Nicopolis. Paris, BnF, f. fr. 2646, fol. 255v, detail, c. 1400–1500. Photograph: Bibliothèque nationale de France.

to the artists working with Froissart's *Chronicles*, who do not depict the Ottoman sultan and warriors as people of color, Bovet amalgamates these racial and ethnic markers. Bovet's black "Saracen" is doubly daunting for his contemporaries. To gauge what he represents requires taking care not to project latter-day conceptions of race onto this figure, as Kristina Richardson underscores.[4] It hinges on distinguishing various attitudes toward people of color in cultures around the Mediterranean, and across the European continent around 1400.[5] This figure is addressed throughout the fiction with respect, recognized as a peer, his prestige acknowledged. Any judgment on the basis of race is conditioned by the rising Muslim Ottoman political force on the European continent. Bovet's invention signals an attentive Christian writer assessing a new and fearsome rival. His outlook is more pragmatic than falsely superior. His character, unusual for fiction in French during these decades, captures the political tensions redefining relations with Muslims after Europeans' first disastrous defeat by the Ottomans on their own ground. Yet this does not necessarily suggest absolute cultural antagonism between them; there was room for less bellicose and more engaging attitudes to develop, political scientist Thierry Hentsch has long argued in his view of a Western imaginary of the eastern Mediterranean.[6]

Bovet was drawing on some familiarity with the domain of Islam to move beyond a crusading mentality. This iconoclastic writer was imagining a strategic political rapport between the French kingdom and *dar-āl-Islām*.[7] His fiction goes so far as to dream a Muslim figure traveling across Christian territories, stopping outside Paris, like several other characters, scientific, Jewish, and Christian peers. *The Apparition* narrates the black Muslim's safe passage.[8]

This fundamental, ancient principle of freedom of movement lies at the heart of this dream vision. It's a powerful idea. This almanach entry pursues it to widen our sense of the knowledge—and wisdom—that fiction of this writer's era invents through its arts.

The dialogue that Bovet imagines between the medical doctor, the Jewish merchant, the Muslim sage and the Christian cleric stages this idea of free and safe passage. What appears first as a dialogue between religious figures resembling a long-attested genre of theological debate is adapted and developed for different political purposes. Bovet animates a debate where each character makes a case that finds no favor with the French court: issues of medical advice for the king in bad health, moneylending, a theological belief about Mary's virginity accused of heresy, as well as defeat at the hands of the Ottomans. Each of Bovet's figures needs safe passage because they're in a precarious position in the French kingdom, and none more than the Muslim sage.

This colloquium in Bovet's *Apparition* traces a political map for the French kingdom in which many players sought to move around. It orients its first public toward Muslim domains in the eastern Mediterranean that readers in French recognized through centuries-long crusading campaigns. Through the route Bovet narrates for the Muslim sage, it extends farther, from lesser known Ottoman territories in the eastern domain of Islam, via Paris, into the southern parts of *dar-āl-Islām*, also little understood at the French court. It draws an expanse visible in the atlas of Abraham Cresques, a Jewish Catalan cartographer, which Jaime I of Aragon had commissioned for Charles V of France a generation earlier, in 1375.[9] With the Mediterranean at its core, the *Apparition*, like the atlas's folios, represents arenas of military rivalry and commercial competition—places where free and safe passage was the challenge.

Bovet belonged to this Mediterranean arena. An Occitan, he grew up in the independent county of Provence. Montpellier, where he had been educated in law, was part of the kingdom of Aragon.[10] Avignon, where he then worked at the university and the papal court, introduced him to unfamiliar groups from eastern Mediterranean regions. Paris, where he entered service to the French king, initiated him into diplomacy. A mission on behalf of Charles VI to the crown of Aragon brought him into a circle and likely into contact with the al-Andalus caliphate next door. By the time Bovet was writing the *Apparition* for the French court, he was primed to assume the guise of another foreign traveler in his fiction, and to address the idea of free and safe passage.

In the writer's own day, this idea did not stimulate much debate in French circuits. It was visionary. Articulated by Bovet's fictional black Muslim sage, when war with the Ottomans was intensifying, it appeared dangerous. It ensured the untimely quality of Bovet's fiction. Yet out of sight, the work remains in the royal library of France. Out of readers' minds, it still epitomizes the question posed by every fiction: will it register for authors and their publics in later periods? This first almanach entry takes up this question because a work that appears lost is not gone for good.

Dreaming, Debating, Negotiating

The dream vision so distinctive of fiction during this epoch is one significant form that writers use to instill a full sense of time. Bovet was in the company of many writers in many cultures who set a standard for this art of dreaming with religious prophecies, political visions, erotic fantasies.[11] The writer takes this art in a new direction. Instead of a dream space nowhere in particular, Bovet anchors his dream in a real place, the capital of the French kingdom. He takes us to La Tournelle, Jean de Meun's address, found on city maps generations later.[12]

By imagining the poet of the *Romance of the Rose* appearing to him in this familiar place, Bovet authorizes his own work. Much as Dante does with Vergil in the *Divine Comedy*, he confirms his vision of the state of the world.[13] Such a configuration of Jean de Meun meeting the author's persona in Paris makes for an original reality effect. From the outset of the dream, Bovet's audience can recognize what is true without having to decode allegorical scenes and abstract personifications.

Bovet's transformation of the dreamer is equally significant. This is a figure who accompanies the powerful; he knows how to interpret what they dream and helps convert it into political action. The scene of Roman emperor Constantine's dream being transcribed on the eve of overcoming his rival in battle epitomizes this persona. Myriad microhistories during this period portray the figure. This dreamer is vigilant—as Jean-Bertrand Pontalis names the figure, and Piero della Francesca paints him a generation after Bovet.[14] In Piero's fresco, this figure sits below the emperor, fast asleep. His eyes are open, giving us a glimpse of this persona's keen awareness. Fixed on us, they relay something of Constantine's dream that otherwise is inaccessible. Bovet's persona, akin to Piero's dreamer, registers all that Jean de Meun exchanges with the other characters.

Bovet's dreamwork conjures possible political alliances during years when battle lines were stiffening once more in the eastern Mediterranean. Rather than call for another crusade as Philippe de Mézières does in his *Dream of the Old Pilgrim*, Bovet takes a nonviolent approach.[15] Instead of debating royal power as the *Dream in the Orchard*, attributed to Evrard de Trémaugon, does, Bovet addresses the French kingdom's disarray directly.[16] The *Apparition* departs from his contemporaries' visions most significantly in *whose* vantage point is adopted to foresee *what* political change. A black Muslim emissary, with three others banished from France, creates an unprecedented fictional lineup for a politics based on dialogue among foreign rivals that extends to the Muslim world.

Such a daring dream confirms what fiction can do. Bovet exploits its mix of time zones for broaching subjects that are hard to address. The *Apparition* encompasses a past long gone, of crusading ideals hardly viable, with a future hypothetical, of direct contact with a new, formidable adversary. His fictional vision incubates a political order as yet inconceivable for the French court he was addressing.

To nurture such fiction, Bovet activates the traditional debate between the Abrahamic religions.[17] He harnesses the argumentative energy of the form practiced by clerics of all three cults around the Mediterranean.[18] Did Bovet have any contact with Muslim clerics? Avignon, a multicultural hub and the seat of a schismatic pope, was certainly a place to encounter them; so was the kingdom of Aragon.[19] There is no evidence that this writer undertook what Majorcan Ramón Lull did, composing his *Book of the Gentile and the Three Wise Men* out of a personal experience of disputation in Tunis (c. 1275).[20] Bovet chooses to turn from the theological judgments of these debates; his figures no longer correct the "errors" of a religious rival. The debate is reconfigured in the *Apparition* for immediate and pressing aims of another order.

Bovet casts the schism splitting the Catholic Church—first and foremost—as a political struggle. It is one with far-reaching consequences. Bovet creates a face-off between the principal figures of Muslim emissary and Christian cleric to address Christendom's power in jeopardy. The so-called Saracen identifies the risks.

> When our people learn about this strife among you, they will no longer doubt or fear that they can terrify Christendom, because people divided in belief will never help themselves to fight the good fight, nor will they ever have victory unless they accept one law.
>
> [Quant nostre gent bien saura / Ce descord qui entre vous va, / Ilz n'auront doubte ne paour / De Crestienté mettre en cremour, / Car gent qui a descort en loy / Ne s'aydera par bon arroy, / Ne ja victoire n'aura gent / S'en une loy ne se maintient.][21]

Christian in-fighting poses a military threat that is more dangerous than any doctrinal conflict because it saps their strength in warfare.

The Dominican cleric is left the task of reckoning with the crisis:

> The time has come when they [the Roman popes] will no longer be believed, for the world clearly sees their folly and their extravagance, and since they have upended the law, many princes and clergy will return it to order so that everyone will have rights.
>
> [Le temps est venus / Qu'ilz ne en seront plus creuz, / Car ly mondes voit par exprez / Leurs oultrages et leurs excez, / Sy feront tant princes et clers / Que, puis qu'ilz ont fait droit envers, / Ilz retourneront l'envers droit, / Pour ce que chascun aye droit.][22]

This duo epitomizes the politicization of a debate with high stakes: a Christian charging his Church with tyranny, in league with a Muslim who indicts Christendom for its self-destructiveness and corruption.

This political reasoning is complemented and reinforced by issues taken up by the other debaters. Bovet's Jewish merchant speaks out about the familiar challenge of the Jews' banishment from the French kingdom. This character represents one of the "Pope's Jews," as they were called, protected as they were by the schismatic papacy.[23] What was a special status in Avignon was a more common practice across southern counties. Merchants, travelers, and opportunists attracted to the city worked across religious-ethnic groups.[24] Bovet knew the advantage of this practice. Introducing a Jewish figure brings to a head the opposing views on the civic status of Jews in Avignon vs. Paris. Through Jean de Meun, Bovet voices the French kingdom's fresh banishment of this community in 1394, the anti-Jewish anger expressed against anyone who ventured back without wearing the stigmatizing badge that the artists depict. Through the Jewish merchant who talks back, the writer promotes a different, inclusive outlook. He advocates for Jews returning to the French kingdom to invigorate the economy.

Bovet's physician speaks out in clear political terms about another school of nonreligious knowledge. With medical doctors under attack at the French court because they are not curing the mentally ill monarch, Charles VI, this character upholds natural science. Through him, the writer pioneers a diverse "scientific" debate. He reinforces it with Latin legal precedent: "God created medicine, and the wise man should not scorn it." ["altissimus de caelo creavit medicinam et vir sapiens non aborrebit illam."][25] The medical doctor with the Jewish merchant construct a united front of *personae non gratae* in Paris, side by side with the so-called Saracen. Together they draw attention to the political consequences of outlawing them and their ideas.

This pair paves the way for what the black Muslim character brings to the debate.

> I am an interpreter, the most free and clear among the great Saracens; for I know how to speak all languages; I am a nobleman, and I am a cleric well versed in our tradition; I understand something of all classes of people, and I also know how to compose in rhyme and verse, and to turn the law all around.
>
> [Car je suy plus franc trocimant / Qui soit en Sarrazime grant; / Car je scay parler tout langage; / Et sy suy homme de parage / Et suy bon clerc en nostre ploy;/ En tous estas m'enten un poy, / Et sy scay faire ryme et vers / Et le droit retourner enver.][26]

Bovet identifies a "*trocimant*," from the Arabic, *targuman*, to introduce an interpreter—in the largest sense.[27] Here is the type of character that Zrinka Stahuljak identifies across literary works in French, c. 1300–1500, whose range of expertise typifies a new group of go-between figures. This is the activist operating in Mediterranean societies that Nathalie Rothman brings to the fore. Bovet invents one of the first such fully fledged characters who moves between the emerging

Ottoman empire and various Christian kingdoms. Master of the various vernaculars of these rival cultures, he also commands a wide-ranging knowledge of their peoples. That Bovet portrays him as the most frank interpreter in all the Muslim world accentuates the truth claims of this character's report. Bovet creates a singular black Muslim character, the dragoman, whose learning and skills broker a new kind of contact between two cultures at war. This dragoman is sent to observe the state of the Christian world, in particular the French. From the new Ottoman stronghold, he travels through Rome, with a brief stop outside Paris, where the debate is held. He is on his way to Granada, with another stop in the kingdom of Aragon. He will continue on "to Belamary," the territories of the Marinids in Morocco-Algeria, "and to the other kings there, those down in southern lands."[28] His itinerary spans both Christendom and *dar-āl-Islām* in all directions, and it takes him through the major centers of each culture before he returns to Ottoman Turkish realms of Sultan Bāyazīd I. This full circle of an itinerary traces what is a *rihla* of sorts, the Arabo-Muslim genre of travel narrative, as Émilie Picherot makes clear.[29] Bovet appears to adapt this form associated with the western side of Islam, Morocco and the Iberian peninsula. Through his dragoman's travelogue, he projects a geopolitical map of Christian kingdoms, such as Hungary, France, and Aragon, in relation to Islam's domain. It traces the contours of the Catalan Atlas, in which the French court saw for the first time the rich and influential Mussi Mehla, named "king of the blacks of Guinea."

Bovet's traveling dragoman brings *dar-āl-Islām* in direct, personal contact with the French kingdom on the European continent. He shows qualities characterizing Muslim intellectuals as Ibn Khaldūn, the renowned scholar, describes around 1375: "the desire to acquire knowledge of the people, of those who don't have much experience."[30] In his *Muqaddimah*, or Introduction to History, travel in search of knowledge was essential. Bovet makes this practice a political affair between sultan and king.

Such a dragoman represented in French reveals the vital importance of free and safe passage. More than any other character outside the walls of Paris, this emissary depends on unimpeded movement to realize his mission. Observing the state of the French is impossible without this right of passage. More than most Muslims, whose travels respond to one of the prophet Mohammed's *hadith*, or "precepts," Bovet's figure goes farther. To serve as a go-between for the Ottomans, he must be able to traverse several kingdoms on the European continent.

In all his traits, Bovet's freelance dragoman personifies the writer's pioneering fictional experimentation. He breaks with existing Muslim stereotypes in French writing: the infidel warrior in epic literature, the merchant or pirate from comic tales such as *Aucassin et Nicolette*. Fleshed out more than the character in Paris's miracle plays who speaks "saracen and Turkish," he plays a larger role than Froissart's translator, the "drug[e]man," in contemporaneous chronicles of the Crusades.[31] Bovet creates a complex character who marks a critical step in imagining contact between the French court and Ottomans. In this, he is a kindred spirit to Boccaccio, who creates a comparable character in the *Decameron*: Saladin, a formidable warrior-sultan, travels across parts of Italy in disguise in order to learn more of Christians, and their abilities to wage further war against his peoples.[32]

Through this fictional character, Bovet creates an effective critic from outside the French court, whose movement enables an expansive and worldly perspective. It qualifies him to interpret the political debacle facing the Christian world in the most cogent detail. Bovet's ethnographer-interpreter becomes the mouthpiece for an in-depth analysis of the state of France following the victory of these Muslims.[33] In military terms, he points out their divided state, as well as their disregard for their soldiers enslaved by the Ottomans. In moral terms, he shows them to be feckless. Bovet's critique extends even to his intended audience at the French court, the party surrounding the king, Charles VI. When the failings of perjury, brigandage, and disrespect for marriage are tallied, the result is a critical ethnography of the people of France.

Bovet's judgment resonates with that of the Italian man of letters Coluccio Salutati.[34] His contemporary was also alert to the dangers; in his correspondence with others, he shares his criticism of the approach that the Burgundian, French, and Hungarian courts were taking with the Ottoman Turks. For a writer to create a fictional character who makes the judgment from an Ottoman point of view, compatible with Muslim tradition, marks a rare, inventive step.

Over and above the shock value of critique offered to the court of France, the dragoman figure serves a tactical purpose for Bovet. Under the guise of this foreign rival, he delivers his assessment to the powers that be with impunity. This black Muslim emissary cum ethnographer is his double. Long before Montesquieu and his *Persian Letters*, as Jean Batany points out, an intellectual deploys a fictional "Oriental" to develop a critical vantage point from without.[35] This character represents a foil and provides the writer with a measure of safety.

With this ingenious tactic, Bovet responds to the fundamental tension between truth and power that defines any dealings between writer and ruler. No figure in the *Apparition* broaches more uncomfortable home truths more clearly than the interpreter-ethnographer; his voice confirms the virtue that Jean de Meun espouses: "If I were as I once was, I'd certainly give my advice to this world full of iniquity . . . I'd speak the truth without lying, for this is a very perilous time."[36]

Bovet counseled the French court to engage with Muslim cultures precisely when the Ottomans were encroaching violently on them. His experience from Montpellier to Avignon and Aragon enabled him to do so. In his campaign to inform them of the scientific knowledge, the wealth, and the growing political force of the Ottomans, this Occitan writer dedicated his work to leaders in the king's circle, as well as to the duchess Valentina Visconti, who was a fellow southerner from Milan.

The two handbooks of the *Apparition* that he had made and lettered in gold substantiate his political project of changing the outlook on the Muslim world and entertaining relations with the powerful Ottoman newcomer.[37]

At the core of that project, Bovet was advocating for negotiating with adversaries. For the dragoman character to establish contact between the French court and the Ottomans on the march into Christian states in Greece and the Balkans requires being able to travel back and forth easily. Bovet's route for his Muslim Turkish emissary takes the character from outside Paris to "Spain to relay some secrets," and to Aragon where he finds "important Saracens."[38] In other words, Bovet charts a path of confidential communiqués between Christian kingdoms and several Muslim powers, with Aragon the flashpoint.[39]

The dragoman's passage through Aragon underscores the issue of freedom of movement of negotiators across the foreign lands of rivals and enemies. Can a Muslim move through Christian Spain without worry, on his way to Granada, the capital of al-Andalus? The question is crucial for every emissary whose task is to foster work with other political, religious, and commercial groups.

Bovet had taken up this question in an earlier work, *The Tree of Battles*, which defined political thinking on warfare for generations (Figure 9).[40] As he analyzes the conditions of "just war," safe passage represents a chief concern; so-called Saracens traveling through Christian lands prove the ultimate test. "In this case of appropriate equity, it is permissible, and in the rights of all Christians [to allow this] so long as he [a Saracen] does not come in such force with men of arms with whom he could harm Christians."[41] Bovet establishes a principle that gives due respect to these enemies as the peers of any monarch—French, Burgundian, or other. On this basis of equal dignity, he sets up conditions for viable contact and negotiations between Muslim and Christian.

The dream vision takes the next step: imagining what can happen when this idea articulated in his military treatise is put into practice. The *Apparition* rehearses the pros and cons through Jean de Meun and the "Saracen" sparring. While the Parisian questions his right to pass through France and accuses him of treacherously relaying information to other Muslims, the dragoman overcomes his initial fear, and answers back. In Aragon, he will travel "safe and sound."[42] In other words, safe passage for Muslims is already practiced elsewhere in Christian

Figure 9. Honorat Bovet, *L'Arbre des Batailles*. Artist Loyset Liédet paints every group in the social hierarchy at war with one another. Brussels, KBR 9079, fol. 10, detail, 1461–67. Photograph: KBR.

territories. Bovet employs the dragoman character to advance this principle and its political value. Freedom of movement ensures exchange with other people.

Aragon's Christian monarchs had learned how to benefit from what was a venerable tradition of safe passage in the Muslim world.[43] After centuries of hostile relations with their rival, free passage had become the Aragonese law of the land. Foreigners—especially adversaries—who were traveling through these societies also confirmed what had been the custom of Christians and Muslims on the Iberian peninsula for centuries.

For writers, this idea of safe-conduct was a particular stake. It distinguished an emerging type: the diplomat. Over many decades, from the 1330s to the 1420s, as commerce and warfare expanded the reach of the world known to those on the European continent, writers were sent out to negotiate at Christian courts.[44] Petrarch, Chaucer, and Alain Chartier are all activists on the move, as much as clerics and humanists holed up in the study. The Occitan Bovet joins them; he goes further, committed to political dealings (*negotium*) in a public sphere that extends on two fronts with the Muslim world, east and west.

The writer's diplomatic word becomes, then, a key medium of contact through negotiation. In the first treatise on diplomacy in the West, the *Brief Discourse on the Ambassador*, which circulated some thirty years after the *Apparition*, the qualities of fearlessness, honesty, and diversity define the ambassador and his language.[45] This type of interpreter, the treatise emphasizes, can assume the name ambassador. These traits clarify the dragoman character of Bovet. They also define his mode for composing this political dream vision. It was courageous to bring all four *personae non gratae* together: a physician under fire, a Jewish merchant banished from the kingdom, a Dominican cleric accused of heresy, and, in an outstanding stroke of innovation, a black Muslim Turkish emissary in transit. A fiction that confronts the many challenges facing the French kingdom through their quadrilogue shows Bovet's remarkable frankness, too. By inventing his traveling dragoman, Bovet ushers a Christian, French-speaking public into an imaginative give-and-take with its latest Muslim counterparts—an exchange that hinges on the idea of free and safe passage for them. The *formal* structure of Bovet's visionary fiction and its characters enable a rapprochement that any crusade makes impossible.

Plain Speaking, Political Truths

The *Apparition* is, finally, an occasion for Bovet to call for free and safe passage for everyone. To underscore the power of this idea, he introduces his own predicament as "someone outside my country because of the war Master Raymond

Roger has waged for so long in Provence."[46] Bovet denounces this invasion as the cause of his exile. The principle of safe passage is advanced twice over because it proves just as important for all those caught in war's maelstrom. This is the writer's final act of political truth-telling to the French court, and it reinforces his alignment with the fictional black Muslim dragoman he creates through experience.

Bovet turns to a second form of fiction to reinforce how crucial this principle is for so many. Breaking the dream frame, he introduces a short tale with the scent of southern and eastern climates. "The Date Palm and the Squash" tells of a mature tree that is overrun by a new plant, and risks being strangled. The palm objects to the invasion: "Would you not weigh me down, or throw me out of my place where I've been nourished and grown every season and possessed in peace for a very long time?" The squash retorts insolently: "By god, I'll send out so many gourds that I'll squash you under them and I won't hold back for anyone who speaks of it." ["Que vous ne veuilliez chargier ne getter de mon lieu la ou je me suy nourris, et en suiz en saisine et possession paisiblemen et de tres long temps . . . Par dieu je getterey tant de courjons que je vous creveray dessoubz, ne je ne m'en lairay pour homme qui en parle."][47] The piquant dialogue at the heart of this exemplum of a tale offers a moral. Those that grow too fast and too big are bound to decline just as quickly. Articulated in the date palm's voice, it takes the long view.

"The Date Palm and the Squash," which Bovet invents for the first time in a European vernacular, is an ancient fable. This Occitan writer was conversant with versions from the eastern Mediterranean that his fellow cleric from Sicily, Bongiovanni of Messina, had transposed in Latin.[48] These vegetal characters, part of Aesop's tales, had long been figured by Byzantine and Persian tales; Ismaili poet Naṣir-i-Khusrau had imagined their debate around 1040.[49] Bovet's story in French marshals the riches of myriad southern cultures, including proverbial wisdom from Languedoc and Lombardy, that would become a favorite detailing knowledge of the natural world.[50]

Bovet transforms "The Date Palm and the Squash" into a political fable for his own day. His two figures each carry rich associations. The palm tree exemplifies power and pedigree.[51] When the Norman Roger II was crowned Holy Roman Emperor, c. 1133–34, the sumptuous mantle he wore featured a date palm embroidered in silk and studded with pearls. It signaled the Muslim and Christian cultures synthesizing under his rule, from Normandy to Sicily. This noble palm was figured in many media around the Mediterranean, on Norman coins, in Ottoman miniatures, and in frescoes in Bovet's Avignon.[52]

The squash, by contrast, was a common, or garden, plant. Its invasive force was described in the earliest known manuals of Islamic natural science. In a notebook of health, the *Tacuinum Sanitatis*, which adapted this knowledge in Latin for publics in Italian city-states, the squash also carried medicinal value (Figure 10). Various cucurbits were easy to cultivate; they proliferated.

Bovet adopts these familiar plants to develop one of the most influential botanical metaphors for the struggle over political dominion. In the life-cycle of political power, the natural forces are represented competing, and their limits exposed. Bovet uses the exemplum to condemn Raymond Roger's conquest of Provence that forced him to flee.

Figure 10. ***Historia plantarum*, first compiled by Ibn Butlân, known as *Tacuinum sanitatis*, Harvesting Cucurbits. Washington, DC, Library of Congress, fol. 86, detail, c. 1400. World Digital Library.**

Bovet delivers a political lesson that extends far beyond this one tyrant's and writer's personal case. In a style particular to scholastic writers, Erich Auerbach makes clear, this plain speaking was well practiced.[53] It enables the writer to take on what is risky, and too audacious for the debate between the black Muslim emissary and the other figures.[54] Outside the dream frame, the fable establishes his license to speak simple truths that concern him directly.

It is the composite of dream vision and fable that explains how untimely Bovet's fiction was: it makes a case for changing course with Muslim potentates, for engaging the Ottomans in the Mediterranean east, as well as on the African coast. His pitch to the French court surpasses what most of his generation could even entertain. The dreamwork of his writing depends on people moving more freely. Both the dialogue of the four outsiders and the fable are the fruit of that movement. When Bovet confronted the French court's first clash with the Ottomans, he responded by opening up imaginatively to that world: reckoning with their political force and experimenting with the cultural riches of Muslim domains. His fiction shows the way.

While Bovet's *Apparition* was forgotten, its central idea came to the fore. Within several generations of the writer's political dream vision, when the Ottomans took Christian Constantinople, contact was established between the sultan, Bāyazīd II, and the French king, Charles VIII. "The greatest Emperor in Asia addresses the most serene and excellent lord . . . our most cherished brother, sending him greetings and brotherly friendship . . . from Constantinople."[55] The sultan's letter, translated into Latin and Italian, with Bāyazīd's initials in gold, makes a stunning appearance in 1488, in a book relating histories of warfare. It was transmitted by Anthony Rericho—a dragoman. What Bovet had imagined was realized, its fiction put into action—in a kind of fundamental political operation that Patrick Boucheron describes well.[56] His fictional character of an erudite, eloquent, and esteemed dragoman personifies the idea of free and safe passage across warring cultures that Bellini portrays in his well-known drawing of a Turkish emissary some ninety years later.[57]

A Fiction Gone Missing and . . . ?

What happened to Bovet's *Apparition*? The two manuscripts he had made remained at the Royal Library in Paris, largely untouched—even by the elite men and women at court who had access to them.[58] They are still there—converted now into thousands of pixels, available and free to digital natives.

Of all the composite parts of the *Apparition*, it's the vegetal fable that attracts attention. Writers engaged with it around 1710, when relations with the Ottomans were well established, and no longer threatened the French kingdom. "The Date Palm and the Squash" emerged again in a circle of Arabists and fellow scholars who translated Avicenna and other early Muslim philosopher-scientists into French.[59] It became an alluring *objet trouvé* of sorts for Jean Boivin de Villeneuve, keeper of the Royal Library.[60] Boivin, who could well have discovered Bovet's *Apparition* manuscripts, makes something of this fiction present.

Boivin enlisted the fable in the so-called Quarrel of the Ancients and the Moderns, a heated discussion revolving around the literary, cultural, and political significance of fiction in this society of Louis XIV.[61] Do writers benefit from reinventing the works of the ancient world? Or does becoming modern require considering their own work unprecedented, invented in their own times? Boivin answers by way of "The Date Palm and the Squash" of 1715 to create an ancient fiction in French of sorts. Placed side by side with the *Iliad*, its "simple, naïve style" ranks as a peer of Homer's epic Greek.

Boivin does not name Bovet. Nor does he touch on the rich ensemble of literary cultures that Bovet was composing around 1400. Yet his circle of scholar-translators committed to bringing works in Arabic, Turkish, and Farsi to French readers in Boivin's milieu could understand Bovet's fable. His dragoman character was recognizable, too; such intermediaries were still coming to Louis XIV's court continuing to pursue relations with the Ottomans.

With that whiff of southern and eastern cultures, the fable that Bovet first recounts in French is enlisted to represent ancient French letters. Boivin makes a French literary tradition that is a cultural composite without identifying it as such—an iconoclastic fiction that looks more and more ironic.

It was philosopher-writer Montesquieu who understood the political significance of the writing.[62] His critique of French absolutism exploits the type of vegetal metaphor in the fable of "The Date Palm and the Squash" that, by Montesquieu's era, had become an emblem for political power: "You can compare empires to a tree whose branches extend out too far and suck the sap out of the trunk, serving only to make shade."[63]

Whether the philosopher was familiar with Bovet's *Apparition* is hard to know at present. The pair of Muslim characters that Montesquieu creates in his *Persian Letters* (1721) to critique French imperial and theocratic absolutism makes this a tantalizing question. One common trait that links Montesquieu and Bovet is clear. For all the differences in their milieux and rapports with eastern potentates, they share an understanding of fiction's potential. Its forms enable writers to represent political ideas that are untimely.

⁎

To introduce Bovet's dream vision now, around 2025, demonstrates how crucial it is to investigate what has been forgotten. The *Apparition* tested what was conceivable during the writer's time. The challenge of entertaining dialogue with those stigmatized, and deemed outsiders was fearsome; so was the idea of their free and safe passage that brought them into full view. The choice to voice the reasons for political weakness through a black Muslim Turkish dragoman was particularly daunting. This combined inventiveness of Bovet, finally, proved too much for his first audience. While monarchs attempted relations with the Ottomans, this fiction would only become legible in fits and starts over centuries.

To gauge what Boivin and Montesquieu could have recognized of Bovet's visionary art and political knowledge is key. It's a first step in this almanach for taking the measure of fiction from around 1400 over various different eras.

1940 1405 1787 1948

Entry 2

Equitable Labor: The Political Dream Vision

CHRISTINE DE PIZAN
AND
ÉDITH THOMAS

Around 1940, as the French Republic capitulated to Nazi forces, the writer and leftist political activist Édith Thomas discovered the fiction of Christine de Pizan.[1] With Paris occupied, and a homegrown totalitarian regime taking charge, Thomas was repulsed by the ideology the Vichy regime began propounding—one they claimed was rooted in a medieval heritage. Trained as an archivist-historian, she could not accept this tendentious version of history, and was compelled to bring out other voices of earlier eras, strong and uncompromised ones that were neither royalist nor intolerant. Thomas went back to work in the National Archives, a place that offered her a haven.[2] It was there and then, during years of escalating violence, that she began thinking with Christine, a fellow writer who had composed dream visions in Paris around 1405. Imagine, if you will, Thomas holed up in these rooms at the Archives lined with books, drafting an essay about this other writer grappling with the intensifying inequities in her society. Her work appeared in August 1943, far from the fray in Paris, in one of the first collections of Resistance literature.[3]

Thomas's "Christine de Pisan," in the ranks with Albert Camus's characters fleeing the plague, enables one of those unpredictable leaps of fiction from around 1400 into another period. Christine's writing takes hold in a new social circumstance distinct from the court of Paris where she composed it, gaining readers such as Thomas with no special taste for this literature.

This almanach entry pursues how it was that political dream visions of this writer—in contrast to Honorat Bovet and his *Apparition*—did not disappear. I'll track these fictions that registered in the writer's own time, works that spoke to Thomas, among others, during later periods of conflict and incisive thinking.

Christine de Pizan was a prolific inventor and voracious reader in the generation following Bovet. Beginning around 1405, she accelerated her pace, writing for people across the French kingdom who were not represented in the body politic, and were increasingly threatened by civic conflict.[4]

Christine was mindful of the model Bovet had set. Much as he had created a dream encounter with poet Jean de Meun to legitimize his vision of a black Muslim emissary advocating for the principle of safe passage, Christine would imagine herself dreaming about Bovet.[5] A "wise and authoritative judge" appears, and greets his "dear friend." Christine invents their meeting in a liminal scene of the military treatise that she begins to compose in a clutch situation of civil war.

Artists working with this *Book of Arms and Chivalry* long after she made it place the dream dialogue in her bedroom (Figure 11). This painting spatializes the close affinities between these two writers. The room filled with books also opens out to the city and the starry sky to situate their common cause in the wider world.[6]

This painted scene brings into view the cumulative, collective power of the political dream vision. These two foreigners at the French court—from Venice and Avignon—exploited it with daring and ingenuity. Bovet's experiment with this visionary form emboldened Christine; she developed over decades her dream visions that would register with publics in her lifetime.

This almanach entry concentrates on *The Book of the City of Ladies* and *The Book of Three Virtues*, two large-scale visions that Christine elaborated, one in relation to the other.[7] These works combine her love of making fiction with her deepening political commitments. She directed every stage of their creation: composing, revising, and overseeing the books being made from 1405 to 1414.[8] The *City* calls up dozens of women from history, from ancient Rome as well as from the more recent French kingdom. Christine links them with many others from the Bible and from Greek and Latin fables. Drawing on the Florentine poet Boccaccio, Christine responds to his stories of exemplary women.[9] She transforms them with her pressing political purpose: addressing the unequal representation of women in both the world of letters she inhabits and the political sphere of the French kingdom she aims to enter decisively. To widen the range of the underrepresented, Christine creates an assembly of skillful and politically active women. She builds from within the polity, not from without, as Bovet had imagined. Furthermore, the second book in the pair that I consider here speaks to the circumstances of women across social classes. Christine's *Book of Three Virtues* offers a guide for women: how to work effectively, in public urban space, in interior chambers, and in the fields. By focusing on what current-day women do, and how their actions contribute to the common good, Christine confirms the political engagement of her writing. In the pair of dream visions, Christine doubles this power, and invests them with her experience, which she engenders though her fictional persona who states, "I who am a woman."[10]

In this entry, I pursue another of Christine's figures who is equally significant: the worker. She begins her *Book of Three Virtues* in this way: "I, as a person worked over by the great labor that I've accomplished, my limbs and my body

Figure 11. Christine de Pizan, *Livre de faits d'armes et de chevalerie*, Brussels, KBR, ms. 9009–11, fol. 181v, detail, c. 1465. Photograph: KBR.

overextended because of long, continuous exercise."[11] Here is a human subject constituted through her labor. Christine emphasizes the physical exertion involved. The laboring of this subject is extreme, bringing her to the breaking point familiar to workers today. Artists focus on the state of Christine's persona (Figure 12). The painting represents her stretched out in her bedroom; this time she depends on three royal figures who take her by her little-used left hand to help her up once more. This artwork sets into relief an ethical quandary for this politically minded writer. Will she figure a worker who is judged for laziness, or rewarded with leisure? Since her worker is chastised for abandoning "the labor of her right hand," the writer makes clear the values at stake. Christine's persona is a manual laborer who ultimately can claim no rest. Pulled from bed—in the miniature—she has to get back to her writing. Pen in hand, she takes up work again on behalf of women citizens whom we see gathered in a circle, "le college feminin," seeking support and practical training.

The opening of Christine's second dream vision personifies a fundamental debate about the worker's condition and the value of her labor. We have here, in

Figure 12. Christine de Pizan, *Livre des trois vertus*, Boston Public Library, medieval ms. 101, fol. 3, detail, c. 1405. Photograph: Boston Public Library.

miniature, several converging theories of the day. On the one hand, she invokes the longstanding scholastic order of social estates, a familiar hierarchy that privileges clerics and a life of the mind, whose occupations do not involve manual work.[12] Implicit is the comparison with the laborers whose existence is predicated on physical work and who are ordained to serve. She updates that order by "humanizing" the scholarly figure who can take breaks from intellectual pursuits with intervals of inactivity. Christine hints at the tantalizing formula promoted by the so-called humanists of her day: *otium*, that is, leisure, balanced with *negotium*, an occupation providing no leisure.[13] On the other hand, she takes up the model of artisan-laborers who work in the arts and sciences with their hands. While their work is rarely evaluated in the same terms, Christine underscores their affinities. Both groups are defined by the physical, time-consuming quality of their labor.

At the center of all these theories, Christine represents her own work of writing as bodily duress that constitutes a dignified occupation. She challenges her readers to think about manual labor as an exercise that is self-affirming. Christine's position is overdetermined. Her French and Italian languages, like our own English, confirms what has proved a focal point for generations of feminist critics: a manual worker's exertion resembles women's labor during childbirth.[14] In several of her books that meditate on the pain and the creative results of this type of work, she emphasizes their shared situation. *Neither* she herself, a widowed *mother* without an inheritance, a *writer* without a reliable patron, *nor* the *laborer* have a choice. Their working condition is a necessity that implicates many of them in a type of domestic service verging on servitude.[15]

Christine's advocacy for workers amounts to a major political provocation. The dream vision enables her to promote the socioeconomic significance of their labor and to evaluate her own working conditions in a similar and unprecedented way. She does so in ethical terms. By compiling stories of exemplary figures across her fictions, she gathers proof of the worth of their labors across historical and legendary time. Industrious women side by side with fieldhands personify the moral imperative to value what they do, to give as much importance to the work of all genders and social estates as to the occupations of military men and clerics.

Christine's political dream visions advance an idea of equitable labor. It's an idea that foregrounds the work of those underrepresented in her society and times. Given the social hierarchy that does not grant equality to all its members and their labors, Christine's idea, in balance, recognizes their worth. She builds on a notion of equity fundamental to an ethical understanding of justice that Nicole Oresme had reintroduced.[16] Christine infuses her dream with it to credit the labor of women and those in the lowest social ranks. By foregrounding the need to assess equitably what this unexpected team does, she points out the necessary work of practical knowledge. That is, she also promotes what those in an Aristotelian line of thinking call *poesis*, making fiction. Her own works for her own age are at stake.

These fictional works would prove prochronous, moving in time. They benefited, first, from the technological innovation of print. When the printers André Vérard and Michel Le Noir began to create multiple copies of the *City of Ladies* and *Three Virtues* several generations after Christine, they made her writing accessible to many more readers.[17] In widening circles, these books went far in creating the material circumstances crucial for such fiction to become timely. As significant as the objects are to this historical process, it is the ideas animating Christine's writing that determine it fundamentally. Her vision of equitable labor is generative. *What* a creator imagines explains *why* other people are drawn to the fiction and begin to engage with it for reasons that make sense to them in their own times. Here I chart one episode in that process as it was played out, off and on, over hundreds of years, among French-speaking generations as well as others who learned of Christine's campaign for women citizens.[18]

It was Édith Thomas, during a period closer to our own, who responded through action to what Christine envisions in *The City of Ladies* and *Three Virtues*. During the combat against Vichy's totalitarian regime collaborating with Nazi forces, and again, in World War II's aftermath, in the campaign for human rights, Christine's ideas about women assembling politically accompanied her at each step. Thomas created her own view of equitable work and equal social relations in writing shaped by the history of struggles as Christine had envisioned it for her own people. The unpublished essay of Thomas, "Towards a Feminized Humanism," is the fruit of extended investigations, and the culmination of her engagement with Christine's fiction.[19]

Considering their political writing together, in the early 1400s, as in the 1940s and 1950s, brings us to the core of this almanach entry: how Christine's fictions registered in her own age, and why Thomas's creative work imagined their ideas of labor as a question of women's human rights.

Laboring Out of Season

Across her writing, Christine develops a phrase that identifies her remarkable fictional persona of the worker whom we meet at the outset of the *Book of Three Virtues*. "The labor of learning" ["le labour d'estude"] characterizes her work as a combination of physical and intellectual work.[20] The phrase has long caught my critical eye as the writer's signature; for Deborah McGrady, it signals the work of writing for a self-trained person with little institutional backing.[21] Christine tests this phrase out first in an earlier mythography, the *Epistle to Othea*, where she uses it to refer to the work she undertakes for one of her patrons, Louis d' Orléans. In her subsequent political prose, she elaborates on it again and again: in the *Three Virtues* incipit; in her autobiographical *Christine's Vision*, where it describes her first work composing poetry; and culminating in her *Book of Peace* where it details her diplomatic efforts. When she dreams of Bovet appearing to her, and calls him Estude, "Learning," in her *Book of Arms and Chivalry*, she winks at her ally who had underscored the difficult, largely unrecognized work that writing had exacted from him when he made his *Apparition* for the French court—the same patrons Christine sought.[22] The phrase gives the work at stake an authoritative cloak. As a whole, her signature "labor of learning" casts all her writing over years as one large-scale act of laboring. Since the phrase incorporates traits of the lowliest of the estate of laborers with the ambitious class of cleric, it composes a body politic as compelling as the numerous schemas in philosophical treatises of the day, and far more real.

In her *City of Ladies*, Christine focuses on key figures who substantiate the close relations between manual laborer and intellectual. Ceres, a goddess in the Greek and Roman pantheon, for one, represents the indispensable cultivator of the "nature of humanity." "The Queen invented the art of working the land, as well as many other arts."[23] The first translation of Christine's *City* (in Flemish around 1475) includes a painting of a dexterous woman at work plowing the fields.[24] Artists make of this mythic woman standing at the origins of agriculture both an expert farmer and a mechanic equipped with handmade tools. They depict Ceres in a landscape in keeping with the nature painting so well practiced in Flanders and the Burgundian Lowlands. For Christine, Ceres humanizes the evolution from nature to culture. She uses Ceres's authoritative knowledge as the gear shifting women and men from an age of bestiality to lives marked by reason.[25]

In the parallel story of Carmenta, Christine introduces a second maker, a woman who originates letters, vowels, and consonants. Far from a purely intellectual undertaking, this verbal invention amounts to hands-on work. Christine emphasizes Carmenta's and Ceres's affinities in the voice of her ally, the figure of Reason:

> Make no doubt about it, that many noteworthy and important sciences and arts have been discovered by women through their subtle understanding . . . both cognitive, speculative science, as writing demonstrates and the arts, as handiwork and manual labor demonstrate.

> [Ne doubez pas du contraire que maintes notables et grans sciences et ars ont este trouvees par engie et soubtiveté de femmes, tant en speculacion d'entendement, lesquelles se demoustrent par escript, comme en ars, qui se demoustrent en oeuvres manuelles et de labour.][26]

Whereas the scholastic social order and the practices of work in Christine's society divide the farmer from the writer, placing them at opposite ends of the hierarchy of estates, she brings them together as related workers. The solidarity she fosters in these portraits of mythical pioneers Ceres and Carmenta is an early sign of her campaign for enfranchising farmer and woman writer, giving their labor its proper value.

In the companion *Book of Three Virtues*, which translates the fabled examples of the *City* into realistic scenarios and concrete guidance, Christine concentrates on the condition of the manual laborer.[27] Her attention to simple women who live in the countryside is exceptional—unique among political commentaries that she reviews. She emphasizes their essential farming work: "their labor sustaining, nourishing, and giving life to every human creature."[28] Food production represents as powerful a model of women's work as any story of origins. While artists depict Ceres tilling the land in one dream vision, Christine's portrayal of female agricultural laborers in the other gives them a comparable significance. Her dream of the equal social value of their work builds force by dint of these reprises and variations.

Women servants in the city, in noble households, are equal key subjects for Christine's thinking. She underscores the labor of Paris's chambermaids because it ensures the function of the entire social structure, including the highest estates.[29] This provides her with the circumstance to critique the disabling repercussions of their working life. Because these women must work for others to make a living, they have no time for their own training. Caught in a type of involuntary servitude, they are deprived of all schooling. Christine launches a new case for educating women workers: instruction for every woman, regardless of her station, offers a chance to better herself and her social prospects. The implicit parallel with Christine's own condition is powerful. An autodidact, she learns from her sustained reading. Her practice of synthesizing the thought of the chief authors in her writing testifies to her determined effort to keep training herself.

It is hardly surprising, then, that the *Book of Three Virtues* concludes with a self-portrait of the writer–worker. "I, Christine, stayed put, fatigued by the lengthy writing, but now taking great pleasure looking at the very beautiful work of their respected lessons" ["je, Cristine, demouray, auques lassee pour la longue scripture, mais tres resjoye regardans la tres belle oeuvre de leurs dignes leçons."][30] The writer at work appears to come to rest like any humanist from the cohort in Florence whom Christine knew, or those in Paris with whom she had already debated Jean de Meun's *Romance of the Rose*.[31]

Does she earn leisure, as they do? She claims it, in fact, in the voice of a servant: "moy, leur servante."[32] Christine is doing more than exploiting a well-known gendered rhetoric; she is diversifying the case that dignifies labor, extending it to all who work, especially those at ground level. While she ennobles her own "labor of learning," distinguishing it strategically in her dealings and negotiations with the dukes, it is never at the expense of her fellow laborers.

In *Christine's Vision*, the brilliant life-writing she composes in this same year as the *Book of Three Virtues* and the *City of Ladies*, she uses her fictional persona to deepen her reflection on work.[33] Here, too, this persona appears, at first, overextended.[34] Her labor requires rest that engenders a familiar kind of marvelous vision. It also entails indefatigable work at writing.

In the dream state, she recounts the story of the First Age in paradise, and the canonical account of agricultural work as the consequence of Adam and Eve abusing the Garden of Eden and losing it as a result.[35] Once again Christine personifies the paradigm of human labor in a postlapsarian state, "a life in sweat," with all its toil and aches. Not only does she continue to reinforce her common lot with manual laborers, but she also links her work with those forced to move.[36] Adam and Eve are the first migrant labor force. So are the so-called wandering scholars. The early episodes in her life-writing substantiate this: the Italian astronomer, her father Thomas de Pizan, who accepts the call from the court of France, as she does, and arrives in Paris, a foreigner.[37]

Christine's thinking about labor culminates in an imaginary dialogue with a figure of Philosophy. The metaphor she uses to translate her fruitful work as maternal labor is made concrete. It becomes, literally, a list numbering the quires and books she composed over six years; in the same way, "just as the worker," Christine is doing the accounts for her labor.[38] In a passage that has proven magnetic for critics, she assesses the socioeconomic value of her writing in a draft that both breaks with the inequities hardened in scholastic discourse and challenges the humanist formulas on equitable relations. The "constancy" of her labor makes Christine's work ethic clear. This description of the books and volumes created for her first patron, King Charles V, represents her at work to ensure house and home for her family. Her constant writing shows her loyalty as well. She labors out of affection for those she has lost and out of respect for others who have never been given their due. Her resolve to campaign for socioeconomic equity across groups rarely wavers. No matter the melancholic tone that Jacqueline Cerquiglini-Toulet captures, Christine's writing is driven by moral conviction.[39]

It is important to take stock of *when* Christine brings her visionary thinking about work to this point. The year 1405 was the banner year of her most intensive writing of the *City of Ladies*, the companion *Three Virtues*, and *Christine's Vision*. This fruitful period coincides with months of polarized conflict at the French court when the rival factions of her patrons, Armagnac and Burgundian, drew arms violently. Christine was reckoning with warmongering that threatened her livelihood and which had already destroyed the lives of thousands of unknown agricultural laborers. The ballads of Eustache Deschamps were already dramatizing the damage inflicted on people being burnt out of house and home: "God help us, the English torched the plains of wheat everywhere."[40] This was the year, too, when she addressed Isabelle of Bavaria, the French Queen, in a letter dated October 5, about the social effects of hatred among warring leaders.[41] Christine's plea: "in times of tribulation, could your powerful highness please give to your poor people some small word and some labor." The writer makes a strategic call to action that translates her vision of work at the highest social level. Pressing the queen into service is one way of actualizing her ideas of equitable labor and implicating all classes of women from the top down.

Such urgent politics plus her personal circumstances moved Christine to outline her position further on the social, economic, and ethical terms determining her work. Christine builds a model that defends the subaltern by esteeming them, and thus challenges the social inferiority of all who labor. Painters in a Paris atelier who illuminated her vision of the *City of Ladies* represent her as a mason, a powerful image that Anne Coldiron underscores.[42] Two generations later, artists painted her as a fieldhand in the Flemish translation of this dream vision (Figure 13). One celebrated artwork, and one lesser known, together depict a profound social solidarity. These painters confirm Christine's dream of removing these laborers, practically speaking, from the baseline of social misrecognition. They show instead the respectable social place of mason and fieldhand. Their artistry reinforces vividly Christine's efforts promoting the inherent and necessary worth of all their laboring.

This is the heart of her vision: an equitable work ethic across sexes and social groups. It is an idea articulated in terms of good action. Any socioeconomic question in the West during this period, Giacomo Todeschini reminds us, is posed first in the conceptual language of moral theology.[43] Espousing an equitable vision of work, no matter its physical demands or mental stress, is an exercise in thinking ethically around 1405. It is also one establishing an early chapter in the history of economic inequality and false meritocracies that Thomas Piketty advances in his *Capital in the Twenty-first Century*.[44] Christine is a pioneering leading voice.

Figure 13. Christine de Pizan, *Het Boek van de Stede der Vrauwen*, London, BL, Add. 20698, fol. 17, c. 1475. Courtesy British Library.

Her conviction about the value of manual and menial work cannot be separated from her experience as a woman working. It is the two converging ideas that distinguish her as a major political thinker, as Cary Nederman emphasizes; it signals a contribution to the history of socioeconomic thought that is innovative and, from our perspective now, far-sighted.[45]

Christine's advocacy for equitable labor takes the form of visionary fiction. She is not in a position to act concretely on behalf of every group of workers. Nor does she promote the emancipation of all workers. Christine is a writer of her age; she bears its mark of a hierarchical understanding of levels of work and political participation that are not equal. Yet she does imagine a fair treatment of what people do in their own station. In her own case, she attends to the constraints she confronted in her writing practice. She devised actual arrangements where "the labor of her learning" gains more than symbolic recognition. Faced with aristocrats in the Valois court no longer investing in producing handmade books, as Deborah McGrady argues, Christine shows her economic savvy.[46] She seeks recompense, as well as other forms of exchange that value the occupation of writing without commodifying the knowledge she cultivates. Around 1405, Christine's attention to her book production and circulation shows her to be as much a pragmatist in the affairs of her writing as a political dreamer in her ideas.

During those same years, this writer was mindful of the prochronous quality of her fictions. She points it out in *Christine's Vision* when her persona debates with the figure, Lady Opinion. When civil war is splitting her society apart, it is no surprise that the idea of the equitable value of laborers' work—regardless of gender, social station, or trade—falls "out of season": "in the time to come, there'll be more talk of it than during your life. For I'll say to you again, you came at a bad time because, at present, the sciences are no longer in favor, just like things out of season." ["Le temps à venir plus en sera parlé qu'à ton vivant. Car tant te dis je encore que tu es venue en mauvais temps. Car les sciences ne sont pas a present en leur reputacion, ains sont comne choses hors saison."][47] Yet Christine adopts the terms of natural history, of seasons, to look to the next cycle. The temporal movement in her dream vision is palpable: the turn or revolution in time as it was understood by astronomers of her day. Champion of all kinds of laborers—the bird-catcher and waffle-maker as much as the writer—Christine imagines when knowledge will put all of them on an equitable footing, and value them as active members of future communities.[48]

Points of Arrival and Departure

Decades into the twentieth century, the surge of revolutionary political action around workers conferred a new sense on Christine's visionary writing. In this different international framework, socialist and communist activist-writers saw how the ideas of social relations of an earlier age were primed to be actualized. What had been taken up as utopian fiction could still come into time, realized through people's work. An idea of equitable labor, for one, could be substantiated in contemporary progressive movements.

Édith Thomas was one militant on the political left whose sense of history moved her to see how Christine's fictions, in its various times, could be part of this process (Figure 14). Her training as an archivist and historian made her alert

Figure 14. Édith Thomas, in the 1930s. Paris, AN, fonds Édith Thomas. Courtesy of Daniel Thomas and Dorothy Kaufmann.

to the potential of earlier works returning to her own times, of other writers configuring their ideas in another "here and now." "Every instant in history is both an arrival point and a point of departure."[49] This is her working principle, with which she begins "Towards a Feminized Humanism." The essay spans hundreds of years, and the activism of numerous women that led to Thomas's day. Her particular historical outlook maintains two directions: extending to women's experience in many ages before her own, and beyond to their circumstances still to be established. Thomas's commitment to egalitarian politics meant that she grasped how her fellow writer's vision dignifying—and crediting—women's work could take shape in her own generation.

Thomas belonged to the generation of 1910 who elected Léon Blum's Popular Front in France and embraced Marxist principles. Alongside many militants mobilized in French and international associations, she was convinced by the fundamental ideals of the Bolshevik revolution's first days, enfranchising working people. She believed their labor to constitute a free and equitable belonging, in the terms that socialist William Morris had considered already around 1893 of "the surviving communism of the Middle Ages."[50] For Thomas, this position necessitated giving women equal civil status with the vote and other human rights by law.

During the Vichy-Nazi years, she went into action, taking the initiative to sustain a key underground group, "The National Center of Writers."[51] After one member, "Jacques Decour," had been assassinated, she organized their clandestine meetings in her Paris apartment. The major role she played in the communist Resistance went beyond the so-called literary one that Gisèle Sapiro identifies. Courier and information-gatherer, she joined dozens of others who fought the collaborationist and totalitarian French state of Vichy day in day out, and yet who did not publicize their militant activism immediately following the war. Thomas stood behind the heroic accounts of intellectuals organizing to resist this political oppression: she was less known than the titular heads of Aragon or Sartre, yet formidable in her writing; less outspoken, yet uncompromising in her nonviolent actions on the streets and at her desk.[52]

Her essay on Christine with which the entry begins took shape in this context. It was part of her activism for a public sphere of free and equal citizens—and against the civil strife building in 1942–43.[53] Thomas wrote about that particular combination of political commitment with a love of writing: "It was not by choice," according to her, "that Christine decided to live by her pen. She was under a double pressure that makes writers, one coming from inside, the other from without. First there was the intimate, almost physiological necessity that pushes people to divulge and express their sentiments. Then there was the response of the outside world that obliges a person to carry on, that encourages her but can often destroy her as well." Thomas's 1943 wartime essay presented a Christine de Pizan in circumstances that were trying personally and threatening politically. Thomas portrayed her without any mentor to support her: a worker with the "will, obstinacy and patient violence of a woman returning to her study in her thirties." This writer was also a person who could not do otherwise, whose strong will enabled her to confront the unequal and untenable social limits constraining her so as to change them. Thomas brought out both sides of Christine's writing activism: by identifying her implicitly as a fellow comrade of sorts, she struck a prochronous link between their work.

Postwar, Thomas gave full form to her recognition of Christine's activism. In her essay "Towards a Feminized Humanism," she enlisted her writing in her own work that militates for freeing women from remaining structures of oppression: "For over a hundred years now, we've been watching a campaign developing in favor of women's liberation. It coincides in time with a push for the liberation of the proletariat. These two parallel movements are conjoined. For the first time, in fact, humanity has in hand the material possibilities for establishing authentic conditions for human liberation."[54] Thomas radicalizes the affinities Christine cultivates between working women and other laborers. With European political leaders ready at last to enfranchise women and negotiate with workers' cooperatives on a par with other social groups, in the summer of 1944 she activates Christine's vision of women's labor in her own intellectual and political work. She does so by writing a new history of women, in a form that takes a leaf from Christine's own books.

Thomas conceives of Christine's writing as part of coming into awareness of the historical process of the combat for women's many rights.[55] By situating various figures in their times, she constructs a history that triggers realizations and cultivates knowledge about the actions of many women. This retrospective account is also pitched into another time.

Thomas's remarkable essay is composed as an anthology that brings together activists of all stripes across five centuries, everyone working toward women's political autonomy. Christine de Pizan is the figurehead at the beginning of the text, the first of forty-five women. Simone de Beauvoir, Thomas's own contemporary and rival, is the last. Thomas approaches them in a style that draws on her second background as a journalist. She "questions them, conducting interviews of their past." The result is a series of biographies that introduces a significant portion of writing from each of them.

In this configuration, Thomas also places her anthology in the vein of the work of Louise-Félicité de Kéralio, a Breton historian active in women's salons, a journalist who would publish bulletins in the heyday of revolution.[56] Kéralio's "Collection of the Best Works in French Composed by Women and Dedicated to French Women," had claimed Christine's writing for women as a peer of authors from around 1787.[57] On the eve of insurrection, Kéralio had made Christine timely as a political thinker on sex and gender through portions of the *City* and *Three Virtues*. Thomas, in turn, engaged Christine's fiction in her own. She shared Kéralio's understanding of the hard work of writing that had cost Christine dearly.[58] Yet for her generation of writers, she also saw how dream visions about women's labor constituted a form that needed not only literary recognition, but recompense. In that spirit, Thomas worked to situate Christine's writing in her own times, to give it credit in a way impossible for Kéralio's age.

Thomas builds what is another *City* that composed and compiled an extended record of achievement of these forty-five women. Her essay is hardly a utopia that Christine is frequently seen to dream; yet it has something of the visionary dimension of her predecessor's political writing.[59] She creates the writing life of each woman out of an earlier age to represent an arrival point of sorts for her generation. Because Thomas is forward-looking, she also sets a departure point for those after her. Her writing is embedded with some still to be fully grasped future that belongs to them.

Thomas calls her essay "Towards a Feminized Humanism" for a specific reason. From her vantage point, "feminism appears to represent only one stage and aspect of women's liberation." She prefers "humanism because it precedes feminism and integrates it while surpassing it." Her choice of humanism as the defining, overarching framework of her writing resonates very differently in the age I inhabit. When "human" is qualified by "post-," when anything "feminized" is part of an expansive, intersectional spectrum of gender, I think of Thomas's humanistic goal in a wider framework.[60] This is one that today's arts and sciences are transforming again as they open up the physical conditions and meanings of being human. I'll return to this point at the end of this entry.

Thomas's essay, set to appear in 1948–49, the same year as Simone de Beauvoir's *Second Sex*, was never published.[61] The reasons were political. She chose to break with the French Communist Party line that continued to support Stalin despite mounting evidence of his violent tyrannical rule at the moment of the split with Yugoslavia's strongman Tito. Her publisher, Hier & Aujourd'hui, defended the line, dropping Thomas from its list of authors.

This soft censorship interrupted the release of Thomas's own visionary work. For some decades it marked this essay as untimely. While it delays this formulation of her ideas about an indispensable historical account of women's combat for labor equity, among other human rights, it did not block her disseminating them in other forms. Thomas was singleminded. She published other essays and reviews, and spoke in many forums in which she propounded the long struggle for equal rights for women, naming Christine de Pizan consistently, as the first woman political thinker at the outset of this movement who worked in French.[62] Over the 1950s and 1960s, in other venues on the left, in publications of National Education, in France-Culture radio broadcasts, and in her own fiction, Thomas persevered in thinking with Christine, and presenting their writing as part of one larger egalitarian enterprise extending over many ages. In this vision of a prolonged and ongoing task, Thomas is akin to Christine. To understand their politically committed work, we must notice the full arc of their writing. Rather than focus on a set of individual books, each one separate and autonomous, we must instead track the return, the reprise and variation of their ideas in different, related instances of their writing. The pair of political dream visions are for Christine's œuvre what the numerous sketches, drafts and other works in the archive are for Thomas's unpublished essay.

Viewed in this way, Thomas's argument for women's economic equality and civic freedom is consolidated, not diminished. Her work on Christine de Pizan's vision of work is pursued, not compromised. Among many such elaborations, she writes, for example, in a review of an essay by fellow militant Clara Malraux (1958): "This feminized humanism that began in the fifteenth century, in France, with Christine de Pizan . . . will contribute perhaps, one day, to establishing the bases for some genuine humanism."[63]

Today, for numbers of people, reading Thomas's essay "Towards a Feminized Humanism" is a powerful operation of time-release. It actualizes Christine's work. When I took up Thomas's typescript in the French National Archives's reading room, having been granted access by her nephew, I conceived my work as one more episode in this historical process.

Thomas introduces three key issues from Christine's *City* and *Three Virtues* into the sociopolitical debate of her day. In her essay, she invokes first the *City*'s call for equal education. "There is nothing that instructs a reasonable creature as well as the exercise and experience of many diverse things."[64] For Thomas as for Christine, the growing contact with different subjects determines how educated a person is. The greater the engagement with ideas, the better the education; the greater the diversity of experience, the more well rounded the educated person becomes. Furthermore, Thomas chooses Christine's writing that claims this diversity for women's education based on their humanity—as people who think—rather than on the basis of their sex or gender. Christine's choice of term, *creature raisonnable*, is deliberate. Her language innovates a gender-neutral precision, as Rosalind Brown-Grant demonstrates.[65] Thomas hears the distinction, and advocates for schooling as a matter of human dignity. In the vision of the earlier writer, what is due to every being within a Christian framework of divine creation is a universal human right in another, secular one.

Their two visions can hardly be taken for granted. During recent years, public education involves an obstacle course. Students in American schools, who are seeking many diverse things, are faced with proposed laws to ban some of their library books; teachers in the French school system have had to confront the events of two of their colleagues, Dominique Bernard and Samuel Paty, killed in action. Christine's and Thomas's work on behalf of women students proves critical for our present day.

Thomas underscores the right to education through the parallel Christine strikes with country people. Their apparent simplemindedness has nothing to do with natural ability, but instead, as with women, is the consequence of a lack of schooling. Thomas and Christine pinpoint the class divide as well as that of gender. Natalie Zemon Davis signaled a generation ago that Christine made one of her most daring social leaps here, and Thomas bounds ahead with her.[66] Together, Thomas and Christine campaign for equal-opportunity instruction in order to advance the overarching argument for women's economic equality. Without comparable training given to all, the labor of some is inevitably devalued, the inequity systematized. As Christine's *Three Virtues* lays out, chambermaids are trapped in this predicament: having to work reduces the occasions for learning more, which in turn limits their type of work and social recognition.[67] In 1948, the year Thomas was set to publish her essay, a year marking a centenary of popular revolutions in Europe and Latin America, Thomas strengthened the rapport that Christine had envisioned between universal instruction and the drive for equality in the labor force.

Thomas also takes up Christine's views on home economics. "How many women are there actually who because of their husbands' harshness spend their lives overextended by the bond of marriage in greater suffering than if they were slaves among the Saracens?" ["quantes femes est il . . . qui usent leur lasse de vie ou lien de mariage par dureté de leurs maris en plus grant penitence que se elles feussent esclaves entre les Sarasins?"][68] Marriage represents, potentially, the most extreme and punishing unequal relation: enslavement. Thomas takes up the dominant rapport that governs women's livelihoods in the 1940s as four hundred years earlier. With clear critical eyes looking ahead, she acts on what Christine recommends in the *City*: "whoever cares to investigate the debate on marriage in order to write a new book in accordance with the truth would uncover new material."[69] Thomas evaluates marriage as an economic contract. Central to her analysis is the imperative that women know about their own household finances and work on them as informed partners alongside their husbands. She reinforces and extends Christine's economic vision of marriage and its political importance for civil society. The situation of the solo writer, which they shared, undergirds why women must learn to do their account books. Without this vital and authoritative knowledge, they would cease to exist, socially speaking.

The final question that Thomas draws from Christine's writing reveals one of the most tenacious "feminine" stereotypes. The "peacemaker" is perennially associated with the gentle language attributed to essentialized women. Christine takes up this role and the strategy of gendered rhetoric, Tracy Adams argues.[70] Christine reconfigures it in the context of reconciling warring parties. Side by side with the received idea is her more pronounced one of peacemaking as work. "So that war can be avoided, she wishes to work hard and labor wisely calling on God for help and good counsel."[71] Once again, Christine shows the travail that such an occupation taken up by women demands. Soft words have no effect if they do not also involve hard work that undergirds good thinking. This is the charge that she places before the French queen in that year (1405), when the internecine violence of factions in the kingdom explodes.

Thomas, in turn, concentrates on this form of labor as a civic exercise: it is urgent yet often downplayed; vital to the workings of any community, yet often conducted by individuals rarely recognized as ambassadors. Thomas draws this thinking of Christine from a 1536 printed version of the *Three Virtues*, known as the *Treasure of the City of Ladies*, that circulated as required reading among European royal circuits from Portugal to England.[72] In other words, Thomas foregrounds the effective action of the history of this dream vision fiction. She chooses it because of the political influence it exerts in another period, several generations after Christine's, when female monarchs, Medicis and Tudors among them, benefited from its practical guidance in conflict resolution.

The figure of the woman peacemaker is one that Rose Rigaud had taken up a generation before Thomas.[73] The first to configure Christine de Pizan's writing and ideas as feminist, Rigaud also turned to the ensemble of dream visions, the *City* and *Three Virtues*, to account for the revolution of Christine's writing. Around 1900, as suffrage movements were gaining momentum, she adopted Christine's visionary work as an exemplar for articulating equal rights of women as political subjects. Before Thomas's more militant feminist understanding of such history of rights, Rigaud's essay enabled Christine's writing to make its leap into twentieth-century political thinking.

In their different ways, both Thomas and Rigaud recognize the pair of Christine's books as a crucial political ensemble. Visionary writing is insufficient if it does not include a compendium that shows how to put the newly envisaged polity into practice: ideas made real. The most demanding and ultimate labor of Christine's writing was following through with a book of guidance. It was Édith Thomas who moved finally to politicize the potential of both the *City* and *Three Virtues* in the public sphere. She acted on it. All her accumulating writing around the idea of equitable labor in Christine's fiction contributed to the campaign for placing the question of women's human rights at the center of political debate: a campaign that would finally legalize the vote for women as well as the right to seek elected office in France in 1945.[74]

✳

Does the writing of Christine de Pizan with Édith Thomas—a case of the historical process of timely fiction—offer us anything for humanistic work today? Naming Christine a humanist according to earlier norms had proven to be a curious flashpoint of contention.[75] She was often disqualified, presumed to lack a mastery of Latin that distinguished intellectuals in her age, especially when viewed retrospectively from the ideological high ground of the so-called Italian Renaissance. For Thomas, the standard set for a humanist was philosophical. It required taking a position in postwar European and American intellectual life. For this generation, the name of "humanist" belonged to Sartre and his company. Thomas was sidelined. Her completed essay, "Towards a Feminized Humanism," appeared virtually impossible to see as humanistic thinking.

Here is one final prochrony of the political dreams of Christine and Thomas for us to weigh. Once we entertain the two writers as humanists based on the labor their writing demands, its becoming timely is clear. Their work does not hinge on language or on a school of philosophy or a particular form of fiction. It is the actual labor substantiating their ideas of social equity that is necessary. For these two activists, it is vital to understand their writing as physical exercise and working for a living; it involves material practice as much as any thought experiment. This understanding registers in a time-released pattern: what Christine's political visions can make happen through and with other writers, what Thomas's essay may still generate. This potential can prove crucial again.

Thomas's typescript of "Towards a Feminized Humanism," currently available to those who seek it out in the French National Archives, brought this home to me. When Thomas chose this title, she cast her writing as one step in an ongoing political process that is historical. As we think now with Thomas, at a time when the experiences of inequities and inequalities are numerous and raw, the challenges of "that labor of learning" that Christine conceptualized are fresh again. I end this almanach entry with one.

When it comes, finally, to the work of Christine, and of Thomas, among many more writers, the challenge involves combating a view of humanist thinking and writing as a nonproductive enterprise of people in their ivory towers, disconnected from the real world. This is at complete odds with Christine's labors in making her dream visions when her milieus were caught in cycles of self-destruction. This was also contrary to Thomas's indefatigable work during wartime that links a history of egalitarian politics for women with equal opportunity in work and education. This is counter, too, to the work of numerous colleagues in schools and universities in 2025–26 who confront political orders and proposed laws divesting public education, actions that devalue their profession and thinking with the next generation.

The "college" that Christine envisaged in her fiction, with its ideas of equitable labor, can incite fruitful writing and action again.

Entry 3

Equality in Dying: Personal Poetry

VILLON, HUGO, HUGHES, MURRAY, AND GLISSANT

In May 2010, the poet Édouard Glissant brought out a collection spanning the verses of François Villon, a balladeer; Dante, a visionary poet; Snorri Sturluson, a saga writer; Li Bai, a Chinese Tang Dynasty poet; and composers of Bambara epic and indigenous American songs, whose names we are missing.[1] All these poems in their variety build a rhythm, making the relations between works of many different eras and places that are Glissant's signature.[2]

Two ballads open his anthology: a 1930s protest song from the United States, Abel Meeropol's "Strange Fruit"; and one of the best known poems in French, Villon's "Ballad of the Hanged Men."

Black bodies swinging in the southern breeze
Strange fruit hanging from the poplar trees.[3]

[Corps noirs qui aux brises du sud mènent leur bruit
Étrange, fruits perdus au haut des peupliers.][4]

You see us five, six, hanging here,
As for the flesh we loved too well,
A while ago it was eaten and rotted away.[5]

[Vous nous voiez cy attachez, cinq, six
Quant de la chair que trop avons nourrie,
El est pieça devoree et pourrie.]

Glissant's combination configures each poem for another situation. We hear Villon's decomposing bodies who address us by way of Meeropol's figures embodying a perversion of nature. We begin to see Black men murdered unjustly in the Jim Crow South by way of those condemned to hang in 1460. In Meeropol, we hear now:

Here is the fruit for the crows to pluck
For the rain to gather, for the wind to suck
For the sun to rot, for the trees to drop,
Here is a strange and bitter crop.

[Voici un fruit que les corbeaux s'affoleront à becqueter
Fruit que la pluie fait fonder et où le vent se désaltère
Que le soleil pourrit, que l'arbre laissera tomber
La voici, étrange récolte, si amère.]

In Villon:

The rain has rinsed and washed us
The sun dried us and turned us black
Magpies and ravens have pecked out our eyes . . .
Therefore don't join in our brotherhood.

[La pluye nous a debuez et lavez
Et le soleil deseichez et noirciz.
Pies, corbeaulx nous ont les yeulx cavez . . .
Ne soiez donc de nostre confrairie.]

Across 1460s Paris and the 1930s United States, Glissant convenes these dead with visceral force. Meeropol's song with Villon's ballad intensify their call for solidarity. They reinforce the act of witnessing the all-too-human remains who are present again. They direct our focus to this unjust dying that is an unrecognized part of living.

By translating Meeropol's lyric into French, Glissant creates more with the two ballads. His poem deepens what Billie Holliday and Nina Simone had sung powerfully, soliciting readers again to take in the ballad's scene for what it is in their context. His title, "Contre les lynchages dans le sud des États-Unis," "Against Lynchings in the American South" makes his protest explicit here and now.

Glissant was collecting the many poems for his anthology as he himself was facing dying. In the wake of his death, they would become his poetic testament. The name for his anthology, *La Terre le feu l'eau et les vents,* "Earth Fire Water and Wind," affirms his affinity with poets in many ages. It evokes the natural elements that Georges Chastelain had chosen too: the raw materials all these writers use to compose a universe of fiction.

This almanach entry begins with Glissant's ingenious triptych of poets because it epitomizes how Villon's poetry can become timely. His choice to set the "Ballad of the Hanged Men" in relation to Meeropol's "Strange Fruit" contemporizes them both. The poem he learned at a French Republican school in Martinique, and the song he heard again in Louisiana, where some four hundred Black men and women had been lynched, are situated in a further era.[6] Every poem, Glissant reminds us, can always be of another time to come.[7] His insight converges with what fellow writer Blaise Cendrars had sensed, whose own ballads propelled Villon into the 1900s; or with what philosopher Jacques Rancière posits—such works making temporal leaps across French-speaking realms in the 1460s, to English and French-speaking ones in the 1930s.[8] Glissant creates a Villon poetry impossible to anticipate in this poet's time: one that reconfigures the ballad for his publics with meaning for their struggle against racist violence in the United States. He reaches for what he calls the trembling of knowledge—an embodied one—as profound as any political act.[9]

Glissant's work takes its place among those of many other poets and artists who also created with Villon's ballad. It becomes part of a rich vein of their poetry that invents with all of Villon's works, especially the *Legacy* and the *Testament* that fictionalize the legal act of taking stock of one's life. The potential of this entire œuvre has a remarkably strong history, in 1920s Japan, as in 1530s France, with people imagining their universe with Villon, in their personal idiom, for their own circumstances.

Two signature traits of Villon will help us take the full social measure of the poetry through its multiple times and places. In the spirit of the "Ballad of the Hanged Men," the major poems configure life's trials, first, under the sign of dying. More than a ritual memento mori, they confront us with this human condition; they go as far as possible in imagining the final experience—the moment of dying. Instead of moving to a spiritual life beyond, they vivify human mortality. Any expectation of another life is tempered with our physical end.

A first-person voice, cantankerous and endearing, transforms dying into an individual experience. "Of my poor self, let me say . . . I mourn . . . I renounce love." ["De moy, povre, je vueil parler . . . Je plains . . . Je regnye amours."][10] Here's a subject who personalizes grievances to protest against violent dying. This inimitable "I" identifies, in the end, a criminal, subject to the death penalty. This persona defies social order and plays according to his own rules; he proves so compelling as to gain an independent force beyond the poetry. This is a personal Villon—Kateb Yacine's incorrigible bad boy of literature—whose life-and-death story engages numerous writers and artists in making sense of their own predicaments.[11]

At the core of this poetry, configured through its mortal quality, and voiced by its outspoken first person, is an arresting idea: dying is the great social equalizer. "Whatever the robber baron might think, / The mortal knife hangs over us all."[12] So Villon's *Testament* says, and numerous images tell (Figure 15). So does the poetic voice of Pauli Murray, a Black American writer and civil rights activist: "in death all men are equal."[13] The *Dark Testament* of this Harlem Renaissance poet confronts and protests the unjust, violent killing of Black people.

Figure 15. Tarot Card from Set of King Charles VI. Death, the apocalyptic figure and great leveler who spares no one, not king or cardinal. Paris, BnF, rés Kh-24-boîte Écu, c. 1460. Photograph: Bibliothèque nationale de France.

In 1930s–1960s Louisiana and North Carolina, it adds to the time table for this poetry emerging in the public spaces of 1460s Paris through its many situations. The question *how* and *why* this act of imagining equality in dying generates such an array of fiction in many voices, translated, and transplanted over five centuries, across numerous cultures, makes Villon's poetry a paradigm for fiction becoming timely.

A Mortal Villon

In a culture where remembering the dead was at the center of public life, Villon's *Legacy* and *Testament* confront dying in all its physicality. The *Legacy* gives us a person who is recording letting go, until his ink freezes, and he loses consciousness. The *Testament* goes further: it exposes the death throes that make everyone "shudder and blanch . . . the flesh go[es] limp, the joints and sinews swell and stretch," only to expose them in the speaker whose heart fails as he draws up a will.[14] This pitiless attention to one person's dying body zeroes in on what's left in a charnel house. "I see them all . . . shoveled together in a heap."[15] Villon's poetry expresses what almost everyone fears about the way we end—and few desire to put into words. The *Testament* relays the only imaginable future in a refrain—poetry's most potent single line: "remember a time will come when you'll die." ["soyez tous recors: une foyz viendra que mourrez."][16]

Such a frank view of dying, paired with its flip side, erotic living, is transgressive. The *Testament* calls it "the spur of love pricking into him."[17] This persona is in constant search of physical pleasure.

> Laughing, toying, dallying, kissing
> Both completely naked for their bodies' delight . . .
> there's no treasure like living high.
>
> [Rire, jouer, mignonner et baisier
> Et nud a nud pour mieulx des corps s'aisier . . .
> Il n'est tresor que de vivre a son aise.][18]

This hetero-eros is by nature excessive, enjoyed with numerous others who are never short on propositions. No one embodies this transgressive pleasure more than the persona, Fat Margot: "stop in again the next time you feel horny / In this whorehouse where we hold our state."[19] The refrain of Margot's ballad expresses the equal-opportunity eros coursing through Villon, its unruly language defying what has been judged "decent" or "good poetry."

Coupling visceral dying with ecstatic living is fundamental to Villon's fiction.

On the one hand, the impulse for more pleasure is relentless: "All to the taverns and girls," the refrain of another *Testament* ballad proclaims. On the other, each new passionate encounter is a reminder of life's deadline. The poem makes the warning and address to others personal: "I mean you, comrades in revels . . . remember / A time will come when you'll die."[20]

This combination of highly sensual living through dying is one key to Villon's fiction becoming timely. Take those companions in pleasure, the *compains de galle*. We find them in the collected works of Villon that were set in circulation again, appearing in 1742, in The Hague, where writers sought freedom from the censorship controlling their work in the French kingdom.[21] The critic-editor, Jean-Antoine Du Cerceau focuses on the licentious energy of these companions. He sees them as "*gallants*," their ballads interacting with the codes of gallantry defining European court life.[22] Situating them in this way, Du Cerceau confirms the unbridled hetero-eros of Villon's fiction: it becomes libertine. Its mix of sensual high living with a sense of mortality feeds the freer, questing spirit of these times that even a Catholic Jesuit editor, Du Cerceau, pursues in his appetite for greater knowledge.

At stake for this generation of readers is the fundamental rapport between a mortal Villon and the irrepressible desire to invent. "You have to admit that in order to joke around in such a situation, to play with a matter so serious, you have to have great gaiety at your core. It's even worse in a way than what the Ancients would call '*pingere sub gladio*,' what we call 'rhyming in the shadow of the gallows.'"[23] Du Cerceau is alert to the gallows humor in Villon's "Ballad of the Hanged Men." His chief discovery, though, involves attributing the force of invention to its view on living as dying. If we're all hanging under a mortal knife, the real choice lies in creating something out of this end. Imagining this, and Villon writing under the noose, flirts with taboo, even more so than the Roman Pliny painting under a sword. Dying is a quintessential opportunity for creating intrepid and liberating fiction.

For the French revolutionary generation of writers, this mortal, sensual poetry was a welcome provocation. It linked them to an era and an aesthetic that fed their revolt against social hierarchy and the strictures imposed on poetry. Théophile Gautier, for one, heralded this libertine quality of Villon's *Testament*. The young poet recognized it in the "Ballad of Fat Margot" that typifies Villon's license: "There is no picture as bold that has been traced by a hand as daring as this one."[24] Gautier sought this "ancient" Villon, for the "freedoms, the frank, liberating charms" of his erotic idiom; the poetry proved an ally for his own experimental expressiveness in a debut collection, *The Comedy of Death*.[25]

It is Victor Hugo who understands a mortal Villon from the inside out.

The challenge of writing freely under the threat of death epitomizes opposition against executing people. Hugo tested the model out—not in his poetry, but in drawing and prose fiction that he published, first, anonymously. *The Last Day of a Condemned Man* chronicles the ruminations of a criminal sent to the guillotine—that instrument of death perfected during the French Revolution.

Over fifteen days, we follow, one by one, "the final thoughts of a miserable person." "It's always a holiday in my imagination," he tells us, "I can think what I want—I'm free."[26] Hugo captures the energetic spirit of a mortal Villon and this sensual poetry. Without ever mentioning the poet's name, Hugo voices the anguish and the gaiety that living freely under the sign of dying enables. Both writers take us to the limit of experience that can unleash a passionate range of human expressiveness.

The end of Hugo's fiction intensifies Villon's mortal poetry. Instead of showing us an execution, it presents us with a copy of a popular song, found in the man's papers. Hugo's fiction creates tantalizing traces of an individual's handwriting postmortem. It makes us privy not only to final inner thoughts, but also to the irrepressible life force of invention. Hugo gives voice to a major social actor during those years, those condemned to death, who compose *chansons d'argot*, songs in slang, as well as anyone.

"Whether you agree or not," Hugo underscores later, "slang has its own syntax, its own poetry; it is a language and we recognize that Villon spoke it."[27] Around 1830, during a second revolution, he was tapping into the talk of the lower social ranks often criminalized. His fiction mobilizes its rich poetic potential that he associated with the ballads of a mortal Villon. It generates "a political idea, a social idea. . . . for abolishing the death penalty.[28] It's one he would later draw again and again, in his *Ecce Lex, The Hanged Man*, in light and dark (c. 1854).

Hugo's idea makes for a striking prochrony of the poetry from 1460. Dying as a social equalizer in Villon becomes a political position against capital punishment in Hugo's ingenious writing and engagement with the poet. The will to invent under the most extreme conditions, yields, during these revolutionary times, an outcry for social equality in life.

Hugo expresses his protest against the death penalty, finally, in his own name. One poet's fiction reverberating—and trembling—with another in violent circumstances.

A Personal Villon

The promise of this poetry to engage other publics in the future depends finally on this personal quality. As Hugo's fiction makes clear, for all the punch of the mortal, sensual poetry, it hinges on an "I" to realize its full force. The particular human character proves decisive for Villon's presence: the voice expressing outrage and fear of meeting a bad end with erotic thrill; the "I" who wills everything from soul, body, and a bit of ginger to friends, and enemies; the first person whose legacy is an idea that dispenses with people's social rank in death. No voice sounds more powerful than the first person confiding a last accounting to us.

This personal Villon is akin to the "we" who speak out in the "Ballad of the Hanged Men." The *Testament* channels the outcry of a collective "we" into one of a single person facing his death. When the two poems are first printed by Levet in 1489, the *Testament* is followed by the ballad, "The Epitaph of Villon." Together they create a final set piece that draws the arc of an individual's life, from beginning to end.

The smallest unit of poetry, a single stanza, captures this personal Villon best:

> I am François which is my cross
> Born in Paris near Pontoise
> From a fathom of rope my neck
> Will learn the weight of my ass.
>
> [Je suis François, dont il me poise
> Né de Paris emprés Pontoise
> Et de la corde d'une toise
> Saura mon col que mon cul poise.]

(STOCKHOLM, KB, VU 22, FOL. 62 C; PIÈCE NON RECUEILLIE, XIV, LL. 1–4, ED. CERQUIGLINI-TOULET, 227; KINNELL, 207.)

This declaration of birth, name, and violent death creates a person in four rhyming, rhythmic lines.

It is hard to underestimate this quatrain's inventiveness. A persona emerges quickly; within a generation of the printed works, the persona of "Maistre Françoys Villon" is circulating, separate and distinct from the poetry. This ne'er-do-well with a new profile appears in several sketches known as "Free Meals" ("Repues franches")—a persona who talks the poet's language without ever quoting it, who frequents the same suspect crowd, surrounded this time by "all manner of farce players . . . all types from strange countries."[29]

This comic persona exists side by side with the personal Villon of the ballads.

Rabelais confirms the figure's appeal. His Maistre Françoys Villon is a theater man aiming to "give a pastime to the people by producing a Passion play in the words and body language of a 'Poitevin'"; devils for the scenes in hell are his favorite creation.[30] This is a persona who mimics the ballads' linguistic verve and plays with their sense of time. Rabelais transforms a fellow writer into a full-fledged character. His "Villon" is one of those influential characters who migrates beyond his original situation, in Umberto Eco's description, sought out and transformed by other writers for their own ends.[31]

As soon as this independent fictional persona converges with the poetry, it gives further impetus to Villon's prochronous presence. Poet Paul Verlaine and his figure of a *poète maudit* provide a matrix around 1880. Through his "accursed poet" shaped for modern times, the migrating Villon persona *becomes* a poet once more.[32] Uncompromising in life and death, this figure comes to confirm a fin-de-siècle cult of absolute art. Life is expressed through a frank language that Villon's poetry cultivates. "If someone wants to object / And say I'm cursing the man . . . Here's the sum of my abuse."[33] The *Testament* persona warns us, with a dose of irony, that he will not hold back. Recounting his death is no less forthright. Villon's final refrain expresses a death wish with one last roguish, erotic thrust. This poetic persona, side by side with the legendary Rimbaud, is beloved because accursed. Although Verlaine never refers explicitly to Villon, his own poetry models the poet. "But to be him, how then to do that?" the poet asks in one short poem.[34] The *poète maudit* is Verlaine's creative answer. With this figure of an outsider poet, this personal poetry makes another leap in time.

Villon's fictional persona is also conjoined with a historical person during these years. Writer Marcel Schwob, known for his detective talent in Paris's archives, brings to light a man sentenced to die, "to be hanged and strangled . . . finally in regards to the bad life of said Villon, to banish him from the city up to ten years."[35] He gives the persona an individual face, an identity, that responds to that search at the core of modern times. Schwob discovers a legal register that identifies the quatrain's "François": here is a known criminal speaking his last who is found again—a *personne trouvée*. The register also links Villon's "Appeal" ballad to an "arbitrary sentence handed down through treachery."[36] This historical record of Villon represents, in Schwob's view, "a little guy, weak, whose subtle perversity is the wellspring of his best poetry."[37]

Schwob's discoveries in the archives touch off a creative flurry among writers and artists who invent many Villon composites.[38] These finds authorize understanding the poetry as a transcript of someone's life. A poet, Ezra Pound, captures it: "Villon's verse is real because he lived it . . . no brew of books, no distillation of sources will match the tang."[39] Many fictions for that someone are licensed by archival details, starting with Schwob's. His imagined life and death for Villon combines documentary details of the young clerk at the University of Paris that he unearthed, with invented episodes of the banished poet on the road. The unprecedented archival find: a list of coded words of working-class petty thieves that both informs the poetry, and feeds imagining Villon's criminal life and death.[40] In this, Schwob joins Robert Louis Stevenson, a young bilingual writer from Scotland, who experiments with a mélange of biographical evidence and invention. His "François Villon, student, poet, housebreaker," fills in the personal profile of a young hoodlum. It goes so far, in the vein of Hugo, as to incorporate the "Ballad of the Hanged Men" as a "transcript" of what the dying poet-persona was feeling.[41] Schwob and Stevenson together accelerated the conflation of person and persona that moved Villon into another era.

Around 1900, many creative people embraced this personal Villon as a model of leading an artistic life. For young men and women, the rebellious and conflicted voice of the ballads called to them as they were making what is always an adventurous life choice. It no longer depends on Villon's poetry. The appeal of this persona registered *without* the ballads. Gaston Duchamp typifies this turn when he first imagined becoming an artist. "So as not to scare off my family, I chose [the name] 'Villon,' because of the poet, and 'Jacques' because of the Alphonse Daudet novel. . . . my father, the upstanding notary, I, the rebel breaking away."[42] For his first drawings, the twenty-year-old Duchamp assumed the alias "Jacques Villon," the persona who freed him to express himself. In the artist's final years, he created a *Testament* that joined their names for the first and last time.[43] The Villon he draws in light and dark is the incipit for François's poem and explicit for Jacques—who died the year the book appeared (Figure 16). The liberating energy that the first poet personifies accompanies the artist to the end.

This fictional Villon identity would extend a current of invention, in poetry as across the visual arts. As soon as writers began to translate ballads, this persona migrates into a world far larger than the one in which Rabelais sent it circulating. This Villon became part of myriad languages in addition to the French that Clément Marot would innovate in 1533. This poor student, "housebreaker" of a Villon is taken up in the wake of political revolutions in Europe, as in the Americas, by writers and artists of various cultures. In the cultural rivalries between French and British empires that condition the hierarchy of literary language, in Pascale Casanova's view, writers working in various English idioms were taking a privileged position; their Villon begins to dominate.[44]

Algernon Charles Swinburne and Dante Gabriel Rossetti, poets enamored of vernacular poetry from around 1460, anglicized the *Lais* and the *Testament* by composing Villon ballads of their own.[45] Swinburne, who wrote in French with

En l'an trentiesme de mon aage,

Figure 16. Le Grand Testament, **Jacques Villon, lithograph, 1962. © 2026 Jacques Villon / Artists Rights Society (ARS), New York / ADAGP, Paris.**

ease, was the kind of writer committed to this multilingual exercise in invention. "I don't know how many times I tried to put it into English verse," he wrote fellow poet Stéphane Mallarmé, "ever since I left school."[46] His efforts focused on the quintessential poem with which Glissant and we began: "Epitaph in the Form of a Ballad which Villon made for Himself and his Comrades Expecting to be Hanged along with Them." Translating Villon was linked, for Swinburne, to the search for a personal aesthetic. He tested his desire to make poetry through the ballad, a form claiming to give voice to all classes of people, as Hugo had imagined too.[47] Swinburne's *Poems and Ballads* (1866) expresses his intimate interaction with this "Villon, our sad bad glad mad brother's name."[48]

However arcane Swinburne's ballads sound to us today, his Villon in British English helped to launch the poetry into another major literary culture. Together with Rossetti's ballads, they established such a poetic force-field, Claire Pascolini-Campbell argues, as to become part of an English canon.[49] The Villon of Swinburne and Rossetti began to move Villon beyond the French-speaking Republic of Letters.[50] Villon was internationalizing, as Marcel Schwob quipped.[51]

Akutagawa Ryūnosuke, composing fiction in Japanese, shows us the transformative extent of the personal Villon circulating in an increasingly wider world. Ryūnosuke's last work, *A Fool's Life*, around 1920, introduces this persona: "Just François Villon alone penetrated his soul. Villon, waiting for the hangman, sometimes appeared in his dreams too."[52] By way of the British English ballads, Ryūnosuke creates another Villon persona under the sign of death, in a set of erotic scenes, voiced in the first person. His fiction, structured around that dying character, appears in a work linked to the writer's suicide. Postmortem, this life in literature situates a personal Villon in Japanese culture and aesthetics, in a time zone as far away from its first creation as is possible.

Klaus Kinski, closer in cultural place, yet distant still in time, confirms the charisma of this personal Villon in German. Two generations later, in the wake of World War II and its genocide, another free spirit began his artistic life creating this persona in Berlin's late-night haunts.[53] *Villon das bin ich*, "Villon so am I," was Kinski's performance number, a declaration of self that also makes for a personal act of creative insurrection.[54]

Both Ryūnosuke's and Kinski's inventiveness signal the far-ranging, multilingual experiments in self-fashioning that Villon's poetic persona enables. They typify young writers and artists in numerous cultures who understood their developing creativity by way of this poetry, and the magnetic identity of its persona. Making fiction was for them, regardless of medium, a Villonesque operation. So was making their personal lives an art form, even to the point of seeking death.

A Contestatory Villon

Another idea invented at the heart of Villon's poetry would register just as profoundly for writers in these generations. More than an art of creating an individual identity, the knowledge articulated and embodied by this persona was at stake. The voice railing against dehumanizing death caught the imagination of young people. These were writers who would exploit brilliantly the idea that Hugo had begun radicalizing in his fiction. Those confronting the inequalities of their social milieus, the drive for totalitarian power in the age of Stalinist and National Socialist movements, would give their Villon a political color that would mark publics deeply. Bertolt Brecht is one forceful case; his "free" translation of the "Ballad of the Hanged Men" and invention of his own for his *Threepenny Opera* (1928) galvanized audiences in Germany as well as in America during his exile.[55]

Hungarian writer George Faludy embraced all the poetry, composing his own ballads in 1937, which would be recited by many during years of cruel polarization between communist and fascist partisans.[56] His Villon made visceral sense to an embattled avant-garde in Budapest. Its personal form became a *cri de cœur* for his generation struggling under Nazi occupation. Transformed again, it became a rallying cry against the oppression of the Soviets, who condemned the dissident Faludy to death by hanging in 1950. The combative force of the personal Villon and its cry of equality in dying was audible still, in English, a generation later, in Toronto in 1981, where Faludy took refuge, and I listened to him reciting his poems by heart with expatriate communities.

It is in the multilingual Americas where poets create songs that give outstanding voice to the potent, political resonances of this poetry. Black American poets re-sound Villon in ballads of uncommon intensity.

Langston Hughes, the Harlem poet of the blues and contemporary of Meeropol, discovered kinship with Villon.[57] Schooled in this poetry at Columbia University, Hughes recites the ballads all his life. He gave shape to his first grand tour abroad through this poetry, his favorite verses capturing the bordellos in Lagos as well as the demimonde of Paris. When he started working at becoming a poet, he chose Villon "of the ragged heart."[58] All his youthful imitation created the circumstances for a North American Villon—a personal one facing the violence of dying almost every day.

When Hughes began composing poems to protest lynching, Villon was with him again. One poem from *A New Song* (1938) gives powerful voice to a teenager dying to live:

> The white folks die?
> What do you mean—
> The white folks die?
>
> That black boy's
> Still body
> Says
> NOT I![59]

Hughes's "Lynching Song" is an original in prochronous tune with Villon's "Ballad of the Hanged Men." The voice we hear, the electric shock of the blues lines, its simple ballad verse all bear something of the poetic scene from long ago and far away. At the level of the line, the New York writer understands the gamble of making poetry out of street talk. His song mobilizes it to express indignation, to draw attention to the assault on Black men and women, and to condemn it.

Pauli Murray, writing in a mode similar to Hughes's, took note. In the epic poem *Dark Testament* (1939–43), the young writer riffs brilliantly on a Black Virginian whom s/he names, and whose unjust condemnation to death s/he contests:

> For the same red earth gives rest
> To the white bones of Tom Jefferson
> And the white bones of Odell Waller,
> —Sharecropper and President—
> in death all men are equal.[60]

As Murray was composing the poem's first drafts, s/he was walking the streets of Harlem, pounding out rhythms during the riots of August 1943.[61] Throughout *Dark Testament,* s/he was giving the verse a particular local tempo; its beat quickened with what s/he called "hobo's slanguage," words that s/he had heard when taking off at age twenty-one, s/he rode the railway in revolt against the kind of "colored woman" that white people, and some Black people, in Durham, North Carolina, and in Baltimore, expected Murray to be.[62] This was one of several versions of popular talk whose poetry s/he would launch ingeniously. Here was another vagabond poet who understood Langston Hughes who understood Villon deeply.[63]

The creative leap Murray's poetry makes into Villon's—and Villon's into Murray's—is surprising. I recognized it when I first heard this poem a few blocks from the poet's childhood home in Durham. *Dark Testament* re-sounds Villon's ballads by taking the radical idea of dying as a social equalizer still further than fellow poets Hughes, Hugo, and Villon himself had imagined. In this inimitable poetic voice protesting Jim Crow, Murray situates the outcry over equality in death at ground zero, in the combat for equal rights for all humans. Still under the sign of unjust and brutal dying, the verse s/he creates speaks for social equality *in living.*

Murray's verse establishes one of those connections, in Rancière's terms, that unleashes an anachronous power to "make history."[64] After Hughes, who calls up Villon to make poetry to protest lynching, Murray configures the death of Odell Waller in what s/he writes; s/he transforms it into a political call for social equality for all humans in a specific time and place of the 1940s American South.

To what extent these poets cast their poetry, and their engagement with Villon's ballads, as political expression varies. Of all the poets here, Murray is the most adamant about poetry being an integral part of the decades-long activism s/he pursued: it took form through legal groundwork defending Odell Waller in Virginia courts, and preparing the case for Thurgood Marshall for universal civil rights in American courts; it was part, too, of political groundwork for articulating the rights of women and trans citizens.[65] Murray's poetry worked in intersectional ways *avant la lettre*. Hughes was clear about his socialist commitments; yet during the years he was composing his "Lynching Songs," his public work was a separate undertaking.[66] Glissant, a generation younger, and some thirty years later, was equally forthright about his involvement in liberation politics in the French Caribbean; yet, of the three, he promoted the singular depths that poetry could plumb that are distinct from any political act.[67]

The political character of their poetry brings us once more to the question of timeliness. In Murray's *Dark Testament*, I recognize one more prochronous turn of Villon's poetry: its artfulness and its wisdom about struggles to live and die on more equal terms. Such a turn signals the ongoing historical process of these ballads engaging creative people to make fiction for their own peoples. It emphasizes much the same process that Murray's poetry undergoes: versions of *Dark Testament* revised and released irregularly in 1944, 1963, and in 1970, each drawing public attention. In today's America, republished through fellow poet Elizabeth Alexander's ministrations, it is leaping again into action for a new generation of politically engaged, trans readers.

A Timely Villon

To consider Villon ballads becoming timely is to promote a dynamic sense of the 1460s poetry that never stops moving in time. Far from texts and performances existing outside of or limited to one era, a timeless tradition, it promises instead a resurgent existence whose poetic form and medium are always subject to change. Far from a collection of anachronistic fiction, rediscovered every now and then, it represents a potential that can spark ingenious creation *in* time, once again, in many places. The ballads composed in French during the 1460s; Bob Dylan's protest song "The Times They are a-Changin," with its "bangs of François Villon echoing / through his mad streets"; or Du Cerceau's libertine Villon: all are autonomous poetic creations.[68] Each one, in its own time, makes history. It does so through the knowledge it bears. The accumulating Villon personae of Rabelais or Ryūnosuke explain the leaps the poetry makes that are particular to their times and places. Of all this personal poetry, the "Ballad of the Hanged Men" is arguably the most recognizable today because it becomes timely in many such situations.

It is the idea of the mortal and personal Villon expressed so vividly that provokes a spectrum of fiction-making. In Brecht's rhythms, the demand for more equal ways to live on rings for audiences. In Murray's ballads, that idea is expressed through the circumstances of violent dying. This is how Villon's personal poetry exists: a time-released invention, with no set expiration date, moveable parts, transmittable across geopolitical zones, cultures, media, and languages. The first poetry is encompassed—in the moment—with its latter-day, latest creations. Villon now, here, is composed of them all. That is why Villon offers a paradigm for the prochrony of fiction.

Freeman Vines made this paradigm material in North Carolina. This blues musician who makes his instruments in an African American tradition builds his "hanging tree" guitars out of found materials, including wood from a tree where a local man was lynched (Figure 17).[69] What inventors compose out of the experiences of their own time and place—no matter how destructive—is a potent means of projecting their embodied knowledge to others still to come.

Figure 17. Freeman Vines, ***Skull Guitar***, c. 2020. Raleigh, Gregg Musuem of Art + Design. North Carolina State University. By permission of the Freeman Vines Collection Trust. Photograph © Timothy Duffy.

Entry 4

Dependence: The Mystery Play

**MARCADÉ AND CO.,
JOLLIVET,
SARTRE,
BEAUVOIR,
BECKETT,
FANON,
FO,
AND
KOLTÈS**

In the first days of 1974, activist Dario Fo created *Mystery Bouffe* for the People's Theater in Paris.[1] The name he chose for his scripts in Italian resonates with the voices of many composing drama in various French idioms around 1450. So did Fo when he performed them solo; so did his troupe of actors, La Comune, when they, in turn, created these familiar scenes. Their acting combined the devotional characters with buffoons who burst into mystery plays with their antics. These dramatis personae ran a gamut: soldiers who squirm when faced with an order to massacre babies; street people who will do anything to stir your compassion, and empty your pocket. Fo and company made their *Mystery* so engaging that it took them off the stage, and out into communities: debating students at the new university campus of Vincennes, and factory workers on an assembly line in Besançon.[2] These actors reversed the steps that had institutionalized many of these scenes over some five hundred years. They brought this particular theatrical action back out into the public arena again to reach people who did not go to the theater.

In the 1450s, great numbers of people whom we will never identify had gathered to participate in a mystery play happening on Arras's town square.[3] Some improvised roles recognizable from biblical books; others took up those from farce. Still others, members of church parishes and workers' guilds, organized large-scale performances that attracted spectators from the environs. Over five holy days in the Christian calendar, they all came together to claim central spaces in their cities for enacting scenarios of cosmic time and human history, dubbed by Victor Turner, a generation ago, "social drama."[4]

This almanach entry takes up such dramas invented in Arras and composed again in Paris and Angers, among other cities on several continents, to investigate the singular power of these fictions in time. Such theatrical ones are quickened by live action. Dozens of actors lend their bodies to invent these scenarios collectively. What they enact—in the presence of other people—bears the force of ritual.

To investigate theatrical fictions, I concentrate this entry on the art of creating dramatis personae. Since the existing scripts relay meager elements of performance, they solicit our critical imagination; they challenge us to consider the physical, collective happenings that escape the record that survives. Four major personae are my focus: two religious, civic figures, and two others who epitomize the trying, and even laughable, conditions of human life.

Justice and Mercy, the first pair, are the type of figure that audiences associate with the mystery play. These virtues or principles appear in an abundant Christian literature, in a well-known biblical scene before a fatherly God (Figure 18).

Figure 18. Arnoul Gréban, *Le Mystère de la Passion*. The Trial concludes by sending Justice into communities. Paris, BnF, f. fr. 12536, fol. 2ter, detail, c. 1548. Photograph: Bibliothèque nationale de France.

Many mystery plays start with these personae debating the destiny of humans. This "Trial in Paradise" introduces the public to their heady arguments over which virtue should prevail. Justice versus Mercy enacts a question contested through the entire mystery play as it unfolds in the time of the Christian story, from the Israelites returning to Jerusalem, through the life, death, and resurrection of Jesus.

A Boy and a Blind Person present an equally prominent pair. With no religious or ethical character, they are rarely identified with the mystery play, yet they too typify its social drama. These are working men and women who struggle to get by. Soldiers, carpenters, prostitutes, cooks, and our pair, do so by serving others. In the absence of any principle, the Boy and the Blind Person distill the perennial power struggle that ensues. As soon as they appear, they start fighting; their spats revolve around their day-to-day efforts to carry on. These all-too-human figures bring the other-worldly ones of the mystery play down to earth and bring the effort to live justly and with compassion closer to almost every spectator. This pair was so popular that artists depicted them in high and low registers in later periods; the two figures were linked to beggars on the street, and even imagined as putti representing their predicament as a lifelong affair (Figure 19a and b).[5]

All four personae who give character to the mystery play are not only compatible, as Jody Enders and Noah Guynn, among others, confirm.[6] The moral figures are akin to the amoral ones who have long been typecast by tradition as the dregs of society—its laughingstock. Together they embody a conflict central to its social drama.

I look to Justice and Mercy enacted *with* the Boy and the Blind Person because they play out dependence in its full dialectics. What the figures in Paradise debate, dignifying a dependent human condition, those at ground level grapple with, blow by blow. The moral case on high involves a match-up that resists any neat resolution. It is put to the test down below in amoral, unfair play. This is a dilemma that people face in every community where this drama was enacted.

Dependence was an idea that intellectuals around 1400 were considering in its various aspects. For Nicole Oresme, whose thinking begins this almanach, translating Aristotle provided the initial framework: the *Ethics* poses the moral issue of people's happiness through their dependent relations.[7] The *Politics* and *Economics* consider dependence without any moral charge, and lead Oresme to examine its most extreme version personified by the serf.[8] His keywords, "servile" and "servitude," come to describe the condition of most people in this hierarchical society; they remain just as true for many in so-called egalitarian ones following the French Revolution, a baseline—and abiding concern—as philosopher Catherine Malabou underscores.[9]

Figure 19a. Jacques Callot, *Les Gueux ou mendiants; l'aveugle et son compagnon*. Etching. Paris, Musée du Louvre, L45 LR/694, c. 1622–23. © RMN-Grand Palais / Art Resource, NY. Photograph: Philippe Fuzeau.

Figure 19b. Unidentified vignette/emblem, c. 1500–1600. Paris, Bibliothèque Estienne. Author photograph.

These four characters will guide us through the social drama of dependence in the mystery play around 1450, embodying and enacting those who have to depend on others, those who live by serving. Their moral, political, and economic ordeals have much to tell us of the search for less unjust and more merciful lives. They do so through a remarkable prochrony. These fictional personae have a centuries-long history with an irregular rhythm. It implicates Molière and his company enacting his incorrigible valet, for example, or community associations in northern French cities around 1900, playing the "Creation of the World."[10] It brings us to another major episode several generations ago: these writers and actors inventing their own personae and scenarios would offer raw material to Fo and his Commune troupe for theirs. I turn to them because, once again, large numbers of people activated the protean social force of the mystery play to create dramas in a matrix far different from its first ones.

This generation during the 1940s and 1950s faced severe threats of servile living; confronted first by Nazi occupation, they witnessed a French Republic eviscerated by its homegrown fascist regime. An unlikely group of writers responded in a surprising way by creating mystery plays, and experimenting with their own mix of moral and political communal action.[11] Simone Jollivet, an actor-dramatist little recognized today, initiated Jean-Paul Sartre into these scripts and characters at Charles Dullin's theater, inspiring him to write plays.[12] The other Simone, philosopher-writer de Beauvoir, took a related creative step: she composed what would be her only drama.[13] Samuel Beckett, a multilingual writer, already knew these fictions from Irish theater in dialogue with the French; his fragmentary scripts in the line of his tragicomic Godot are an outstanding tribute to the Boy and the Blind Person.[14] More unlikely still are two major writers—one, Fo's contemporary, and the other, closer to us. Frantz Fanon, best known for his political and psychiatric work in the 1950s, began his writing in a theatrical mode.[15] His revolutionary critique of the social repression of Blacks and Arabs, French citizens living outside metropolitan France, took its first form through dramatis personae. Bernard-Marie Koltès, the other writer, ignited the theater milieu in the 1980s with his iconoclastic creation shaped by this comic duo.[16] His scripts configured their struggles to expose a status quo that is gender-repressive as well.

By investigating this chapter in theater history, I foreground fictions of creators who understand how reckoning with dependence was activated through both abstract, symbolic personae and roguish invalids. This entry explores myriad different ways these various creators transform these characters in their ongoing dialectic. They reset the time of the mystery play by enlisting these personae in battles over sociopolitical tyrannies that gripped them and their publics.

The Trials of Justice and Mercy

ARRAS 1430, PARIS 1452, VALENCIENNES 1480, MONS 1548

We go first to Arras—a commercial crossroads and significant crucible for theatrical culture. Its people who committed to mounting a mystery play almost every year, pioneered the Trial in Paradise scene.[17] In a region where city burghers were militating for political autonomy from powerful Burgundian nobles, French kings, and Flemish counts, where working people rose up in insurrection, their productions were more than a religious practice organized with Christian clerics.[18] They were a seedbed of civic ideas for their many communities. Performing their mystery plays over years fed experiments in imagining and adjudicating civil conflict in more balanced and clement ways.

On Arras's main square, around 1450, the people working with the script of lawyer-cleric Eustache Marcadé usher in the characters Justice and Mercy straightaway.[19] Many of the players and their audiences recognized these figures from a widely recited psalm that joins them with Truth and Peace.

> Kindness and truth have met; righteousness and peace have kissed.
> Truth will sprout from the earth, and righteousness will peer from heaven.
>
> [Misericordia et veritas obviaverunt sibi; iustitia et pax osculatae sunt
> Veritas de terra orta est et iustitia de caelo prospexit.]
> (PSALM 84: 11–13)

For Christians, the debate among the four characters echoed what they had heard in their parish churches. For Jewish townspeople, Justice's words were shot through with commentaries of Talmudic scholar Rashi and his rabbinical school renowned in the region.[20]

The script gives us a playbill for a particular theatrical production, as Laura Wiegert demonstrates with clear-sighted analysis.[21]

In this earliest surviving mystery play in French, artists portray Justice armed with her sword to cut to the quick of transgressions, and Mercy, bearing her book, who extends her olive branch to seek pardon. They face off in vigorous debate. Both are wearing the dress of the day: Justice in her courtly gown and Mercy in modest clothing.[22] To the public, these principled, biblical figures are also city women whom they would see in their midst.

Marcadé and the actors cast their debate as a moral reckoning with unruly people who do wrong. Mercy, lamenting over the five-thousand-year exile of humans as the Bible's first books recount it, calls for humane understanding. "While I must wait, I will do all that I can with my father, I'll find a way to lift humans out of their misery."[23] Justice counters with absolute force: there is no end to the punishment of people who have transgressed. Writers, artists, and actors dramatize the fundamental opposition between a human need for compassion and the necessity to judge their wrongdoing. What many see today as the legal operation of plea-bargaining, Marcadé and company regard as a moral impasse: Justice metes out her sentence, while Mercy accommodates human failing by calling for compassion in the Christian language of redemption. While Marcadé's script gives prominence to the moral virtues around Mercy, it cannot foreclose the debate. It is Wisdom or Sapience embodying the utmost knowledge who emerges; framed in scarlet, this highest of human authorities delivers the final, divine sentence to Mercy, with her olive sprig offered, and Justice with her sword laid down (Figure 20).

How did people enacting this Trial speak to those assembled in Arras? The actors creating Justice, Mercy, and company in this opening scene do more than prepare the audience for the biblical scenario of Jesus dying before them that is to come. They humanize principles that condition the lives of the play's participants. Their theatrical action bodies forth what women and men were reckoning with in their town. In the final scene of Wisdom's judgment, they also hear another persona, Truth, the usual ally of Justice, who pleads to release them from servitude: "the king of heaven . . . wished him [Jesus] to become human and die in this way in the world to buy back humankind whose sin had placed them in servitude."[24] The Arras public were party to the moral arguments of Justice and Mercy over their liberation from a servile life. It is worthwhile imagining critically whether the townspeople understood this debate cast in a Christian language to speak to their social condition as well: personifying this call to end servitude in their midst could register as a political act.

This social drama was work in progress over many generations. In the four scripts of the Trial that survive, various writers invented complex mystery plays that alter the balance between Justice and Mercy. Since actors animated the Trial more frequently in the public, civic space of urban communities, the scales tip more often toward Justice.

Figure 20. Eustache Marcadé, *Le Mystère d'Arras*, Wisdom Rendering Judgment in the Trial in Paradise. Arras, BM 625 (697), fol. 13v, detail, c. 1450–80. Photograph: Bibliothèque municipale d'Arras.

The later script attributed to Arnoul Gréban, master of theology in Paris, drew on the prestige and resources of the capital of the French kingdom to enact more powerful moral personae.[25] In "The Beginning and Creation of the World," the opening of the splendid mise-en-scène in 1452, Justice gains a stronger juridical appearance. She's a prosecutor making a case: "listen well to my arguments. I'll conclude with actual laws and demonstrable reasons."[26] Peace, who regains her place in the debate, advocates for "delivering humankind from servitude" and their freer action.[27] Truth takes her place alongside Peace to argue for a more livable future for humans: releasing them from a servile life becomes a "civil cause," a matter of equity.

Several generations working subsequently with Gréban's script create a new character who intensifies this tension between Justice and Mercy. Humankind/Humain Lignaige appears before the Trial begins and approaches the otherworldly figures once they start debating. Their physical connection is close throughout the play since Humankind never leaves the stage. The actors performing this script around 1500 made this persona even more prominent.[28] Humankind, moving nearer to Paradise, heightens the moral debate over the future: will the persona be judged justly or treated with mercy, liberated from servitude or not? This "strange" figure standing in for humans fleshes out their quandary for the public to whom it belongs as well.

For this mise-en-scène in Mons, one of the chief cities in the Burgundian state, the dramaturg gave the role of Humankind to the permanent representative of the city elders.[29] Leure Bultet, who was well known to the spectators, brought the social drama home to them; he enacted their struggle over the values that would prevail, and expressed a common desire to break free from servile living.

Across its changing casts and scripts over decades, the Trial in Paradise points to townspeople taking greater charge of these productions. Clerics continued to ensure the theological purpose and religious function of this scene. Yet actors who personified Justice and Mercy, and their competing deliberations over Humankind's future, were working to make a scenario for their fellow citizens. This was a developing municipal social drama. In Arras, Paris, and Mons, all these various enactments were bringing the moral question of shaping fair and merciful lives to the heart of their civic cultures. Embodied, written, painted—often with gold leaf—the scenario engaged many groups in creating a theatrical fiction that renegotiates the balance between the principles of Justice and Mercy again and again.

In Valenciennes, when these actor-citizens of various ranks enacted the Trial in Paradise scene, they also spoke to the ordinary disputes between people, the sort of causes appearing in the regional law courts of the period.[30] Their staging of the mystery in 1457 has Justice coming down to earth, and the Trial plays out simultaneously over several scenes where royal authority and common law were at stake. This collective theatrical work was shifting the locus for testing these moral principles. Actors were creating a face-off between Justice and Mercy that was also being recast for a secular, political scene, one reinforced by these personae sculpted on the façades of buildings that the public passed by day in, day out.[31] The theatrical art in this commune addressed the people's welfare—how working communities respond to the search for more just and merciful and less servile lives.[32]

Valenciennes, another urban community in the Burgundian state, was home to writers who extended the political character of these personae. Jean Molinet, whose prognostications we have considered, experimented with all kinds of fictional forms in his work for the court.[33] Around 1480, he creates another Justice, giving her a leading voice in his *Resource for the common people*.[34] Molinet introduces her through Truth, who exposes "the miserable violence oppressing Justice."[35] He places his persona side by side with People, a character akin to the mystery play's Humankind, with a stronger political voice.[36] Both characters are in a disfigured state. Molinet invents his People and Justice when the dynastic warfare between the rival French and Burgundian states reached a paroxysm: Valenciennes on the brink of siege from without, and its communities fractured by popular revolt within.

Molinet's public encounters a Justice beset by Tyranny and pleading for women and men.[37]

> I am Justice deprived of solace,
> Oh
> alas!
> By false tyranny,
> For I've lost—through war and debate,
> Beaten down . . .
> I'm completely stripped
> Of people and my household . . .
>
> Daughter of God, very wise young woman,
> Handmaid,
> And the one
> In whom faith confides,
> Who purifies malice
> Who rectifies misdeeds
> Who pacifies wars

When I am valiant
Who sanctifies the laws
Who honors the good with pearls
And finds justice for hearts
In the scales. . . .

[Justice suis, privee de solas,
Ez las
helas!
De fausse tirannie,
Car j'ai perdu, par guerres et debas,
Esbas . . .
Je suis fort desgarnie
De gens et de maisnie . . .

Fille de Dieu, tres sage jovencelle,
Ancelle,
Et celle
En qui foy se confie,
Qui les maulx purifie
Qui torfais rectifie
Qui guerre pacifie
Quant j'ay vaillance
Qui les loix saintifie
Qui les bons perlifie
Qui les cœurs justifie.
A la balance. . . .] (LVIII)

In this dramatic monologue, the voice of the Trial's intransigent debater echoes. The persona recounts her moral virtue, her civic sway. She even shows her weighing scales and militant prowess that affiliate her with Roman law. Here, by contrast, she is in dire straits. Molinet's art gives her a full lament:

I'm stretched out in a bed of discomfort,
My strong
Comfort
Leaves me perishing.
I barely exist—for my hope is dead.
Death gnaws at me
And I am diminishing,

I'm diminished, languishing
I languish, wailing
I wail, crying . . .
Ladies of the court, who enjoy a good time
Come,
Turn
Your pity toward me, face me,
And you, darlings, who sing and dance
Think,
Look
At the misfortune that is erasing me . . .

[Je suis couchee ou lit de desconfort,
Mon fort
Confort
Me laisse perissant,
Je vis envis, car mon espoir est mort
La mort
me mord
Et suis amenrissant
J'amenris languissant
Je languis gemissant
Je gemis en plourant . . .
Dames de court, qui le bon temps menez
Venez,
Tournez
Pitie devant ma face.
Et vous, mignons, qui chantez et dansez
Pensez
Visez
Au mischief qui m'efface . . .] (LIX)

This poignant persona has the voice of a tragedian that draws us in through Molinet's cadences and rhymes. Not only has this Justice lost her characteristic rigor, she is abused by the court she oversees. She is no longer able to maintain laws and rid society of wrongdoing. A much reduced persona bemoaning her state calls for pity: Justice *becomes* Mercy. In Molinet's scene, she demands compassion on behalf of the largest and most underrepresented group of people. Instead of her fellow debaters in the Paradise scene of mystery plays, she addresses women in Burgundian circles, challenging them to take up her just cause.

In a brilliant improvisation, Molinet secularizes that debate fully to direct its force toward the different goal of advocating for a working population confronted with constant deprivations. This hybrid figure of Justice speaks to the trials of day-to-day living. She offers succor to the public through the People: a political persona who is the forerunner of one representing a Republic. By the same act, she condemns the tyrannical rule of Valenciennes's nobles.[38] Molinet's *Resource* rallies the community in extreme penury; the writer works to make his town more responsive to more of its people.

This struggle over Justice was also played out in a sardonic mode. The predominant figure of virtue and principle who is politicized increasingly was paired with a persona we associate more with our amoral pair of ordinary people. Justice confronted by a fool is a scene that has generated improvisation as prodigious as that of the Trial in Paradise. The first, famous version of this fiction, created around 1494 by lawyer-writer Sebastian Brant, and Albrecht Dürer's atelier of artists, radicalized the struggle, with the so-called lowlife persona duping the high-minded one.[39] Pierre Rivière created his *Ship of Fools* for French speakers in a region near the heartlands of the mystery play.[40] The Justice he depicts is failing; she appears as demoralized as any figure Brant and Molinet had represented.

This Justice facing this Fool brings the moral and amoral figures from the mystery play together in one scene that catches Justice in a double bind (Figure 21). Once the Fool is in the picture, blindfolding her, Justice is shown to be corruptible. Any notion of her blindness as proof of her impartiality that lawyers defend today is upended.[41] Justice was already subject to ridicule in morality plays in French, as Estelle Doudet points out; writers were mocking her supposed equitable judgment.[42] For French- and German-speaking communities who knew the *Ship of Fools* and the Trial in Paradise, this was unnerving; for some few foolhardy, it was worth a nervous laugh. The scene extends a critique of the law courts in towns like the one we glimpse outside the window, where people are beset by fraud, and tomfoolery compromises Justice.

Brant and Rivière's scene cuts to the quick of the social drama that generations cultivated across northern European towns. Writers, actors, and their publics were exploring various states of dependence in this and multiple scenes. They were personifying an ethical challenge through theatrical fiction: how to live justly and mercifully with others. Their work was a political affair, too, that kept changing character. Since power becomes unjust and merciless, as Molinet had represented for Valenciennes, and Rivière had shown, servile living is a perennial danger.

Figure 21. Sebastien Brant, *La Nef des Folz du monde*, trans. Pierre Rivière, Dresden, SLUB, INK 4114.2, fol. 63, c. 1498. Photograph: Sächsische Landesbibliothek und Universitätsbibliothek.

The Travails of Poor Guys

ARRAS 1270 AND 1430, ANGERS 1456, SEURRE 1496

To pursue the dialectics of a dependent condition, I turn now to a second major pair of dramatis personae in the mystery play.

The Boy and the Blind Person, also first sighted in Arras, epitomize the consequences of a servile condition.[43] These characters who typify fundamental human relations keep changing shape, their traits shifting over centuries in several scripts. What remains constant through their play: the interminable combat over dependence on others that is their raison d'être.

This duo gives spunk and sweat to the abstract ideals and talking heads of Justice and company. They turn the trial of virtues and principles meant to resolve human iniquities and liberate people from servitude into the travails that ordinary people face in everyday life. Their struggle—who serves whom?—reveals the crucial role of the Boy and the Blind Person. Through these personae, writers and actors develop one sociopolitical promise of the mystery play: *inter*dependence.

We meet this pair in a situation that is systematically unfair: they start out life as invalids—in a physical sense as well as in a social one. Today we recognize two disabled characters whom Julie Singer interprets lucidly.[44] Around 1270, they were considered unfit and unlucky. Unable to see and climb society's ladder, these personae are stigmatized. The Blind Person meets the Boy, whose shape changes easily into another unfortunate, a Lame Person. Together they represent a significant character type who elicits insults without any just cause or mercy.[45] One of them, more trusting—or more gullible—takes them on the chin. The other, true to character, mimics this downgrading, calling himself in the first script we have of their antics, "a poor guy"—*un pauvre triquemers*.[46] They are left to play those who scratch out an existence in towns and countryside. Numerous writers and actors created multiple profiles of these struggling personae who offer a counterpoint to Justice and Mercy.

The first version of *The Boy and the Blind Person*, like the Trial, comes down to us in one script, from around 1270. It presents a degree-zero of dramatic action: these two hapless personae at a crossroads. One needs guidance to see where he's going, the other, with no social advantages, needs a job. Joining forces out of necessity, they settle on a basic arrangement: "you'll beg, I'll sing, and we'll have enough money and bread."[47] The Boy turns out to be the opposite of the reliable servant or valet he claims to be. After robbing his partner and beating him up, he justifies his actions as he takes off: "Sir, didn't I settle up well with the blindman, who doesn't have money or a coat too?" he gloats to the public.[48] Left to their own devices, these two characters behave without mercy. They mete out a crude type of justice attributed to so-called lowlife.

Since there is no surviving account of what this involved for actor or audience at the time, our critical imagination is solicited once more. It is not difficult to see how this script takes us right to the edge of our ideals. Let's face it, the personae tell us, your efforts to make life a little more fair, more merciful, and a bit more equal, may well blow up in your face. The anonymous creator of this *Boy and the Blind Person* responds to the Trial in Paradise with a caustic scene that leaves little room for illusion.

When this pair appears for the first time in the mystery play from Arras, many years later, they no longer appear hard-bitten.[49] Once the writer Marcadé brings them into the story of Jesus's life, this character trait changes to respond to the drama's moral purpose. Their one testy exchange gives way to an uplifting outcome. Marcadé "saves" the Blind Person through a miracle script that restores their sight (Figure 22). The artists who created images for the playbill accentuate the cure. The Blind Person is depicted doubly infirm—lame as well—while the Boy, characterized again as a valet, is doing double service by carrying others who also need help. All of them appear healed by Jesus's touch. These miraculous acts override the merciless core of *The Boy and the Blind Person* script.

Marcadé, artists and actors still retain a sense of ideals. The Blind Person emerges as their principal poor guy, who is treated with mercy and receives some modicum of justice—an exemplary figure in the clerical alphabet of storytelling at the time.[50] This person is able now, at last, to see what life entails. Their play creates a fiction of divine intervention to address an otherwise unjust and pitiless situation. A theatrical god, a deus ex machina, ensures that this happens.

Arras's communities give us the two versions of *The Boy and the Blind Person*: one enacting merciless human action in a single sketch, and the other, softer one in a mystery play scenario. Together they dramatize the tension over having to depend on others and acquiescing to servile lives. The comic faultline separating them makes each one distinctive. Whether their creators imagine a miraculous act for the Boy and the Blind Person, or a hard-bitten one instead, their characters sharpen the differences between these types of dependent relations.

André de la Vigne, a prolific writer who was Molinet's contemporary, keeps the dialectics of dependence in play.[51] His two personae embody both the desire to believe in justice and mercy changing their lives, as Noah Guynn demonstrates, as well as a more opportunistic view.[52] Their protracted struggle becomes

Figure 22. **Eustache Marcadé, *Le Mystère d'Arras*, Arras, BM 625 (697), fol. 108, detail. Photograph: Bibliothèque municipale d'Arras.**

ludicrous. La Vigne's Boy, who is lame, is carried by the Blind Person. Every audience sees the contentious imbalance between the two right away. The Lame Person blocks all talk of marvelous outcomes. This character literally on top leads them both to voice contradictory wishes. "I don't want to walk straight." proclaims the Lame Person. "I'd prefer that great misfortune be my lot than someone restore my sight."[53] La Vigne gives voice to the desire to stay a physical invalid and play on people's sympathies. This perverse wish is a type of opportunism that offers a way out of the travails of life. It appears even to validate their servile circumstances since remaining a down-and-out beggar can yield more money and better food than working under someone else. It's an act that appears to win out, as the pair heads for a tavern—the permanent address of fools.

André de la Vigne's script that entertains people's contrary behavior creates an edgy comedy of sorts. On the one hand, the Blind Person is cured despite running away from Saint Martin. His ultimate place is on the side of the fault line where miracles can happen, not by desire, but by (mis)fortune. On the other, the Lame Person is also healed in spite of himself, and his resistance to divine intervention. In the absence of values governing his day-to-day existence, he carries on with his playacting: "I'll be the person who does the desperate number . . . I'll say . . . look, this poor guy is tormented by great extortion, you see how!"[54]

The actors embodying the Lame Person and the Blind Person become *gagsters*. One actor wields his cane as a slapstick, blow after blow. The other actor times his resisting assault—and his surrender—just right. It's a comic tour de force that itinerant commedia dell' arte troupes and Molière's players would make their own a few hundred years later.[55]

For La Vigne's actors and their public, such comedy confronts the social risks of servile living: it meets this negative dependence with insurrectional verve that is audible in the witty rhyme of both characters complaining:

THE BLIND PERSON
My poverty will be complete
If I don't find a servant in a short time.

THE LAME PERSON
Misfortune has followed me so much
That I'm having to serve her.

[AVEUGLE
Ma pauvreté est assouvie
S'en brief temps ne treuve ung servant.

BOITEUX
Maleurté m'a si fort suyvye
Qu'a elle je suis asservant.][56]

The clownish feistiness of these characters is a first response to their situation of having to serve others. La Vigne lays bare the contradictions inherent in a life of involuntary service.

These two struggling characters at loggerheads dramatize Oresme's political commentary on service and servitude.[57] Both are dealing with what their physical misfortunes necessitate. Here is one unjust reason, according to Oresme, why a human is forced to become a serf, serving another.[58] It's La Vigne's Lame Person who epitomizes the response to such an unjust circumstance when he has little choice but to work under a blind master. For the first public of La Vigne's play in

Seurre, Burgundy, around 1496, his outcry would have resonated for some; the strategy of appearing to serve the master so as to reverse his superior position and ride on top of him was likely familiar.

La Vigne brings us to the opposite end of the moral spectrum of the mystery play. We are at a far remove, too, from the idea of service as a defining sociopolitical relation that Jacques Dalarun analyzes in Franciscan thought.[59] In these theatrical fictions, any chance that the misfortune—and combat—of such characters could be alleviated miraculously comes invariably with more merciless slapstick. As for the alternative, getting out of a servile situation by playacting, it offers some comic relief, but no certain act of liberation. La Vigne's dramatis personae place the social drama of those two poor guys in the arena of social justice for all. It is hard fought.

The drama of this duo's struggle over who serves whom was also developed in economic terms. A generation earlier, in Angers, in 1456, writers and actors unknown to us mounted an elaborate *Mystery of the Resurrection* and created characters wrangling over a fair salary.[60] This time, the Blind Person and his Valet attempt working together in a way that has more to do with making a living than surviving. Their social predicament takes precedence over their physical disabilities. In this situation, they argue over a plan to sell written copies of the songs they sing after their act. The Blind Person is concerned with the servant's skills, his literacy, while the Valet, Saudret, is focused on his service. The drama of the two personae develops, this time, over establishing an equal and fair commercial exchange. For a brief moment, both parties are satisfied: "I'm thrilled with this marketing," the Blind Person crows. "You've bartered well," Saudret says, "to take care of such an affair because, let me assure you, I'm well suited to leading you."[61]

This type of economic justice is short-lived; the face-off between the personae that ensues comes to a new breaking point; who stands to profit? A third character who enters the fray, a buyer, complicates their commercial relations. "It certainly suits me to buy your song, to carry several copies with me, and to sell them again," the persona tells us.[62] This Messenger goes on to hawk what he's bought and make his own cut. The trio of personae extends the familiar contentious scenario, transforming it through a scene of proto-capitalist activity. Their songs turn into commodities, and the written copies into capital to be controlled. They enact the struggle over inalienable labor. With it comes the demand for a just wage:

SAUDRET
You have enough to pay
'Cuz you've received
big money, as you know

That comes from my industry.
I defy your mastery
If I'm not paid at least for
The labor that comes from my hands.

BLIND PERSON
Listen Saudret . . .

SAUDRET
Ha! What a marketer!
You don't believe in God or man
I'll get paid, that's the sum of it.

[SAUDRET
Vous avez bien a quoy payer
Car icy recëu avez
Grant argent comme vous savez
Qui vient de mon industrie.
Je dy fi de vostre maistrie
Se je ne suy payé au mains
Du labeur qui vient de mes mains.

CECUS
Enten Saudret . . .

SAUDRET
Hau! Quel marchant!
Vous ne croyez ne Dieu ne homme !
Je seray payé C'est la somme.][63]

The showdown between the pair of characters combines two fights: one over the value of what Saudret makes, another over the future profit margin of the commodity bought and resold. The Valet turned worker protesting the Blind Person turned marketer dramatizes what happens when people monetize their relations. This duo reminds audiences that this social drama is played out between people on the bottom rung of the social ladder: those with no choice but to serve the higher echelons in French or Burgundian realms. They enact a challenge to their dependent condition as physical invalids with no valid social means. At play: devising political and economic relations that are fairer.

At this moment of fundamental power struggle, fiction enters in. The ancient technique of one dramatis persona creating another before us enables the Valet to create the character "Fictus" out of thin air. "Friend, come here. You seem like a good man."[64] The stunt involves ventriloquy, introducing a different voice that convinces the Blind Person there's a third person in their midst. Saudret with Fictus are an unbeatable new pair. Their slapstick shows how sheer wit can overcome anyone:

> BLIND PERSON
> Since I've cried for mercy
> And given in to you
> Without hardly waiting at all . . .
> I believe that should suffice for you. . . .
>
> SAUDRET
> Done! . . .
> You'll be promising clearly
> That I'll be able to pay for everything
> With what I make with my hands,
> No more no less,
> On all the money I'll gain . . .
> Even so, it'll be as if I could be
> The true lord of your wealth.
>
> [CECUS
> Puisque je t'ay mercy crié
> Et qu'à vous je me suis rendu
> Sans avoir guere actendu . . .
> Je croy qui te doit suffire.
>
> SAUDRET
> Faictes! . . .
> Vous prometrez expressement
> Que je m'en porray par mes mains
> Paier du tout
> Ne plus ne mains,
> Sur l'argent que je gagneray . . .
> Toutevoies comme se jestoye
> Vray seigneur de vostre monnoye.][65]

Transforming the conflict of the Boy vs. the Blind Person into one over political and economic autonomy marks another ingenious creation.[66] Both writer and actors deploy fiction, in a general sense, to arbitrate the conflict over who controls the purse strings. The persona Fictus, like Wisdom between Justice and Mercy, proves a crucial intermediary between these two poor guys.

It is worth dwelling for a moment on such fiction. The character, a figment of

Saudret's imagination used to deceive the Blind Person, has real effects. This fiction in action addresses the imbalance between the Blind Person and the Valet. It substantiates the idea of a servant's just worth. While the Valet is not liberated from servitude, this person is dignified in service. Here is an outstanding example of the artfulness of theatrical fiction that cultivates a particular knowledge. It experiments with social rapports that are more equitable and comprise a reciprocal dependence of one persona on another.

This sophisticated script that responds to economic and social injustices with comic, insurrectional energy brings all the actions of the characters into a mystery play of the Resurrection. It takes place after Jesus's Passion and Crucifixion, when people are left to sort out how to live when a Christian savior has come and gone; when people want miracles to happen. Its particular social drama enacts people's conflicted efforts to carry on in an unjust society. In a mystery play that does not include the Trial in Paradise, it falls to these all-too-human characters to play out their struggles to make living less servile, more just and merciful. This unidentified writer focuses inventiveness on those people in unfair and unequal circumstances acting to redress the balance.

Here the public encounters the most radical version of our amoral personae. In the streets of Angers, around 1456, the two poor guys are transformed into spokespersons for the serf, the most underrepresented class of worker of their time. The Boy in the first sketch, who responds to his servile situation through merciless action, becomes in this sketch a vociferous servant militating for his due. Both servant and master work against the servile conditions determining their livelihood.

In a final inventive twist, the Angers writer and actors link this struggle on all fronts to their own situation. Saudret, the literate servant, writes for a living. His outcry over a fair salary is an early sounding in a campaign for author's rights that Deborah McGrady has brought to the fore.[67] The invalid physique of the characters also makes them kindred. The line of authors who are blind or lame or marked by some other stigma is long, as Jacqueline Cerquiglini-Toulet demonstrates, including Jean Molinet who is fictionalized as another lame guy, among the so-called low life in Burgundy.[68] Saudret, the Valet, and the Blind Person exemplify the alliance between writer and militant worker. Their comic theatrical art enacts what Marxist thinkers and trade unionists would conceptualize many hundreds of years later: people militating for a just price for their labors.

Dependence/Interdependence

What happens when we consider the Boy and the Blind Person alongside Justice and Mercy? It brings into relief how creators of the mystery play developed a fundamental idea of dependence that is double-edged.

The Boy, or shall we say the Valet, and the Blind Person, or shall we say the Lame Master, are bound together through their strife over who serves whom. Physically, one cannot advance without the other. This pair enacts how people come to rely on one another because of their infirmities. Psychically, too, their destined position makes them dependent. Life demands dealing with their invalid condition in the sense of both weakness and inferiority. Yet their desires to assert themselves as political and economic agents are unquenchable. When the Blind Person says "we," we here recognize how the dialectic of dependence and service that they body forth looks impossible to resolve. The two characters personify an ongoing debate over a freer and more compassionate condition defining human relations. They bespeak a desire for a particular type of independence, too; as they make their lives, they have no need for other people who could debase them.

In the case of Justice and Mercy, keeping these virtues—and principles—in play together is crucial. While Catholic theology appears to judge in favor of Mercy through the interventions of Charity, the ongoing improvisations of the Trial scene counteract any such resolution. Wisdom, who remains a pivotal intermediary between the two vying characters, decrees some sort of balance between them. This tenuous equilibrium has much to do with their addressing the human condition of dependence. Mercy calls with Peace for relaxing the extreme form of servitude to counterbalance the stringent judgments of Justice with Truth. Yet Justice and Mercy prevail; this principal duo exemplifies *inter*dependence. Molinet's hybrid figure that melds them together reinforces their symbiotic state.

In Oresme's work on Aristotle's *Ethics*, the thinker takes up the positive aspects of dependence. It is a necessary relation linking two people or beings together, a condition of happy human lives that are an end in themselves.[69] Both the trials of Justice and Mercy and the travails of the Boy/Valet and the Blind Person/Lame Master reveal people bound indefinitely one to another. In their perennial efforts to break out of a negative and debilitating form of service and servitude, what remains is an affirming type of dependent rapport that puts the actions of people on a more equal footing.

Dependence is also crucial for the writer Albert Memmi, active during the 1970s; it involves a "constraining relation, more or less accepted, real or ideal, that satisfies a need."[70] Both a plus and a hindrance, it offers support to people all the while that it holds them back in various limiting conditions. Memmi's idea is the culmination of his lifelong thinking about human relations marked by antisemitic and racist attitudes, by the power dynamics too between colonists and those subjected to this unjust regime, all of which he experienced in Tunisia under French rule. He joins Frantz Fanon who wrote decisively against any facile association between living under colonial rule and an inevitable disabling and negative version of dependence.[71] In *Black Skin, White Masks*, Fanon makes his critique in psychological terms that are also theatrical, a point to which I shall return. In Memmi's case, his view of dependence is also the fruit of his physical experience becoming weak and an invalid. Memmi distills all his thinking about dependence, its positive and negative aspects, into two figures, lifelong adversaries and begrudging accomplices. They are, for him, "an agitated duo."[72] Memmi's pair give us a precise portrait of our Boy/Valet and Blind Person/Lame Master—their indispensable, conflicted dependence on one another.

It is the two pairs of fictional characters, moral and amoral, in the mystery play that cultivate—in miniature—this social drama in all its limits and contradictions: how to adjudicate the perennial injustices, how to confront and overcome servile circumstances. The writers, actors, artists, and townspeople faced with civil conflicts in Arras, Valenciennes, Paris, and Seurre pioneered an art of impersonation to test what is experimental knowledge about human dependence. By creating characters who depend on each other willy-nilly, they respond imaginatively—and viscerally—to those who contend daily with an arbitrary lot in life that is physically debilitating and socially degrading.

The Trials of Justice and the Travails of Poor Guys

PARIS 1940s, 1955, 1974, 1986

For further generations of writers and actors, beset by a plethora of repressive regimes, this theatrical fiction with its interdependent characters made sense. This view runs counter to the tenacious received idea that the mystery play's religious orthodoxies disqualified it from any ongoing experimentation. Those steeped in a French revolutionary tradition, and its anticlerical fervor, consigned it to an incorrigible past, seen as hierarchical in its cruel power. Many of its fictions, then, had to be rejected ideologically. Yet this same tradition cast political action in theatrical terms.[73] This received idea licensed another view: that creating fictions collectively was one way to express indignation and imagine alternatives to unjust relations imposed by force from without, or internalized poignantly within. In the case of the generation from the 1940s and 1950s, to whom I turn now, the mystery play was politically promising. Its theatrical fictions were, for them, part of combatting the authoritarian French state of Vichy, and fighting in the wars of liberation in its wake. Some writers responded to the disenfranchisement and tyranny through this form they knew well. Simone de Beauvoir, Jean-Paul Sartre, and Samuel Beckett, found its structures of trial and travail potent, once again, for pursuing a twofold question: how do people reckon with living in a violently unjust society? How to carry on without becoming servile?

Simone de Beauvoir's *Useless Mouths* was the first play from this group of writers to be enacted publicly. Set in 1400, in a town resembling Calais or Arras, it focuses on a bargain that people confront during wartime: to accept or refuse sacrificing something of yourself in the fight for the common good. That is, any individual action depends inevitably on other people.

Beauvoir's choice to transpose the moral quandary of her generation to a long-ago situation appears, at first, expedient. Numbers of writers chose to negotiate the double jeopardy of Vichy in that way. At the peak of the war, in 1943, Beauvoir had been working for Radio Vichy doing scripts steeped in farce and other festive forms typical of Arras drama around 1270; "A Medieval Fair" was part of this writing-for-a-living.[74] It also offered indirect, modest resistance to Vichy and Nazi oppression in theatrical form. *Useless Mouths* was an effort to experiment in stronger, intransigent ways; its dramatis personae exemplify how resisting proves demanding and poses the ultimatum of interacting justly with everyone.

At the play's center, we meet citizens in a town under siege. This age-old military scenario that still generates fictions during states of emergency was, around 1429, one political subject of mystery plays.[75] Beauvoir creates personae who challenge the town councilors over their merciless course of action toward the community. In her script that puts life in the balance, the councilors decree that all infirm people, women, children, and the elderly will be sacrificed to save the larger number. The powers that be impose this mandate on the sole basis of authority they attribute to themselves. As veteran freedom fighters who won autonomy for the town in the past, they claim a legitimate position to condemn some citizens for the hypothetical benefit of others. "It's not about you or about us. It's about our community and the future of the entire world."[76] The councilors become willing executioners; in choosing to obliterate individual humans, they disavow responsibility for securing justice for all.

Beauvoir reconfigures the symbolic moral figures from the mystery play; instead of Justice and Mercy, she creates individual female characters who voice these principles. They do not tolerate any travesty. While the men query whether it is the moment to be concerned about justice, the women act on it. They take charge of combatting this unequal, sectarian view of the common good and a self-serving, tyrannical notion of the community's future.[77]

For Sartre, the question of how to live in a violently unjust society had already led him to theatrical fiction. Such an intellectual and writer on the anticlerical left, who would seem allergic to the mystery play, turned to improvise one. During the first months of this war, under the shock of French defeat, he had composed *Bariona or Play of Pain and Hope* while imprisoned in Germany; he enacted it with fellow prisoners in 1940.[78]

Once back in Paris, he began working again at Charles Dullin's Théâtre de la Cité. He joined Simone Jollivet, an actress who was also his childhood friend, and together they taught theater history to the latest cohort of actors. In their seminars, they gave pride of place to the drama of mysteries in French, over and above the tragedies of Greece and the comedies of Rome. Sartre taught plays "born out of religion, the Christian religion, what it is, what it will become."[79] He was professing a historically minded view of drama already tested by leading theater people and propounded by medievalist Gustave Cohen during the 1930s.[80] It would take him many years before he would acknowledge his writing and acting in this so-called medieval vein, as if this were an aberration in the public, creative life of a Marxist intellectual. He did so at a time when he returned again to invent with this powerful theatrical form of fiction.

The Bet, as Sartre and his comrade Colette Audry imagined it, exists in a draft.[81] It, too, is structured as a trial over the future of humans. Justice vs. Mercy has faded away, but their debate, in an undetermined time and place, is keenly pursued. The symbolic personae of the mystery play mutate into legal actors who make their cases: the Defendant, the Accuser, and the Arbiter who supplants the mediator in the Trial scene, Wisdom. Sartre transposed the theological debate from Paradise in another mode of theatrical fiction. "I'd prefer telling you a story," the Defendant says to us. This scenario raises the curtain on a couple in a miserable state, when "all of a sudden: a thunderclap, a special fantastical effect in the style of medievalizing theater."[82] A supernatural, malevolent figure appears to take a place beside the other five personae who each were present in the performance space in Valenciennes 1480.

Sartre creates characters who bring to the fore the challenge of reckoning with weak human relations, alongside the extreme state of dependence and prospect of servitude, which open the earlier mystery play. What he had been thinking through in his philosophical writing *Being and Nothingness*, published under censorship in 1943, he configures for theatrical action.[83] The dramatis persona Sartre foregrounds, finally, is a profile of Humankind/Humain Lignaige who stands beside Justice and Mercy during many mises-en-scène of mystery plays in French-speaking towns around 1480. "Thanks to what he brings in his person, to his choice, and his sense of liberty, he makes what is an atrocious life metamorphose into one that is sublime."[84] Sartre invents a persona of Humain Lignaige for his wartime generation, a subject freer in his thought and action, if not in his political position and social condition. This profile, as John Ireland argues, suggests an autobiographical persona of sorts for the central role in the most familiar and celebrated mystery play.[85] Sartre reconfigures the Passion. He transforms its culminating act of self-sacrifice, which becomes, in the throes of war and its wake, a person's voluntary choice to serve others. Sartre transforms the culminating act of this mystery play in another powerful way: this persona liberates himself by making a choice to serve others. Sartre reconfigures the struggle over human bondage leading to a type of freedom of voluntary servitude that Étienne de la Boétie had envisaged.[86] His dramatis persona embodies a complete interdependence in choosing to live—and to risk dying—for the welfare of others.

Of all the writers in this wartime generation experimenting with the mystery play, it is Samuel Beckett who brings us to the limits of any moral sense. More playwright than philosopher, he conceives of his *Rough for Theater* as an endgame of sorts. "So it is not a dream. At last! Nor a vision. They are mute and I am mute before them. Poor wretch. Now I may go back. The mystery is over." ["Ce n'est pas donc un rêve. Enfin ! Une vision non plus. Elles sont muettes, et moi je suis muet devant elles. Pauvre. Je peux rentrer. Il n y a plus de mystère."][87] In the nowheresville Beckett imagines, there is no miraculous show-and-tell of Justice and Mercy. What's left: two poor guys, utterly dependent on one another as they carry on living in spite of themselves.

Bet, Bargain, and Deal

It's the amoral Blind and Lame duo who provide all these writers basic human matter for scripting the travail of making lives freer of servile relations. In response to a host of pressures brought to bear on people, they imagine the bruising negative experience of dependence, as well as the encouraging one of interdependence that comes with comic bursts.

Beauvoir creates characters who become beggars in their hometown. The siege of an entire town coupled with the famine it causes moves everyone into this extreme situation. Beauvoir radicalizes the danger of being condemned to servitude. Her characters address it head on: "No! No! it's too unjust. We shall not beg for their pity."[88] The more their confrontation with the town councilors escalates, the more they refuse to plead, the more their fellow citizens feel enslaved. Beauvoir gives her play a name that signals this impasse with sardonic irony. Their mouths are anything but useless because they alone express the uncompromising combat for freer lives in a just society. In her scenario, this struggle enacted by two infirm characters in the earliest mystery plays is refracted through several vociferous women—for whom the combat proves fatal.

Useless Mouths was staged at the socialist Théâtre des Carrefours after the liberation of Paris and the end of the war, at a time when the public understood at skin level the desperate situation of these characters.[89] They knew some of the terrible risks of not submitting to tyrannical Vichy and Nazi authorities—but not all. The program warned: "For if you start treating certain people as things, it's humankind who appears to be nothing more than a thing; justice and liberty denied with force alone in command."[90] Beauvoir's transposed mystery registered a small part of a momentous social drama over violent, merciless injustices in their own town: the deportation of tens of thousands of people.

Sartre's draft of a script does not give us any characters resembling the Blind Person and the Lame Person. By giving *The Bet* the form of a passion play, he privileges the quintessential Christian religious scene for his society. Nonetheless, he reconfigures it with Humankind, underscoring that this persona, like you and me, make choices. It is a life-affirming bargain. The absolute value Sartre gives to individual freedom or independence no doubt surpasses what actors body forth in the mystery play in Angers or Paris, around 1460. This is his iconoclastic way of scripting characters in solidarity with those invalidated during years of violent dehumanization.

What is absent is any mise-en-scène of Sartre's *Bet*. We're in the realm of the hypothetical here. If actors had convinced Sartre to enact these sketches that he had disavowed for years, would his transformed mystery play have engaged a public? It is hard to gauge the effect of the *Bet* script, published in Paris 1955, whether its version of the bargain of lives depending on others would have registered or not.

By contrast, Frantz Fanon took on the social drama of the mystery play directly through one of the poor guy characters. In his earliest writing, the militant Martinican psychiatrist confronted the social and moral issue of negative dependence. While studying medicine in the late 1940s, he drafted several plays in a milieu saturated with Sartre's dramas.[91] Fanon's first play, *The Drowning Eye*, adopts a fundamentally different approach to the question. He composes a psychodrama that casts a new situation for several combative characters who fight against a degrading and self-debasing existence with words and actions. Among them, Fanon personifies this struggle through a blind servant.[92] The script that survives is missing the blind servant's part. Fanon's fragmentary theater manuscripts ask us once more to use our critical imagination: how did Fanon's dramatis persona critique the dangers of a servile condition for Black and Arab French women and men? What his *Drowning Eye* would have created for the public in postwar Lyon where he was studying is difficult to ascertain. We do know Fanon's conviction about the servant persona's language. It articulates the struggle over a just, more independent, and expressive human existence: "take the words of the vagrant," he says, "and renew their teeth."[93]

It is the Blind Person next to the Lame Person who together spur Samuel Beckett on to his experimentation. During those postwar years, the duo represents, for him, as for the clerics around 1300, an ABC of theatricalizing the desperate human comedy of life in the wake of genocide.[94] In Beckett's minimalist style, he names his personae A and B. Those who recognize their prototypes from the mystery play fill in the letters in French: **A** standing in for Aveugle, Blind, and **B** for Boiteux, Lame (Figure 23). Several years after creating their kin in *Waiting for Godot*, Beckett was still distilling, in essence, the predicament of this hapless duo. In *Rough for Theater*, his A and B are survival artists. They tell us as much:

> A.—After all those hours in the darkness, you don't— . . .
> B.— . . . perhaps it's soup or baked beans.
>
> [A.—Après toutes ces heures d'obscurité, vous ne— . . .
> B.— . . . c'est peut-être du potage, ou des flageolets.][95]

Beckett's way of representing the necessary bargain of living together, again, is punctuating the sobering situation of his characters with comic outbursts. When it comes to the perennial risk of servile living amid power struggles, he entertains both sides.

Figure 23. Milo O'Shea (B) and David Kelly (A) in Samuel Beckett's *Rough for Theatre I*, dir. Kieron Walsh, in *Beckett on Film*, prod. Michael Colgan and Alan Moloney, 2002. Author photograph.

> B.—Wait, you're not going to do me a service for nothing? *[Pause.]* I mean unconditionally? *[Pause.]* Good God!
>
> [B.—Attendez, vous n'allez pas me rendre service pour rien? *(Un temps)* Je veux dire sans conditions. *(Un temps)* Mon Dieu!][96]

Rough for Theater equivocates between the kind of service that amounts to a charitable act and those unequal, unfair, and merciless relations that breed resentment, even hatred. Here are the two sides of dependence, one more nourishing and generous, the other a servile and hostile codependence. In Beckett's version in Paris, during the late 1950s, or in *The Boy and the Blind Person* sketch in Arras, 1270, writer, actors, and public play with our profound anxiety over autonomy. All of them kept on converting it into droll scenes that make us wince and, maybe, laugh a bit as well. A tough act of interdependence.

Comedy for the People and the Blind Injustice of Friends

PARIS 1974, 1986

Over the last generation, the two characters in the mystery play are matter again for playmakers to respond to the chief social injustices galvanizing their milieu. I come back to Dario Fo, with whom we began, because his work at the Popular Theater in Paris for the New Year, 1974, was operating explicitly within this tradition. More than any of the other writers, Beauvoir, Sartre, Fanon, or Beckett, Fo was drawing on both a script and a mode of action seen in Angers, 1456, and in his own environs of the Italian Lake District. In a particularly powerful prochrony, his acting was transforming the Blind Person and the Lame Person from the inside out to politicize a social drama that revolves around working people.

In his *Mystery Bouffe*, we meet characters who are not the expected, major biblical figures. Fo displaces Justice and Mercy and their Trial in Paradise to begin his play instead with minor figures from the Massacre of the Innocents scene at the beginning of the story of Jesus's life.[97] These are local characters who speak out against the injustice of killing babies. Fo creates mothers who block the violence with their bodies, as well as soldiers whose stomachs finally turn against the authorities requiring them to butcher the youngest. The final word is spoken by one of them in protest:

> The Mother.—Cruel pitiless God it's you who ordered this massacre . . . it's you who wanted this sacrifice in exchange for the coming of your son: a thousand kids whose throats are slit for one of yours . . . you could have kept him close to you, your son, if his coming had to cost us other poor people such a big sacrifice. . . .
>
> [La Mère.—Dieu cruel et sans pitié c'est toi qui as ordonné ce massacre. . . . c'est toi qui as voulu ce sacrifice en échange de la venue de ton fils : mille enfants égorgés pour un des tiens . . . tu pouvais bien le garder près de toi, ton fils, si sa venue devait nous coûter un si gros sacrifice, à nous autres pauvres bougres. . . .][98]

Fo focuses on ordinary people living through merciless events that erode any moral high ground: individual women and men facing an increasingly debased existence.

In this situation, Fo introduces the other duo of characters to unleash their *bouffe*—their wit—through their antics. His Blind Person and Lame Person, improvised from La Vigne's play, give full rein to their contradictory impulses and rebellious verve. "These two creatures now formed into one" are moving toward happiness when, faced with the possibility of a miraculous intervention and cure, they attempt to escape. Their argument over working conditions stops them in their tracks.

> The Lame.—"Start working, vagrant," they're going to yell at you, "it's down in the ship's hole for those arms that aren't working . . ." That's how you lose the big privilege of the salt tax we share with the rich and the bosses: they set up the law, and we exploit pity . . . one and the other cheating assholes!
>
> [Le Boiteux.—"Va travailler, vagabond" ils te crieront, "Aux galères les bras qui ne travaillent pas . . ." Et de cette façon on perdra le grand privilège du droit de gabelle que nous partageons avec les riches et les patrons: eux en arrangeant les lois, nous en exploitant la pitié; l'un et l'autre en truandant les couillons!][99]

Fo is irrepressible in unmasking exploitation and hypocrisy. The invalid pair he impersonates are wily protesters just as much as skeptics who contest any action that could be deemed servitude in the marketplace; their roles and characters are reconfigured to lambast well-intentioned democracies for their policies exploiting workers. Fo's Blind Person and Lame Person speak out for themselves again in the fight over labor practices.

Drawing on his militant activities on the communist left, Fo marshals their voices from different episodes in social history. He devises scenes for his characters as a provocation to the Italian class-based society he inhabited, where Catholic authority was often heavy-handed. The centuries-long theatrical form combining high and low offered him something liberating; Vladimir Mayakovsky had already tested it with his version of *Mystery Bouffe* during the heyday of the Russian Revolution.[100] Fo's dramatis persona is the latest political actor, appearing by turns as the People, Agitator, Ruffian, and Worker, marked by the various social movements and strikes of the 1960s.

Fo is the only inventor of mystery plays to perform solo. In numerous public venues, he synthesized all the dramatis personae into a single one. Impersonating this composite character, improvisation by improvisation, was his original formula for creating a compelling representative of people. His type of one-man show did more than travel. Whether Fo spoke his own dialect from the north of Italy, or mimicked Parisian French or American English, he worked to make his personae understandable to many different groups. This theatrical lingua franca that he created, known as *grammelot*, was another of his original strokes, one entirely in harmony with the multilingual energy of actors around 1300 and commedia dell'arte troupes. It typifies his political commitment to popular expression.[101] Fo champions the itinerant actor who moves to any place, and plays for any public, in a manner that institutions, including national theaters, can never contain.

In the months leading up to performing in the Paris theater, Fo was playing *Mystery Bouffe* with workers at the Lipp watch factory in Besançon, 1973. We find him bringing these transformed characters of the mystery play into social action for one of the largest popular mobilizations against a business in a capitalist economy.[102] Fo enacts this situation during the strike with truculent humor: people militating for more just, more autonomous conditions, facing off with their handicaps, and giving insurrectional verve to their efforts to get by. His composite character of the mystery play models interdependence and all it involves. Fo's theatrical activism would be recognized by the Nobel Committee with the Prize in Literature in 1997.[103]

A decade later, Bernard-Marie Koltès, a maverick spirit, appeared in Paris's theater milieu with characters who take us as far away as one can go from any drama resembling the mystery play. He pursued a kind of creative destruction of writing, intent on deconstructing any moral ambition of theatrical fiction.[104] The personae he invents are often down and out. His play *In the Solitude of Cotton Fields*, revolves around a Dealer and a Client.[105] His pair alchemizes something of the poor guys in an uncanny way. Through the situation of a commercial transaction, Koltès radicalizes the basic struggle for an autonomous existence in economic terms that writers and actors had been testing in Angers around 1456. Since everything is up for sale, bargaining is the lingua franca of everyday, and commerce is the only way of life that Dealer and Client can make for themselves.

Koltès zeroes in on what generates every deal: desire. Instead of trading in materials, as the Blind Person and the Lame Person do with handmade copies of their song in Angers's Resurrection play, Koltès's characters trade in the molten energy of what they want, moment to moment. Their contest is driven by attempts to satisfy their desires that, regardless of substance, mean sparring over superiority. There is no resolution here. On the contrary, the Dealer and the Client take turns in intensifying their ongoing struggle.

Koltès dramatizes the give and take of desire in personae who are far from individuals, with psychologies of their own. He creates character types in the guise of many composed around 1450: their social drama reveals the risks of desire that in the civic space can invalidate you as strongly as physical handicaps. Such risky desires pose challenges that are formidable because they are out of anyone's personal control. Koltès's duo of Dealer and Client battle the arbitrary lot that societies impose upon them: "If the true injustice of this world is that of the chance of a man's birth, of time and place," the Dealer warns, how to respond?[106]

Koltès focuses on such accidents of birth that condition our relations with others—and our elementary desires. In response to the unquestioned character of race in his French society, he cast the Dealer as Black and the Client as white.[107] He titles his play with words echoing Carson McCullers's "lonesome cotton fields," a scene that, in Georgia during the 1940s, she associated imaginatively with the struggles of people over their color.[108] Koltès too, in his own time and place, was characterizing those entrapped by the everyday bargaining of their desires through racialized and racist relations. Koltès shared an understanding with Fanon; they both unleashed an explosive language to recount that bargaining. From his vantage point in 1980s France, Koltès creates a theatrical situation to challenge his publics with a duo whose color-coded struggle against such injustices is violent.

Koltès also riveted attention on the chance of sex at birth imposed by his society, and all the sexualized consequences that followed. He was alive to the vagaries of feeling that made life a travail for anyone with desires outside heterosexual norms; his pair of personae have no gender fixed. The "solitude" enacted expresses what a gay person in Koltès's generation knew from the inside out since homosexuality, as it was designated at the time, was a criminal offense. This repressed spectrum of relations and desires was integral to the struggle between his Dealer and Client. It makes negative dependence visible and visceral to his audiences.

Above all, Koltès understood, in the vein of Fanon, that the greatest challenges for those deemed invalid are self-induced. This internal tension intensifies the social drama as it was personified by the first duo we met in Arras. In a French society that claims all its citizens are free, yet denies the pressures that push some to debase themselves, Koltès brings out just how unlikely it is that these characters can come together. The act of interdependence is, for him, exquisitely rare.

In the end, the Client pitches an improbable proposal:

> THE CLIENT
> Let's be equals. Equality of pride, equality of impotence, equally disarmed, suffering equally from some cold and some heat.
>
> [LE CLIENT
> Soyons égaux, à égalité d'orgueil, à égalité d'impuissance, également désarmés, souffrant également du froid et du chaud.][109]

It's a double-edged bargain: "let's be two zeros, perfectly round, impenetrable zeros."[110] Koltès's personae continue to fight on ground they can make equal at the lowest level. At degree zero, they can appear to become codependents again in a negative, psychological sense. Or, in this open-ended situation, they can become positively interdependent.

Koltès creates their dilemma in a comic mode. He makes this clear by resisting directors' attempts to create absurd or tragic characters. In the theatrical mode he favors, internalizing a servile role is never a done deal. The chance of fraternity between the two is ever present; this is what the Dealer proposes with ironic zest, "the blind injustice of the friend."[111] Whether the Client brings desire for such friendship to his relation with the Dealer in the next round, or a weapon, is unclear. Your guess is as good as mine. This unpredictable game can veer from supreme feelings of elation to a nadir. That's why director Patrice Chéreau, who created the first mise-en-scène of this script with Koltès, called it the work of a "joyous desperado."[112]

In the Solitude of Cotton Fields suggests an unlikely rapport with the mystery play, and its social drama. Throughout his creative life, Koltès made allusions to this theater. It was a form he knew well in his hometown of Metz, a heartland of mystery plays during the 1460s, as in his Catholic family's circles during the 1960s.[113] Through his travels in the Americas, he detected versions of it, especially in the Brazilian culture of *capoeira*, which he discovered.[114] All the while that Koltès rejected any moral claim of theatrical action, and lambasted the destructive hypocrisies of religion, his *Solitude* recoups something of two dramatis personae from the mystery play. He updates them for the social drama of his generation over race, gender, and sexuality. His duo offers brilliant witness to the shape-changing creative force of the Boy and the Blind Person.

✳

In the present times and places that this almanach marks, there are signs of these theatrical fictions around dependence.

Koltès is back in force on French stages, as political life has reached a contentious impasse, and denunciations of all manner of injustices are shrill. Beckett's fragment of a play experimenting with the remains of the mystery play registers again with English-speaking actors. During the pandemic confinement in 2020, Bill Irwin took to *Rough*.[115] This theatrical piece responded to the anxiety over our utter dependence that was running very high, as humor was running low. Irwin's acting took a new turn when he performed it solo, online, creating a fiction that was no longer distinguished by actor and public physically present in a shared space, yet still animated by the wish to be together. An occasion for both acts of dependence. During a time when people were also taking to the streets in large numbers to call for justice for Nahel Merzouk and Adama Traouré killed in Paris and George Floyd in Minneapolis, the power of theatrical fiction in its many transmuted forms was palpable.[116]

2001 1200 1900 c.1475 1938

Entry 5

Living Together in the Animal World: Graphic Narrative in Ivory

INUIT AND FRENCH-SPEAKING REALMS

Alongside hundreds of fictions composed in words, and inscribed in manuscripts, there are hundreds more made with ivory. Such artifacts are palm-sized or long and curved; some are figurines, others are shaped as small books with two leaves. Hewn from tusks of animals from various climates, many are incised with the finesse that working on a small scale requires. Scores of unidentifiable people working in ateliers across the European continent took to this material coming from elsewhere to shape and engrave stories for their own cultures.[1] So did many others in regions where ivory was plentiful, in northern climates, and around the Mediterranean. In sheer numbers of artifacts and creators involved, these graphics in ivory rank as a major form.

Such an object makes a stunning first appearance in fiction in French around 1100. *The Song of Roland*, recounting the last stand of the emperor Charlemagne's forces against the so-called Saracens, or Muslims, highlights the ivory horn of his chief warrior. In search of support, the count blows it "with difficulty, suffering, and great pain."[2] Roland's "olifant," composed in words, resonates with no small irony. This horn is a cardinal artifact of Islamic artistic traditions, its ivory engraved with ornate flora and fauna. Painters Jean Fouquet and Simon Marmion, following poets of the epic fiction, depict Roland, inseparable from his horn; several hundred years later, they make it a focal point of the story of Roland's death for the history of the French kingdom.[3] Their warrior who personifies heroism in French-speaking realms expresses his struggle against Muslim forces in a form and matter identified with their formidable rival.

Over centuries, ivory was integrated into many fictions.[4] Objects are foregrounded through artful description in romance and mystery play scenes, too. An outstanding example in the *Romance of the Rose* gives us a human shape that an artist figure, Pygmalion, carves out of ivory: a beautiful, feminized image.[5] For poets and artists working with the sumptuous substance, ivory became a raw material for a quintessential creative act and a prized medium for knowledge.[6] More and more abstracted from its animal matter, it becomes more and more a matter of fine art. Courtly and Christian fictions made with it abound: a hair parter shaped as Tristan embracing Iseult, for example, or boxes bearing scenes of the Passion.[7]

The range of artifacts attests to a significant practice that commands an international public, as Sarah Guérin demonstrates for Parisian ateliers.[8]

Graphic ivories of another equally ancient, rich tradition were featured at Paris's Museum of Man when it opened its doors in 1938.[9] These are Inuit artifacts in ivory. For the peoples of this northern circumpolar culture, these are belongings made for a very different purpose that substantiate a distinct view of their environs, far from the Trocadéro where the museum sat above the Seine. In the French setting, they were part of a presentation of Arctic culture that aimed to lay out the life cycle of men and women in Greenland.[10] At the beginning of human culture, according to the hypothesis of anthropologist André Leroi-Goerhan and ethnographer Paul-Émile Victor, Inuit were incising intricate lines on ivory that Leroi-Gourhan called "writing."

This almanach entry takes up a set of Inuit ivories on their unique cultural terms. It approaches them in the specific locales of the central, high, and eastern Arctic that Inuit peoples have been inhabiting for millennia.[11] As generations of Indigenous communities and archaeologists demonstrate, these pieces are signature creations of particular communities on their lands.[12] What these peoples incise on walrus tusks represents a distinct account of their nomadic hunting cultures in the darkest—and still the coldest—climate on Earth.

To offer an almanach entry on Inuit ivory artifacts is surprising for several reasons. Standard Western periodization and nomenclature have long kept the Inuit from being considered alongside the plethora of cultures around 1200–1500. Among cultural historians, it has been uncommon to examine such Indigenous forms of knowledge and techniques from these eras. To reverse this longstanding habit, I draw further critical, imaginative attention to them. This almanach places these artifacts and all of the other works it considers on a single temporal continuum. The cultures of the northern pole are part of the Earth's natural history of time. Their works are marked by the historical process of prochrony, too—in earlier years, as now, in our era.

To do so requires contending with the ideological frameworks that still obscure such ivory pieces in public view. Many of these artifacts moved as a result of numerous first encounters between Inuit and non-Inuit that have braided their histories together. Over centuries the artifacts were objects of barter and extortion. While the climate conditions proved extreme for non-Inuit attempting to settle—the Norse, around 1260, the English around 1570, before the Danes took hold of lands on the eastern and western coastlines of Greenland, in 1723—Europeans and North Americans kept coming to the Arctic. Their commercial ambitions coupled with their appetite for claiming "the unknown," put ivory pieces into circulation far beyond the area.[13] The result: significant collections of such artifacts in Scandinavia, Canada, and Russia, among other countries adjacent to polar regions, as well as collections in France and other parts of Europe.

For decades, museum curators and researchers, joined by artists and activists, have been responding to this checkered history by returning artifacts to their communities, and designing new modes of exhibition that represent Inuit cultures on their own terms.[14] Indigenous perspectives establish the frame of vision. Pia Arke creates a critical one on Paul-Émile Victor's ethnographic mission in Greenland in 1934–35, among the least familiar and considered of such collecting ventures.[15] Her pioneering artistic research foregrounds what Kalaallit, Inuit Greenlanders, observed of Victor's expeditions, and the ill-fated voyage of his nautical collaborator, Jean-Baptiste Charcot, as she trains a critical eye on the oddity of four white men coming off a hundred-foot schooner, the *Pourquoi Pas?*, to spend a year in their midst.[16]

This almanach entry reviews, then, the received ideas with which many of us first encounter Inuit ivory artifacts in museums and galleries. What of the value system that removed numbers of them from their lands, and assigned them to curiosity cabinets where European collectors had begun placing them around 1550?[17] What of the cultural hierarchies that put them in anthropological collections, such as the French Museum of Man, starting in the 1930s, while other ivories made in Paris and Montpellier workshops around 1400 are given their place in art galleries? These questions add to the steps taken to clear the ground of some basic presuppositions. They direct more attention to the Inuit matrix of culture and history of their ivory pieces. This matrix has been accruing over hundreds of years. Since the last century, local communities have been examining it, and excavating it with other archaeologists and anthropologists.[18] It provides the basis of this entry.

In situ, at ground level in the Arctic, in Nunavut and Kalaallit Nunaat/Greenland, Inuit graphic ivories become more clearly legible. Their particular knowledge comes into focus; so do the techniques used to make them. Small scraping implements are made with walrus tusk. These are deemed more difficult to work with than elephant tusk; they bear a few, short lines that depict sea mammals on the horizon, and common houses or *iluuvigaq*. Inuit who make their ivory pieces for several purposes represent the particular relations they cultivate with other animals. Their pictographs depict a balance or equilibrium between themselves and the animals they hunt for basic sustenance. They narrate a fundamental, indispensable idea of respect between species within the cosmos they all inhabit.

These graphics do so in and through the animal material that transmits them. The matter bears the close relation between the people who incise ivory, and the animals who supply it. This convergence of Inuit pictographic form and ivory matter is at the center of this final entry.

The effects of this combination on their graphic narrative are significant and influential. They entail another conception of creating objects that differs from the poetics informing the works of dream vision or drama in other entries of this almanach. What this time-honored Inuit idea brings to understandings of fiction that prevail in Euro-Mediterranean and other Western cultures is the last question this final entry will consider. Inuit artists who innovate it today through their singular creative practices show the way.

Inuit Storylines

To begin looking closely at Inuit ivory artifacts is to open your eyes to the distinctive graphic form of these small objects. The Inuit use line as the basic unit for depicting and recounting the animals they see in their environs, the interactions with them.[19] The basic tools of their hunting culture—knives, drills, and scrapers of animal skin—offer a medium and surface for storytelling. Inuit incise simple lines on them that are not based on the human body, often without any trace of a human image (Figure 24). Their signature Y-shaped sign, representing the whale's enormous tail, is a motif Inuit have traced for as long as their material culture exists.[20] Here, on the ivory tool, the three slight strokes catch six of these animals in motion. On many such implements, Inuit incise them on a horizon that makes animals and things more visible.

These outlines representing such animals, and delimiting a place common to all creatures, are narrative elements that Inuit compose with various materials. We find the Y-shaped whale-tail motif tattooed on the faces of two mummies of women buried around 1475 in Qilakitsoq, on the western Greenlandic coast, north of the Arctic circle.[21] People incised this simple animal shape on their own skin in a fundamental exercise of storytelling. These incisions duplicate the physical rapport humans have with other mammals. Drawings of women's tattoos from a hundred years ago detail this linework done over centuries.[22] They underscore the significance of marking their close rapport.

String was likely used in this way as well.[23] People stretched it between their fingers to create intricate patterns that told of whale and walrus in a characteristic game. Since little of it survives—or has yet to come to light—we're challenged to imagine critically how working with string composed a narrative about animals.[24] Inuit artists today invite us to visualize these string games: Manasie Akpaliapik, from Ikpiarjuk, Nunavut, in the high Arctic, captures the deft movement involved in his piece *The Woman Storyteller* (2003), which he composed with sinew, whale bone, and antler.[25] All these materials, including gut membrane, point to their sparing work: Inuit use every animal part to make implements that bear the idea of their species coexisting in balance.

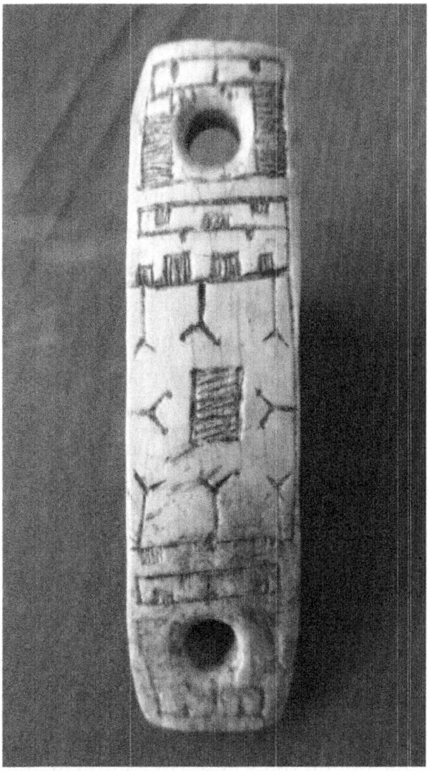

Figure 24. Ivory scraper, date unestablished. Paris, Musée Quai Branly, Inv. 71.1949.39.39. © Musée du Quai Branly – Jacques Chirac. Dist. RMN Grand Palais / Art Resource, NY.

Some of these animals, known to peoples on the other, eastern side of the Atlantic around 1200, were figures in their narratives. The bowhead whale, for example, had become recognizable to publics far from the ocean, a figure in the tales of Brendan, Irish *imramma* or tales of wonder, that made its way through Norman scribes into bestiaries, in Latin, French, and other vernaculars.[26] The whale of Bernardus Sylvestris in his *Cosmographia* is drawn from what Breton sailors had seen and recounted along their coast.[27] The gigantic presence and formidable movement of the sea creature had become a part of zoological knowledge that natural philosopher Albert the Great was codifying in Latin by 1250.[28]

Other animals, found only across Inuit Nunangat lands in the Arctic, were unique to the storytelling of these northernmost Inuit cultures. The narwhal, for example, with its single spiral of an ivory tusk, is named in the Inuktitut language as "one turning back on itself": *qilalugaq qernertaq*. By the time knowledge of it reached Norse and Norman, French-speaking publics, it had metamorphosed into another animal.[29] What the Norse called a seahorse became a horse with a horn on its head—a unicorn—with the result that a semblance of the Arctic animal was strangely familiar to many who listened to romances and read natural philosophy.[30]

These two outlooks on Arctic animals fed distinct imaginations. They generate two types of graphism developing in parallel. Inuit graphics are minimalist. Their drawing conforms to the shape and size of walrus or narwhal tusk, resulting, often, in small pieces of such ivory.[31] They make something out of this constraint, condensing their natural world into a few storylines. In contrast to the carvings of the *ivoiriers* in fourteenth-century Paris, Inuit graphics are an integral part of the tusk. Their lines are incised in the matter of the animals they hunt, on the very drills, harpoons, and knives crucial to surviving in the northern circumpolar climate. Miniature in scale, they represent how nomadic hunters used the portable tools on which they are inscribed. Matter, form, and function are fused. These graphic narratives in ivory substantiate how Inuit creators understand and value the delicate, necessary balance of animal coexistence.

Prehistory and Thule Culture

To look closely at the ivories' graphic form from Inuit vantage points also means attending to an order of time that governs Inuit practice of incising their implements. This natural time situates them in a cosmos lit by stars and moon.[32] A starry sky offered a first means of telling time, as it did for many peoples on and around the European continent and worldwide, during Oresme's and al-Din al-Ṭūsī's era.[33] The moon was another. Inuit peoples share their measure of lunar phases with the Arabo-Muslim calendar and, through a set of figures, with the first almanach in French as well. Across northern circumpolar regions, however, Inuit know the greatest variation of light and darkness made by the moon's orbit around Earth. At 64.2°N latitude and 84.8°W longitude, one of the northernmost continuously inhabited communities, Ikpiarjuk, or Arctic Bay, knows periods of darkness that extend through seventy-eight days of no light at all, or polar night, and periods of light with no darkness extending through ninety-four days of the midnight sun. This radical light and dark are the stuff of story, represented through a rich vocabulary in the Inuktitut language that specifies units of time according to the fluctuating light, including names for the shortest and longest day.[34]

This finely articulated order of natural time conveys an important sense of cohabiting the Earth with other animals. Instead of naming temporal units after humanized gods, the Inuit chose names of the animal species most important to them: February, for example, "*Tirituraliut*, the time when the small walrus swims toward our land."[35] This particular naming is all the more significant for the way of life of these peoples. Their time revolves around the life-sustaining activity of hunting such animals—whale, walrus, or other mammals—during particular periods. We have here a principal storyline incised on their implements.

This longstanding Inuit order of natural, cosmic time that conditions their graphics in ivory would confront several other systems of time. During the 1720s in the eastern Arctic, and the early 1800s in the central and high Arctic, people outside Inuit culture, Qallunaat, would begin attempting to impose their temporal regimes and to situate Inuit in Western cultures. Prehistory remains the dominant one.[36] This capacious category for the beginnings of human culture characterizes Inuit as an origin of sorts, as anthropologists would argue initially. Curiosity about them intensified, as if these peoples carried living traces of a primeval era.[37] They were identified with a system of time that acquired a mythic quality of sorts, one that appears static and, for some, even unrecorded, as Benoît l'Estoile demonstrates.[38] As a consequence, Inuit conceptions of time locating them and their material culture in the cosmos are displaced, the unique cultural significance of their graphic narratives distorted.

Prehistory also characterizes these ivory pieces in relation to the advent of writing, canonized by Western cultures. Consigning them to eras "before" verbal literacy, or considering them as writing, is a value judgment that privileges written, textual cultures. While this notion of a prehistoric period continues to serve as a general label for nomadic hunting peoples of cultures around 1200, it still carries this presumption. Archaeologists and anthropologists, as well as historians and cultural critics, have called for another conception for organizing historical time, one that is not a standard-bearer for a normative written language that had been used to qualify Inuit graphics.[39]

Releasing Inuit implements in ivory from these ideas around prehistory is a formidable undertaking. In museums, as in teaching/research programs and popular culture, this temporal order has a life of its own so deeply institutionalized that it is not easily revised. "Prehistory" had been reinforced by the category of "the primitive" as well.[40] Its charge was brought to bear on peoples of the Arctic around 1900, identified by their Western name, Eskimo.[41] "Primitive" aesthetics typecast Inuit work. Henri Matisse, for example, was taken with "Eskimo" drawing, and delighted in imitating its linework; writers and artists calling themselves surrealists, or modernists, collected Inuit artifacts with gusto.[42] In the process, these pieces were transformed in a way that bears little relation to their creation and function in Inuit life. Claimed instead as muses for Western and European aesthetics, they served an originary function for a culture little aware of the full spectrum of Inuit Nunangat cultures.

At the least, it's crucial to account for what these temporal categories have long presumed about Inuit cultures—ideas received and tested that still bear the mark of modern colonial histories in Danish, British, and French guises. Being mindful of the implications of such systems is the first way to move beyond their limits.

For readers of this almanach familiar with the ideologies of Medieval and Renaissance periods, it involves a comparable step. These periods that continue to frame Euro-Mediterranean vernacular cultures are also freighted with teleological presumptions about what cultures serve as precursors and what peoples represent progress in time.

It is the so-called Thule period, 1200–1500, that represents the most tenacious category characterizing Inuit cultures.[43] This Greek and Latin term, introduced by ancient geographers to designate the northernmost climes that they imagined only through writing epitomizes the reflex of those outside Inuit cultures to identify them.[44] Knud Rasmussen, an ethnologist who traversed the northern circumpolar area from Greenland to Beringia, on dogsled, with the help of Arnarulunnguaq and several other Inuit guides, modernized this tradition around 1900: he gave the name "Thule" to an area in northwestern coastal Greenland—where he began studying ancient structures and artifacts.[45] The name he gave to his expeditions evolved into an accepted term for a first stage of Inuit culture.[46] Thule came to designate a time and a space. However alien to Inuit, who call the area Qaanaaq, it became a marker of culture with scientific authority still used by archeologists. The challenge, as ever: to consider the Inuit understandings of this time/space.

Over recent decades, when Inuit peoples have seen the various Cold War adversaries occupy their lands and jeopardize their ways of life, the category has gained renewed force. Used across the ideological spectrum, it expresses the tensions between Indigenous and others, the political conflicts between Inuit and foreign aggressors and occupiers that threaten again in 2026. *Ultima Thule*, an essay by anthropologist Jean Malaurie, who spent a lifetime researching the Arctic, casts his advocacy for autonomous Inuit cultures in these terms.[47] Thule combines the classical Latin sense of the farthest zone imaginable with something of a last-stand defense. Today, an American military base that is re-arming operates in the vicinity of the early Thule sites on the coast, near Pituffik, its name changing back and forth from the Indigenous to the americanized Thule.[48] In the wake of far right movements in 2020s America that falsely instrumentalize the Thule term for racist ends, as they had done in 1930s Europe, accounting for all the misguided uses and distortions of the term proves indispensable. Ethnologist Peter Whitbridge lays them bare to dispense with them once and for all.[49]

It is nonetheless important to recognize that the unique Inuit graphic ivories are one Indigenous form among others. Indigeneity is often assumed to refer to non-Western cultures alone. Yet it can refer to contemporaneous forms developed on the European continent, to take one example. For artist Mark Rothko, around 1940, it often seemed to have been measured first in terms of longitude rather than latitude; an "Eskimo" piece need not be considered more acceptable as an ingenious Indigenous form, in his view, than contemporaneous ones made by French artists.[50] Étienne Anheim points out that the conception of primitive art has a European history; Quattrocento frescoes from Assisi rediscovered by art connoisseurs in the 1850s represent one prominent case.[51] Flemish painting from the Burgundian realm, contemporaneous with the theatrical scenes and fiction in other entries in the almanach, is another.[52] "Primitive," meaning "first" in chronological time, organizes such history. It is the sense, too, of 'First Nations,' the legal phrase in Canada for the political states of Indigenous peoples.

Once we dispense with these distorting implications of prehistoric peoples and their material culture, and think in terms of Inuit-Thule, as archaeologists, other researchers, and critics do, beholding Inuit artifacts in ivory on their own terms is a better prospect.[53]

Verbal language provides a way into Inuit points of view on graphic storytelling in this animal matter. One Inuktitut word used today, *unikkausinnguaq*, identifies imaginative stories.[54] Whether Inuit hunting stories were incised in pictographs, or composed in words, they represented happenings without needing to specify their truth value. Pauloosie Kasukluak, who carved animals in stone during the 1970s, is clear about this understanding.[55] Such micro-narrative forms are not "made up." There's nothing "marvelous" about them. Manasie Akpaliapik gives pride of place to his artwork as an expression of his Ikpiarjuk community in Nunavut.[56] His pieces recount happenings central to the life of this particular Inuit group during many different times.

This conception of composing pictographic stories makes clear that such Inuit ivory artifacts do not correspond to fiction in any contemporary Western sense. Nor are they considered as fine art first and foremost by these peoples. When we turn to the few earliest surviving Inuit-Thule pieces known today, they appear to be made primarily for hunting.[57] To see them in this way confirms how their graphics are integrated fully into their use. The knives of Iñupiaq peoples, Inuit inhabiting the Bering Strait that are known in Alaska today as "story knives" exemplify this integration during a later period.[58] The storyline incised on the blade is intrinsic to and inseparable from the knife being used to cut up whale blubber: the merging of ivory matter, form, and function.

With the Inuit sense of these implements in walrus and narwhal ivory, their pictographic narrative forms come into focus. In the Inuit temporal order, their function in natural time is clearer, too.[59] It draws out ideas about animal relations in their natural environment particular to these cultures—what they call, in Inuktitut, *qaujimajatuqanjit*, "longtime knowledge." These are bonds between humans and other animals that depend on respect and determine survival.

Storytelling Tools

To investigate these ideas, we turn to an ivory artifact incised with some of the most intricate Inuit Thule graphics known today (Figure 25).[60] Ever since it was taken out of its community and environs in 1959, it has generated much interpretative energy in non-Inuit circuits of archaeologists, anthropologists, and art historians.[61] This piece of walrus tusk is slender, and 43 centimeters long. It tells its stories on both sides of the hewn tusk. On the more fully preserved side seen in Figure 25, the maker who worked the ivory incised two sets of episodes separated by a vertical border with a V-shaped motif. Whether we decipher episodes from left to right (Figure 25a to b), or right to left (Figure 25b to a), we begin to follow various animal movements. Ikpiarjuk/Arctic Bay community members, Inuit elders and students, along with anthropologist Janet Young and archaeologist Matthw Betts, describe fundamental events in a hunt that are engraved in precise detail: in Figure 25b, we see caribou and humans in their kayaks, paddles raised, along the bottom of the implement, and other hunters in their *umiaq*, or larger seal hide boats, at the top. In Figure 25a, we see a human figure, accompanied by a dog, and hunters with their tools raised. The various storylines are simultaneous and extend in both directions. In both Figure 25a and b, on the far left and right, we follow people coming out of their *qargi* or communal structures, who frame the hunt.[62] On the other side of the implement that is not

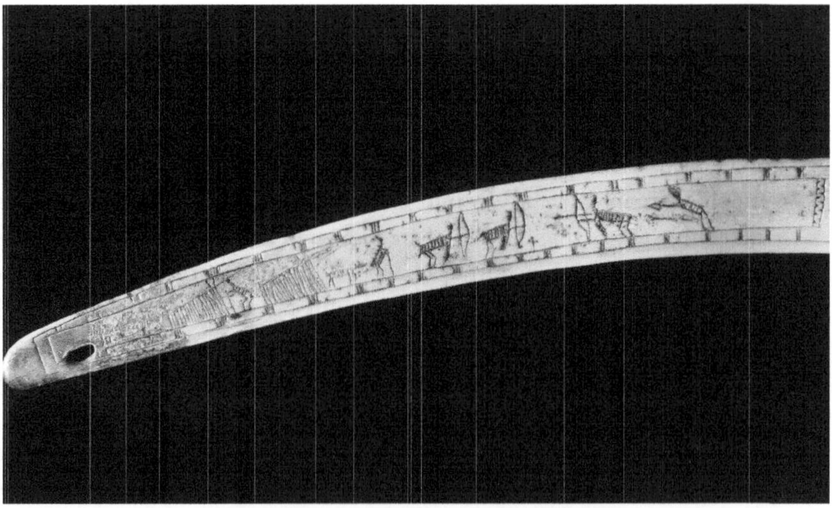

Figure 25a,b. **Ivory bowdrill, panel on left, and on right, c. 1200. Gatineau, Québec, Canadian Museum of History, PgHq-1:1. By permission of the Inuit Heritage Trust.**

shown here, similar episodes are repeated: those in the *qargi*, and others with people out on the waters, in their *umiaq*. Whales are hunted, the skins of other slaughtered animals are laid out.

On both ivory surfaces, the side we see in Figure 25, and the other one we don't, the maker incises a strong central line. This Inuk, or single person, traces the narrative along this horizon line where the animals are moving. The stories unfold for us by following the hunter's line of sight.

In creating such a narrative, this Inuk geometrizes his environs. The graphics are determined first, in situ, by landscape. They trace what Inuit view when they look out across the tundra, and see whatever light makes visible on the horizon line. The human figures, which most non-Inuit would look for first, are not the most important.

This Inuit ivory implement, with its miniature graphic storyline, is a bowdrill, a tool called in Inuktitut *iquutak*, used to pierce small holes in the ice, in search of animals coming to the surface to breathe.[63] This function links it to a variety of objects made with walrus tusk and other animal parts: fishing lures, harpoons, and the various small knives used for hunting. The smaller the object, the more limited the surface to incise, and the more remarkably condensed the narrative lines. On one lure, for instance, a whale is shown harpooned by a tiny human: the hunter is barely visible compared to the whale.[64] We have here the chief traits of Inuit ivory artifacts: minute graphics narrating the close relations with animals

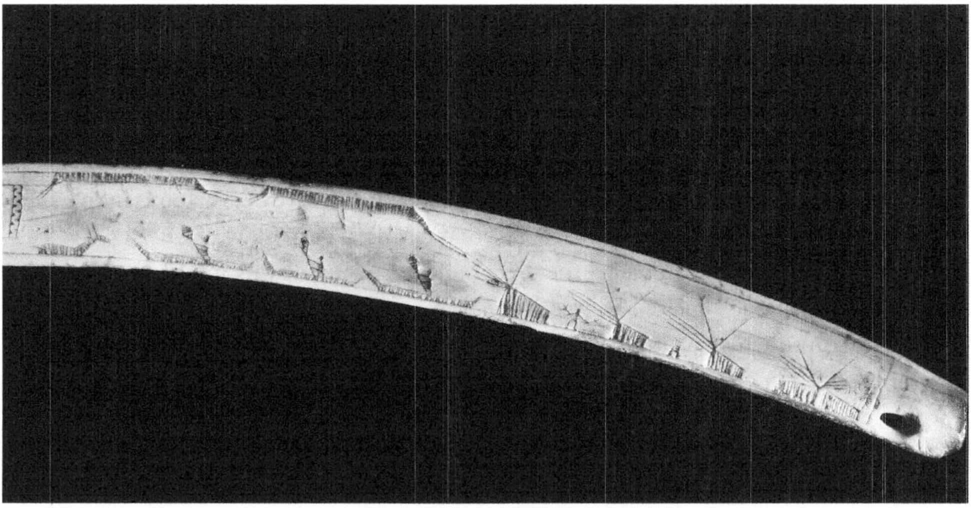

on the principal tools used to hunt them. These are stories that relate elementary ways of coexisting in the northern polar climate.

What makes the bowdrill in Figure 25 remarkable, and uniquely important for the creative work this almanach brings together, are its historical circumstances that are now established. The Inuit community of Ikpiarjuk worked to determine who made this bowdrill, and when, in this place above the Arctic Circle, at latitude 73°N, some thousand miles from the North Pole.[65] Through the ancient resources of oral tradition, combined with the contemporary techniques of radiocarbon dating, the Inuk carver has been identified by name, Nuvumiutaq, and the implement that he made for hunting has been dated to around 1200, according to our conventional calendar.

This graphic narrative represents human beings in a sequence unusual for the period. We find here storylines that personalize the paradigmatic scene depicted of hunting bowhead whales or caribou.[66] We see a human figure moving from tent to a hunting boat outdoors in Figure 25b. Here too, in Figure 25a, are the rare outlines of domestic scenes: a child is being tended to inside a house, while the man walking out from his tent with a stick appears to be an elder in the company of a dog. This narrative extends from childhood to maturity.

For the Ikpiarjuk community, as well as for Young and Betts, these pictographs are the work of an individual Inuk who "had carved his autobiography into the ivory tools."[67] The incisions are thought to relay a story about Nuvumiutaq's own actions. Separate and distinct from any Western genre of autobiographical writing and its notion of a human subject, this ivory tool offers the fullest narrative sequence that has come to light so far. Its graphics detailing human lifelines accentuate, as ever, those of various coexisting animal species. We follow here an arc of a hunter-kayaker's daily life, including the episode of an elder with a stick.[68] Through one person, it recounts how vital the relation is between hunter and hunted, how precarious—and indispensable—the balance between a vulnerable human and another fellow animal harpooned. We have here an outstanding graphic narrative of Inuit culture—one of the earliest currently known.

The challenge is to gauge the exceptional character of this implement. The numbers of such incised walrus ivory pieces from around 1200–1500 held in permafrost across Nunavut are difficult to account for. When we open up the investigation toward the east and Inuit lands in Kalaallit Nunaat/Greenland, the evidence is sparse. When we take the step to cover the entire circumpolar Inuit expanse, we are, in effect, retracing migrating Inuit along routes taken from Beringia eastward around 1200.[69] Along all these ways, the implements we do know thus far are few in number.

Two small pieces offer examples. A fragment of walrus ivory discovered in an excavated site in Qaanaaq recounts a whale hunt (Figure 26).[70] Four humans are

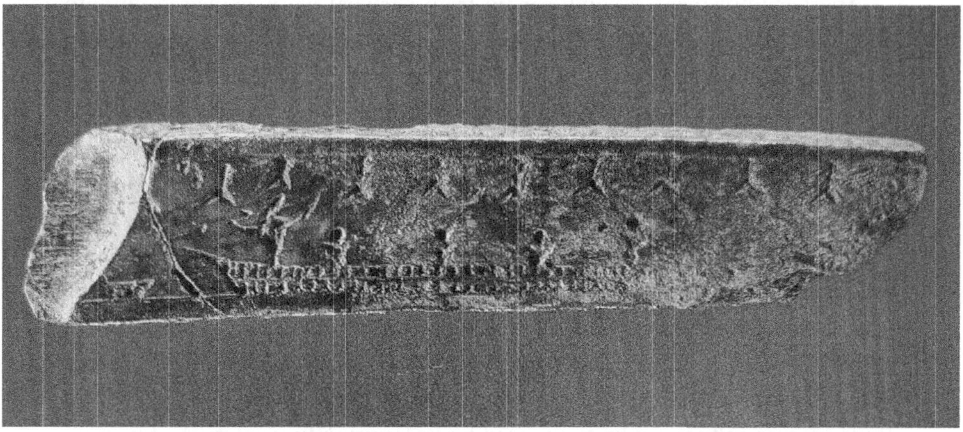

Figure 26. Ivory implement fragment, c. 1200–1500. Nuuk, National Greenland Museum and Archives. Photograph: John Lee. National Greenland Museum and Archives.

in their *umiaq*; a hunter with harpoon in hand is primed to strike the whale whose tail is visible above the waterline. These pictographs are framed by the Y-shaped whale tail motif on the second graphic plane. The piece is incised with minute lines that trace even the intricate structure of the boat. Its small scale makes its use unclear. Found in the midden of a Thule house, it could have come from, and been made, in any number of places. The site in northwestern Kalaallit Nunaat/Greenland locates the object on a route across the water from Qikiqtaaluk/Baffin Island, some four hundred miles from Ikpiarjuk, a route that Inuit following the ice floe current traveled in search of animals. This is a singular Inuit Thule artifact, found in an area rich in ancient history. The ongoing community archaeological work that Mari Kleist organized there, along with the photographic analysis of the Thule house, may yet yield further knowledge to contextualize it.[71]

Another implement, a comb carved from narwhal ivory, is incised on both sides, like Nuvumiutaq's drill.[72] On one side, in an *umiaq*, a hunter, his harpoon raised, and three other figures are holding their paddles. On the other, a hunter in his kayak is on the verge of harpooning an animal. The likely one, a whale, and another human figure are difficult to discern. This artifact, which came to light on Salliq/Southhampton Island, in Nunavut on the northern shore of Hudson Bay, shows the signature storylines of a whale hunt.

Dozens more such pieces that have been collected and are now in Greenland, Denmark, Norway, Russia, Japan, the United Kingdom, and in Europe as well as across North America, have yet to be examined comprehensively or dated; Igor Krupnik's ongoing collaborative work is crucial to this effort.[73] The more teams that can pursue such a comparative study, the more this phase of Inuit Thule graphic culture can be recognized for its longstanding practices of incising narrative in ivory.

As it stands now, this history, being put together by Inuit communities working with archaeologists, anthropologists, and curators, substantiates ideas about animal relations developing over hundreds of years, over thousands of miles halfway around the Earth. This is the graphic culture that caught the eye of John White, an adventurer-settler and artist known for working in Walter Raleigh's expedition to Roanoke Island off the Carolina coast, who likely accompanied others exploring Arctic coasts (Figure 27).[74] This Inuk drawn by White is holding a longer type of bowdrill that is both carved and incised with Inuit graphics: a piece as crucial to the hunter and Inuit Thule culture as the seal skin he's wearing. With Nuvumiutaq's bowdrill, the Qaanaaq fragment, and the Salliq comb, he too signals the artful techniques and "longtime knowledge" of Inuit Thule culture, around 1200–1600.

To begin to gauge the historical significance of this provisional set poses the

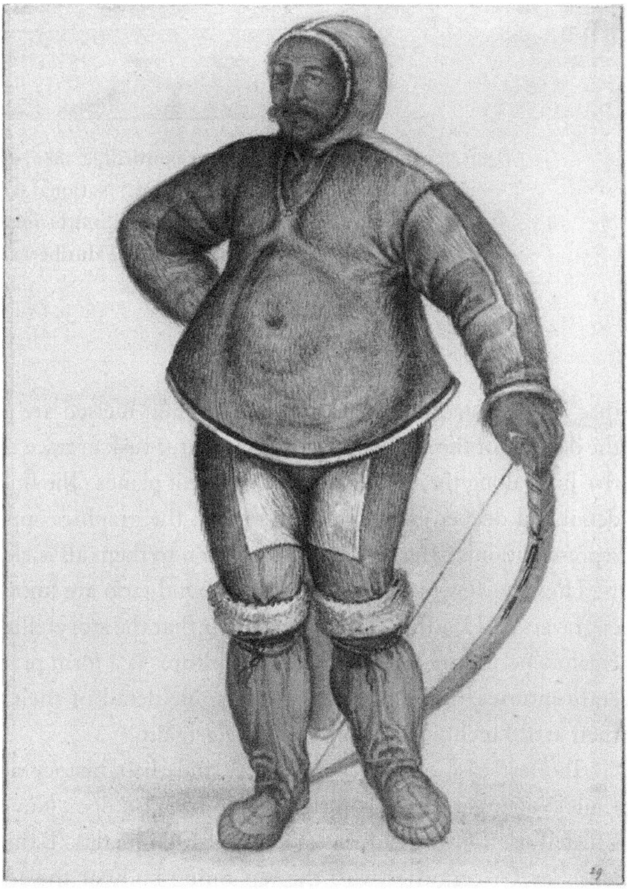

Figure 27. **John White, An Inuk, watercolor drawing, c. 1580–95. London, British Museum, 1906, 0509.1.29. CC BY-NC-SA 4.0.**

question of their situation during various eras. It is worthwhile turning to Iñupiaq culture in Beringia and Alaska, where engraving ivory tools is a defining trait that has long been recognized for its graphic arts.[75] Many bowdrills made by several generations over the last century are incised with the signature graphics and demonstrate the same fusion of form and matter.

To take one example, the bow of a Pitiksiaq bowdrill from the coast near Nome, Alaska, and likely made during the 1880s, shows whales at the horizon, sharply incised; the Y lines of the tails, as well as the sea mammals' bodies, are filled in more thoroughly by inlay (Figure 28a, b).[76] The graphic depictions of hunter-kayakers

Figure 28a,b. **Bow of Pitiksiaq, ivory bowdrill, c. 1880, detail. Edward W. Nelson Collection, Washington, DC. National Anthropological Archives, Department of Anthropology, Smithsonian Institution, E44398-0. Photograph: Donald E. Hurlbert, Smithsonian Institution.**

that Nuvumiutaq and other anonymous Inuit incised are also in evidence. So is the deft use of the entire surface of the walrus tusk to trace multidirectional narrative lines along the horizon on two different planes. The linework involves greater detail and deeper etching into the ivory; the graphics appear, as a whole, more representational. The storytelling common to them all is clear.

However few incised pieces from around 1200 are known at present, Iñupiaq engravers and Phillips-Chan make clear that the storytelling tools of Indigenous creators on the western side of Inuit cultures is a form practiced for at least several centuries.[77] The knowledge in graphic detail of their natural environs and their artful techniques can prove timely again.

The test case of such ivory pieces and their history needs to be studied in Inuit Nunangat: place is formative. What else does Nuvumiutaq's bowdrill in situ tell us? On the northwest coast of Qikiqtaaluk/Baffin Island, this incised piece lay for centuries with the remaining body of the adult man identified as Nuvumiutaq, a baby, and some thirty objects made of walrus tusk.[78] The graphic ivory bowdrill was a grave offering. In this setting, it was part of a cache of goods including knives incised with animals and humans, a fish-shaped lure for fishing, an arrow, and many figurines of birds. All of them were accompanying these Inuit dead laid out on the tundra and buried in a rock cairn. The site was likely a choice one on the Uluksan peninsula, viewed, as the name "Ikpiarjuk" indicates, as a pocket of land, surrounded by water. The graphic ivory bowdrill was embedded in a place of passage for some eight hundred years.

During the summer of 1959, Iperk, an Inuk from the region, guided Guy Mary-Rousselière, a vocational archaeologist, and Lawrence Oschinsky, an anthropologist at the then Museum of Canadian Civilization, to this gravesite.[79] His Indigenous knowledge of the locale was indispensable for their work; without it, any such expedition, as a non-Inuit archaeologist remarked a generation ago, was a lottery.[80]

Their decision to remove the grave goods from Qikiqtaaluk to Ottawa, where they became part of the museum's collection, took the objects out of place, and reinforced the break with Inuit Thule cosmic time/space.[81] What was justified in the 1950s by reasons of science imposed consequences on the local Inuit community. In effect, these pieces were not only wrested from their locale likely chosen for the dead, but they were also relocated in another Western order of time, one of "prehistory," largely regulated in the 1950s and 1960s by a logic that did not attend to the specific circumstances of Inuit cultures. This was a "timeless present" of sorts, in Alice Conklin's trenchant assessment, one that had been cultivated by museum display during these decades.[82]

Today, a generation later, the repatriation of Nuvumiutaq, his ivories, and all the grave goods to Qikiqtaaluk, which the Inuit Heritage Trust is pursuing with the Canadian Museum of History, is responding to these multiple disruptions to Inuit culture and community life.[83] It restores the social relation between the Inuk maker of the bowdrill and the Ikpiarjuk communities, situating them again in their times and place. It contributes to the ongoing, in situ transmission of Inuit knowledge that making these ivories and placing them in an Inuk's grave represent.[84]

Nuvumiutaq's bowdrill and the other Inuit Thule ivory pieces considered here continue nonetheless to exist in double-edged circumstances. They continue to be defined by two orders of time, an Inuit cosmic time overlaid with a Western chronology that functions in Nunavut as it does in Greenland, Canada, the United States, France, or any other country.

Inuit artists of the most recent generation are acutely sensitive to these circumstances. When they make their work, they're taking another unprecedented creative step alongside that of repatriating objects of their peoples. Over the last several decades, a significant number are engaging with the time-honored forms and matter of Inuit peoples, vindicating their cultures' prerogatives. They transform them through digital media, metal, and raw material from outside their environs. In creating their art, they also re-present some of the most ancient Inuit Thule artifacts known today.

Alignments for Today

Artist Germaine Arnaktauyok, who draws, etches, and works in video animation, creates with Nuvumiutaq's bowdrill (Figure 29).[85] In her etching *Then and Now*, she transposes the line-drawing and miniature scale of its graphic narrative in ivory. Arnaktauyok goes in a vertical direction. She changes the narrative line, and the sequence of our vision. The bowdrill that she draws is divided into four different pieces and graphic panels. While she draws the domestic scene from the ivory, its human figure and small animals around the *qargi* tent house, as well as other figures in combat, she configures Nuvumiutaq's individual story in her own way. While she draws the outdoor scene of hunters in their *umiaq* boats, Arnaktauyok's graphic "then" relates something else, something that goes in a different direction. In the fourth piece at the bottom, the animals are gone. The movement that Arnaktauyok traces is technological, a mechanized and electrical one of snowmobile, plane, and boat resembling those seen in Greenland, Ontario, Québec, and Manitoba. At the center of her graphic is a woman in her *silappiaq*, or parka, and boots. Arnaktauyok's "now" goes figurative, and in a realistic style that creates an eye-catching image of an Inuk in motion.

Then and Now issues a subtle provocation about the timeliness of Inuit graphic narrative in ivory. On the one hand, the machinery that Arnaktauyok draws underscores the radically different relation of her people to their Thule culture, fellow creators, and their earliest known practices. This major change in Inuit life may not seem to be as desecrating as was the removal of Nuvumiutaq's remains and grave goods to a museum in the Canadian capital. It is certainly as consequential. *Then and Now* makes visible the effects of removing the ivory bowdrill from its cultural matrix, marooning its graphic narrative. Arnaktauyok describes her limited knowledge of the hunting culture in which the tool was first situated; the techniques of working ivory for its use are largely unfamiliar to her.[86] This is the case for an increasing number of Inuit today.

On the other hand, drawing Nuvumiutaq's bowdrill with such precision expresses her resolve to transmit Inuit storylines in her inimitable way. It's a commitment to the graphic practices of her culture—a call to take note. Her drawings of women's ivory combs with the basic graphic unit of the Y-shaped whale tail and *qargi* testify to the same commitment.[87]

Arnaktauyok innovates these forms to address the transformations her com-

Figure 29. Germaine Arnaktauyok, *Then and Now*, etching, 2001. By permission of Germaine Arnaktauyok. Photograph: Inhabit Media, Inc.

munities have been undergoing: the accelerating Westernizing pace of Inuit life. What she chooses to draw updates Nuvumiutaq's bowdrill and directs it to the current circumstances of her people. It involves claiming these timely ivory artifacts for their milieu, and making work that responds to the fast-moving changes in their environment.

Arnaktauyok's *Then and Now* issues a different challenge to its non-Inuit publics today. It involves recognizing Inuit Thule graphic practices exemplified by Nuvumiutaq's tool, to make them part of the spectrum of cultures, from 1200 up to our own day. At stake as well is the knowledge incised on walrus tusk about animal relations in the Arctic. This has everything to do with the *untimely* character of Inuit Thule graphic narrative in ivory for audiences stretching far beyond Inuit communities. To what extent will they get to know the singular artful techniques and knowledge of these ivories? Arnaktauyok's etching activates finally the potency of these ivories to draw attention to the precarious quality of the culture they represent. Can the art world that is promoting Inuit cultures also integrate the history of Inuit graphic narratives, and their particular wisdom, into its aesthetic understanding?

David Ruben Piqtoukun, an Inuvialuit artist who works with stone, bone, and sinew in different forms, is alert to Inuit artifacts accompanying their dead.[88] In the line of Nuvumiutaq's ivory, he transposes a site such as the one on the Uluksan peninsula. His installation, *Remains of Ancient Civilization* (1997), at the Art Gallery of Ontario brings a human face and body into view. A figurine lies at the center of the outline of an arrowhead found in many such sites. Piqtoukun makes grave goods to pay homage to the first Indigenous peoples of the northern circumpolar area, including the Dorset who created masks. In the same way, he cultivates Inuit Thule practices for dignifying their dead.

It is Tim Pitsiulak whose drawing situates Inuit graphic narrative in ivory in a new framework. This artist, who was also a dedicated hunter, depicted close relations with the animals he tracked; art activist and historian Pat Fehely emphasizes how Pitsiulak's two practices share this view.[89] His work bears vivid markings of this closeness between the bowhead whale and Inuit hunters (Figure 30). Large and small masks of the so-called Dorset peoples who inhabited the central and eastern Arctic before the Inuit, whales, and hunters are all drawn in minute lines on the animal's back and tail. Pitsiulak composes his own set of ancient cultures. He imitates and transforms the practice of incising lines on walrus tusk, drawing a whale he cherished that now bears these objects on its body. The relation between the two animals could not be closer. Pitsiulak creates a brilliant graphic of the balance he sought with the whale he hunted. He reconfigures their idea of intimate respect for the animal world as a whole.

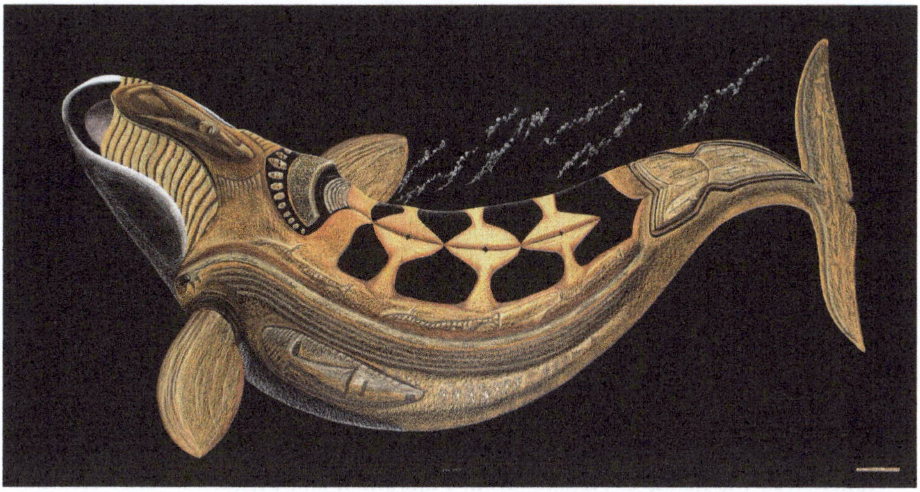

Figure 30. **Tim Pitsiulak, *Ivory Atquik*, colored pencil, 2013. By permission of Dorset Fine Arts.**

Pitsiulak's homage to the whale resembles a tattoo, a name he gave to another drawing. It, too, fuses parts of different mammals together. With minimalist human representation, his Inuit graphics mimic the linework incised on ivory yellowed with age. It gives this creature pride of place in a dark field as devoid of light as many nights in the polar regions they share. This artwork was part of his sustained engagement with the artifacts of Inuit Thule culture, including drawings of incised tusks. Pitsiulak was supremely attentive to their long and vital coexistence with fellow animals, and showed it in what they made.

✳

What is the effect of the artwork of Arnaktauyok, Piqtoukun, and Pitsiulak situating the earliest known Inuit Thule graphic ivory pieces in contemporary culture? It's an open question for several reasons. In a world where Inuit people interact with those from the "South," or others at a greater distance, their narratives are caught in a force-field of multiple, competing claims. In the current regime of time, which breaks long Arctic days and nights into seconds regulated by smartphones for "productive" use, these ivory objects can appear inert—and long surpassed. There are many consequences.

For one, the matter of their ivory is at stake: over some two centuries in the central and eastern Arctic, Inuit have contended with the threat to walrus and the prospect of fewer tusks. Activists on many fronts have long advocated for communities whose way of life hinges on cohabiting with walrus. They've been sounding the alarm about the destructive effects of a Western luxury market of ivory that endangered these animals' survival.[90] Since the Inuit Heritage Trust was established in 1994, Nunavut's political sovereignty recognized in 1999, and Kallaallit Nunaat/Greenland's home rule enacted in 1979, activists have dedicated special energy to safeguarding their cultures.[91] They confront the perennial commercial and military risks to Inuit practices that undercut close relations among all animals of the pan-Arctic, especially the walrus.

Furthermore, the function of these graphic ivories is altered. Fewer Inuit are making bowdrills and incising pictographic narratives because they use them less. As their ivory implements are increasingly separated from hunting day to day, they lose their practical value. Yet the tool that is disappearing gains another function in the hands of Arnaktauyok, Piqtoukun, and Pitsiulak.[92] They create fine art with their work—an Inuit one—solicited by an international market. Those few who do work with ivory are mindful of its functions for Inuit culture. The miniature poles that Adam Alorut or Aron Kleist made, for example, transform the earliest known Inuit Thule graphic forms in ivory for today's public.[93]

To contemplate such Inuit pieces today from outside their culture is sobering. The double jeopardy of less matter and changing function casts their untimely quality in a stark light. So do the current environmental circumstances.[94] These artifacts that had been carried by Inuit across vast expanses of land and water, preserved in the tundra, are in sites that are eroding. In some seventy years, Canadian, American, Soviet, and European industries intervening in the Arctic have triggered damaging changes to Inuit communities existing for thousands of years. Archaeologists describe the effects on Inuit Thule sites as turning bones as soft as butter. Such destruction surrounds these artifacts in situ with an aura of urgency. Betts likens it to book burning.[95]

The potential of these graphic narratives in ivory to generate new work exists nonetheless. First and foremost this involves Inuit who create for their communities—without any need to engage with others. What is unavailable to non-Inuit represents a potent resource for Inuit. In the cases of Arnaktauyok, Piqtoukun, and Pitsiulak, who do work across cultures, their creativity makes the earliest known Inuit Thule ivory tools visible to a broader public.

These pieces have their place in this almanach for this reason. I join Inuit artists, archaeologists, anthropologists, and other researchers to draw further attention to this time-honored form of graphic narrative incised in ivory. The promise of these implements for Inuit cultures is unique; their time will tell how they engage the next generation in the circumpolar Arctic.

For readers more familiar with the contemporaneous fictions from Euro-Mediterranean regions of the other almanach entries, Inuit ivories contribute a powerful model of testing ideas through form and technique. These small pictographic pieces representing interaction between animals crucial to survival do not represent humans as central, often not figuring them at all. Inuit creators depict sentient beings of several animal species along the same lines, cohabiting in their natural world.

The resulting wisdom, Inuit *qaujimajatuqanjit*, or "longtime knowledge," is materialized. Their graphic narratives recount it efficiently in its cosmography of thousands of moons ago. The proof of the extended creative activity of the nomadic Inuit circulated among peoples that they encountered along the way. These artifacts testify to Inuit Thule culture among others, c. 1200–1600.

By investigating something of the long record of Inuit Thule ivory artifacts, this almanach entry opens up our notions of fiction. Their graphic narratives of animal life turn from a dominant paradigm to innovate a distinct tactile one, a solid ensemble of form and matter. Composed with animal parts that are dignified as such, these ivories bear much of the natural world; their narratives substantiate what the carver-engravers know of it through experience. The knowledge—or science—we understand fiction to relay is transmuted in another way that proves vital and necessary for all manner of life.

Closing Entry

Compost

The ensemble of works tracked in time brings this almanach full circle. As we encounter them today, the historical process of their composition comes clear. Some that had engaged the public right away did so again when different writers and artists transformed them for communities far from their first situations. They may still. Others proved untimely in their initial circumstance; no matter the creators' ingenuity, their imagined ideas have yet to register to their full extent in fictional forms. Still others, from Nunavut, Kalaallit Nunaat, and the expanse of Inuit territories once called *terrae incognitae* from a Euro-Mediterranean vantage point, enlarge the scope of the Earth and its inhabitants, as they forge another narrative model for their cultures.

In this final entry, I return to the 1493 *Calendar and Compost of Shepherds*, and one of its chief ideas. "Compost" is integral to the almanach—as crucial as the calendar. I introduce it to conclude this almanach because it specifies another conception of making fiction more responsive to our current circumstances than the one that has long dominated.

"Compost" signifies here something other than what readers expect today: in French, in its earliest known use around 1100, it can best be translated as "compute."[1] "Compost" is a calculation that describes lunar cycles. Rather than the mulch of materials we understand it to mean in English, as in French today, the 1493 almanach defines it as a model for measuring time that involves leap years. "Compost" organizes dates that are moveable. Christian holy days are explained by complex diagrams that, according to one writer, "are not said or written in any calendar."[2]

Philippe de Thaon introduced this sort of long-attested computational method in one of the first vernacular, so-called scientific treatises around 1110.[3] His *Comput* accounts for time by combining natural units with religious ones. In the spirit that would come to distinguish the almanach, it explains seasons of hibernation and rebirth together with liturgical seasons of Advent and Easter. This numerical calculation is an early exercise in what proves a perennial system of computation for the human sciences that is, once again, taking precedence.[4]

Thaon's treatise also reveals how "comput" was fused—confused—with "compost." Words in play signal the issue. Translating the Latin *computus* for a wider public with little or no access to the learned language generates a range of variants.[5] In multilingual Norman courts and schools in England, the one word, *comput*, passes more commonly into English, and the other, *compost*, into French vernaculars.[6] Whichever the case, another model for planning time emerges that complexifies the calendar.

This "comput/compost" combination helps set the terms for knowledge about sun and moon that poets and other creators used to establish days and years, and shape the sense of time of their work. Eustache Deschamps deploys "compost" in his literary treatise, just as Simon de Phares does in his art of astronomy and commentary on the stars.[7] Almanachs in French codify "compost" as their second name. Different types of the form proliferate, the result of exuberant and zany experimentation, designed for women and men, across many social groups.[8] Year upon year, its method is used to recalibrate time, right through to the 1780s and 1790s when revolutions were accompanied by declarations of a new time in the name of the people. "The Singing Almanach," a palm-sized sheaf of pages printed for Year Two of the French Republican calendar (1793–94), began the year anew, with a different month named after the harvest season (Vendémiaire).[9]

"Comput/compost" captures the full sense of timely fictions in all its semantic permutations. The formulas devised for our experience of time represent, first, how writers and artists situate their works and account for their fictions, and this over many hundreds of years. These various temporal phases continue to accumulate. Through myriad other works, they are compounded. They resemble the kind of compacted levels that archaeologists dig through in every excavation. Their work exposes layers sedimenting any object in situ, in the earth. These are layers in time that, peeled back, show the matter of multiple periods; excavating a common site, the refuse heap, known as a midden, makes them visible.[10] In a comparable way, verbal fictions are embedded in time. Literary critic Mireille Séguy in dialogue with archaeologist Laurent Olivier brings this analogy to the fore.[11] When we encounter these fictions in other circumstances and phases than those in which they were first made, we find their materials and forms bearing all sorts of temporal marks. These marks are incorporated in the ongoing existence of fictions.

It is hardly surprising that these temporal phases of fictions do not occur to the public; nor do they even necessarily register with their creators. Creatures of their day, they operate, first, in the framework of their own lifespan; they approach works in their own time. The critical practice today of juxtaposing works from the past with those of the present is yet another sign of this reflex. Yet, whether people recognize a fuller temporal existence of fictions is irrelevant to the historical process underway. We are not master of it. At any given moment, their fictions are the sum of many transformations in different ages. The result is a singular admixture. We have here a sense of fiction as a temporal compost.

"Compost" carries a second important sense. This fertilizing mix of materials that we recognize was already appearing by 1300 in the countryside on either side of the Channel, on the islands as well as on the European continent.[12] Oresme extended it to describe a human makeup.[13]

Like all compost makers, fictions are distinguished by their multifarious components. Language is a fundamental one; the fictions around 1400 relay to us the occitanized French of Honorat Bovet, and the Franco-Flemish jargon of those composing theatrical scripts in Arras and Valenciennes, or, over the years, translations of Christine de Pizan into Castilian Spanish and of Villon into Black American English. All these idioms diversify and enrich the linguistic ingredient. Animal matter is another component: the sheepskin cured for folio pages, walrus tusk and whalebone hewn for making other durable surfaces. These elements from species inhabiting several climates constitute a remarkable medley of media for inscribing work. We have here, with many of them, fiction's material compost.

The temporal conjoined with the material makes for an outstanding figure for timely fictions. This compost figure is one I advance to represent the historical process of composing such fictions, to show their particular makeup as well. It extends the poetic concepts introduced in the opening entry. The prochrony that Cendrars attributes to the fiction of Villon's personal poetry represents time's movement propelling the ballads; the anachrony that Rancière posits for ideas involves leaps in time, ones retained, in English, in the expression "leap years." The compost figure takes us in a different direction. By combining fiction's accruing times with its diverse matter, it accentuates a generative potential. This can be activated in varying degrees during different eras, informing both the techniques of its arts, and its experimental ideas, its knowledge. Compost highlights this formative character of fiction—in untimely and timely states. It does so by giving it a sensual character. While time is an abstraction, with no visible shape, taste, or odor, as historian Graham Chapman reminds us, this figure for timely fictions imbues it with the feel of humus.[14] I associate the figure with this organic substance made rich through matter that is changing constantly.[15]

Those who enjoy working with words and images will recognize the compost figure and its fundamental context as one of their own: it bespeaks composition across all the arts—literary, performing, visual, musical. What is commonplace today signals a principal way of working for creators of fiction around 1400, for those making political dream visions, drama, personal poetry, and graphic narrative.

These writers and artists work according to the rhetoric of composition. Christine de Pizan, for one, turns to *composer* in systematic fashion; that is, to order words into various meaningful units, as Sarah Delale reviews.[16] Christine was one among many in perfect step with these Latin arts, deploying them to give shape to their fictions. It is hard to overestimate this rhetorical understanding that defined the activity of numerous generations across centuries, regardless of the form or medium they chose. Knowledge or Science, and Clear Invention, the ladies introduced in the Prologue exemplify its versatile power.

Alongside this elementary creative activity of composition, writers and ateliers of scribes in Paris, as in Cairo and Baghdad, were pursuing compilation.[17] To engage with other authors, they amassed the variety of their writing. This practice of composition operates on a larger scale that results in handmade books.[18] We have only to look at the anthology from Arras, in which the first sketch introducing the Boy and the Blind Person is wedged between dozens of songs and short stories, to gauge the ambitious composition these compilations represent, or the miscellany of poetry put together around 1475 in which Villon's ballads find their place.[19] The attention focused on the aesthetic construction of such manuscripts is revising—and surpassing—the received idea that links "creative writing" to individuals alone. Instead of zeroing in on original work of single authors, I direct attention to what is the fruit of a collective of people, many remaining unidentified. Once we consider composing and compiling with composting, generations of writers and artists come into view: those who create fictions for their particular seasons and places. Their works appear as part of larger composites that can grow further.

The compost figure integrates fictions in their many times into the natural world. Jean Froissart, who likens his compiling the history of the French, English and Flemish realms to rivers converging, shares a similar understanding.[20] My figure reminds us that creative work is also subject to the cyclical temporal orders in nature. Over time, what is composed also decomposes. Its components disintegrate so that in the hands of more writers and artists, they mutate and, in turn, can give rise to something else. Take the scrappy pair of the Boy and the Blind Person, for instance, who, over the course of centuries, transmogrify when Beckett, Fo, and Koltès invent their dramatis personae for societies at war struggling against servility. Writer Anne F. Garréta names this temporal cycle explicitly in her novel *La Décomposition*; breaking down Proust's *In Search of Lost Time* is fundamental to creating her own fiction several generations later.[21]

The compost figure poses a fresh alternative to the palimpsest. Literary critics have long assimilated this figure to describe how fictional invention and writing in general exists in time. Anyone who has seen or felt the rough surface where one inscribed text has been scratched out to make space for a new one is liable to find it convincing; anyone who has passing knowledge of a formalist school of criticism entertains Gérard Genette's palimpsest for what he dubs literature in the second degree.[22] The compost figure is different for several reasons. It is not text bound; that is, its figurative force leads beyond objects made exclusively with words. Nor is it human-centered. This figure accommodates various genera and species characterizing the natural world. It comes out of the lexicon of various writers around 1400. It epitomizes their inventiveness in the very language with which they are making fiction. In this, it contrasts with the rhizome of Gilles Deleuze, a natural image adapted from botanical science around 1800.[23]

The compost figure, then, makes clear that creative people at work composing and decomposing participate in a system much larger than themselves. We can critically imagine this system surrounding them through the elements—air, water, earth—that philosopher Brunetto Latini describes in his book of knowledge, the *Treasure*.[24] These are the same natural elements that Édouard Glissant evokes to name his last collection, his poetic testament published postmortem.[25] Call this the environment—the watchword adopted around 1920 for an idea and a movement dedicated to the nature of our planet.[26] Or if you prefer, consider it in still larger terms. Call it macrocosm and conjure up the universe. Poet Gervais du Bus did so around 1350, when he configured it in his fiction, the *Fauvel*, imagining an enormous space inhabited by phantoms.[27] Whatever the scale of this natural world, people's work operates within it as an integral part. While today's researchers acknowledge that contemplating the universe and its absolute time strains the human imagination, they also underscore the vital resource of cosmologies that writers and artists narrate to configure this largest scale of nature.[28]

The compost figure represents, finally, how timely fictions contribute to "renaturalizing culture."[29] It foregrounds what has been sidelined by the engines of so-called modern cultures, what philosopher Augustin Berque sees through an Eastern perspective on the West. Writers and artists are key agents of this fundamental shift. For those creators around 1400 whose works are the starting points of this almanach's entries, this is especially significant. Neither the central agents, nor the only ones involved, they nonetheless see themselves within temporal cycles that situate their work in that largest natural circumstance of the universe.[30] They understand what they make and use in these terms. Christine de Pizan deliberately dates almost every one of her works. This choice is more than attending to the relative time of composing her *Book of Three Virtues*. In the guise of an astronomer, she situates her fiction in the time-scale of the universe. So too her contemporary, Alain Chartier. To begin his *Quadrilogue Invectif*, he evokes physicists' knowledge, and the period of time in the universe.[31] He does so to account for the duration of human communities, to assess the decline of empires like the French in terms that reach scientifically, to those of absolute time.

This is true for the subjects and matter of many more writers and artists. It is equally true for their activity of making fiction. Deschamps was already espousing this view in his treatise canonized as the first art of literary composition in French: poetry is, for him, a natural music.[32] His understanding points us toward recognizing fiction and its forms in time within a cosmic framework, as they say, of the spheres.

Visual artists working around 1450 shared this critical imagination. Those who pictured the treatise of scientist Luis de Angulo, *On Figures and Images of the World*, represented this natural circumstance of the universe brilliantly in a later rendition of an image and work that accompanied the emerging almanach (Figure 31).[33] The round Earth is composed of fertile land and an alleyway of trees in the foreground, and, in the background, another composition made by humankind, a walled city. Two figures go around the Earth, explaining their positions as well as the changing light and dark with raised finger and lantern. Readers discover how they—and the Earth—are positioned in the blue, light-ringed cosmos.

Two generations after artists working with Nicole Oresme drew this sphere in abstract lines, these confrères configured more of its geological, botanical, and animal life. Two generations after Oresme imagined this sphere, and considered those circumnavigating it with his marvelous tale, Luis de Angulo imagined this in greater astronomical and geographical detail. This scientific thinker places his two humans on an Earth identified by its two poles, Arctic and Antarctic, as well as its directions, east and west. He too tells the story of their roundabout travels; his narrative refines Oresme's question of the time differential by representing a cosmography in which human activity takes place.

De Angulo's imaged tale enables us to visualize fuller natural environs and history for timely fictions. That great blue yonder incites us to ponder such a context for what humans do, including what they make with words and images, transmitted on skin, bone, and vegetal matter. I see these travelers who circumnavigate the globe confirming and extending what the compost figure demonstrates: the various cosmic cycles of time that shape the fictions of humankind, and the diverse earthly matter they use to make them.

A generation later, one of the first *Calendar and Compost* printed in French depicts the most elusive segment of temporal cycles that preoccupies thoughtful people: the future (Figure 32). The *Shepherdesses's Compost and Calendar* addresses the almanach's subject and matter by introducing two women sibyls who recommend thinking ahead. These prophets, equipped to work in the fields, make their

Figure 31. Ludovicus de Angulo, *De Figura seu de imagine mundi*. Kantonsbibliothek Vadiana St. Gallen, Vadianische Sammlung der Ortsbürgergemeinde, VadSlg Ms 427, fol. 11v. Photograph: Kantonsbibliothek Vadiana St. Gallen.

Figure 32. Compost et Kalendrier des bergeres (Paris: G. Marchand, 1499); Paris, BnF, Res-V-275, fol. 7. Photograph: Bibliothèque nationale de France.

forecast, in dialogue with the shepherds. This agricultural metaphor of throwing seeds has everything to do with the natural circumstance of ideas and materials presented in their *Compost and Calendar*—at ground level, and that of the starry cosmos. All of them will change and can become fertile again in time.

So too with the works gathered here. I make this almanach during years when astronomers are advancing knowledge about the universe's historical time. In 2022, they released photographic evidence that made its 13-billion-year past visible as never before.[34] Their images radicalize our sense of time. Once more, it is a question of computing temporal phases. Accounting for the times of the literary and graphic works put together here changes again. What creators of all stripes have imagined and thought around 1900, as around 1400, indeed as around 2000, we now can perceive and better understand in the context of this vast time-space. In this situation, how inventive people compose the forms of fictions then, how and why they'll generate further artful, knowledge-rich ones in time to come remains to be seen.

Acknowledgments

This book has been taking shape during years punctuated by natural disasters and political divisiveness in the corners of the world I inhabit. All this turmoil makes it even clearer that crafting such a book is a collective venture that can never be taken for granted.

When it was first a glimmer in my mind, Alice Kaplan, Peggy McCracken, Helmut Puff, and Don Reid supported the idea and emboldened me to think big and write with relish. When it became a jigsaw of pieces, Anne Garréta spent a day probing my prose with me, proving again how exhilarating it is to pursue writing in tandem with others. When a manuscript emerged, Julie Singer organized a workshop with Christine Bourgeois, Noah Guynn, Andrea Marculescu, Deborah McGrady, Meghan Moore, Jeannette Patterson, Charlie Samuelson, and Karen Sullivan: an invaluable thought-fest and memorable exchange. Daisy Delogu and Vincent Bruyère engaged with the work so fully, giving me both precise and expansive ways to envisage the scope of the book as a whole. I thank all of them for their insights and challenges that helped me to bring it to fruition.

All along the way, colleagues have accompanied me with their questions, and suggestions from their own research. Michele Lamprokos is an ally in all matters involving Arabo-Muslim cultures. Didem Havlioğlu, Asli Niyazioğlu, and Émilie Picherot have led me deeper into the shared histories of writers in French, Ottoman Turkish, and Arabic. Dorothy Kaufmann introduced me to Édith Thomas, at a juncture when she was editing her œuvre still largely unknown.

For numerous conversations about literature in circumstances that are increasingly "remote," I thank Yasmina Foehrs-Janssens, Nathalie Koble, Amandine Mussou, Mathias Sieffert, Dominique Demartini, and Christopher Lucken. The book bears many marks of their camaraderie. Sylvie LeFèvre's linguistic precision as her professional solidarity, is invaluable. Lucien Dugaz, Sarah Delale, Charlotte Cooper-Davis, Chloé Gumy, and I came together for a spirited confab on the shores of Lake Léman that added new facets to my sense of Christine de Pizan. In a league all her own, Jacqueline Cerquiglini-Toulet always models for me what we can ask of literature. Her queries about Villon, Christine, and the color of French words deepen my thinking. Years ago, Mark Webb initiated a college student into Villon by way of American poets. Better late than never, I thank him for this gift.

The theater milieu continues to nourish my work. The circle of Jelle Koopmans, Estelle Doudet, and Marie Bouhaïk-Gironès was a crucible for much of my thinking about mystery plays; I'm grateful for their generous engagement over years. Bob Clark was always up for another discussion about manuscript images; I miss his wit. Gabriella Parussa and Darwin Smith were welcoming interlocutors: working with them and Véronique Dominguez refined my work. Metteur-en-scène Denis Guénoun, actor Barry McGovern, and lighting designer Olivier Oudiou inducted me into the transformations of performance in French, especially of Beckett and Koltès. In North Carolina, as in France, I am lucky having Darren Gobert as a colleague whose knowledge of the history of theater is so much a part of him that the smallest exchange always offers food for more thought. Without Mauricette Berne, the manuscripts of Simone Jollivet and Sartre would have been out of reach.

My choice to begin working with Inuit cultures would have been impossible without many colleagues and friends. My first thanks go to members of Ikpiarjuk /Arctic Bay communities for their willingness to respond to an outsider. I am all the more humbled and inspired by them now. They model integrity in the face of wanton greed and ignorance.

I am also endebted to Janet Young at the Canadian Museum of History for sharing her ongoing work with the Ikpiarjuk community. That heady discussion with her encouraged me to continue my work. Karen Ryan and Pierre Desrosiers fielded my questions with generosity. Peter Tost welcomed me to the National Museum of Denmark. The excavation drawings of archaeological sites across Nunavut that he brought out incited me to embark on a comparative study. He gave to me a sense of common investigation. Frederik Fuuja Larsen was an incomparable guide into Inuit/Thule archaeology. His discussion of artifacts in Nuuk, at the Greenland National Musuem, is all the more precious, because he tempered it with a sobering reminder of misguided, destructive American interventions. André Delpuech, then at the Quai Branly Museum, Paris, introduced me to European circles of archaeologists working in the Arctic. In Washington,

Igor Krupnik, Bill Fitzhugh, and Stephen Loring opened up a Smithsonian collection of Iñupiaq and Yupik bowdrills. I thank them for instructing an unknown scholar and sharing their experience of collaborative projects. A powerfully good exchange with Igor Krupnik defines intellectual inquiry for me.

Pat Fehely did not hesitate to share her deep knowledge and commitment to Inuit artists. In her activism, she was always ready with the next lead. Leslie Howse was an irreplaceable colleague at the Inuit Heritage Trust whose advice came at the right times; Kelly Ward-Wills was an indispensable intermediary with Germaine Arnaktauyok. Paul Gooch and Pauline Thompson connected me with activists in Kinngait. It was Deirdre Baker and Jane Burns who impressed on me my responsibilities in working with communities: they are my ethical compass.

During years when our institutions were subjected to increasing, severe pressure, I am all the more grateful for the support my work received from the Guggenheim Foundation. At Duke University, Dean Kevin Moore had my back. The chair of my department of Romance Studies, Martin Eisner, understood what time off meant for making a book during the pandemic.

Colleagues who participated in my presentations in Paris, Sydney, Ann Arbor, Nashville, Kalamazoo, and Berlin are too numerous to identify; they have all contributed in detail to my work—whether they know it or not. Roland Betancourt was an incisive colleague at a key stage in the book. Andrew Griebeler knew just how to direct me in tracking date palms across the Mediterranean. Ann Rigney gets to the quick of every subject we discuss, from Dingle to Belleville.

The student researchers I'm fortunate enough to work with enriched this book in many ways with their own expertise: Matthew Melgoza, Unglid Paul, Daria Kozhanova, Shreya Hurli, and Halle Wagner.

Librarians and archivists in several countries, ever ready to answer another question, are the collaborators of all my work: the many at the Bibliothèque nationale de France, the Archives nationales, the Library of Congress, the Schlesinger Library at Radcliffe Institute for Advanced Study, the Royal Libraries of Sweden and Holland, Harvard University, the Smithsonian Institution, and the National Library of Greenland. Comrades at my home institution's Bostock, Rubenstein Libraries and the Bibliothèque Estienne are due special thanks, especially Andy Armacost and Claire Hilfiger.

In the final stretch, Mark Olson, Ezgi Ozturk, Lys Weiss, and Victoria George helped me shepherd the book into production, with Erica Wetter and Caroline McKusick, caring editors.

At the heart of my efforts are those whose company I cherish. They energize me when I begin to flag or lose sight of my goal: to cultivate intrepid and courageous thinking with the next generation. Bonnie Krueger, Ann Marie Rasmussen, Jean Delabroy, Carla Puppin, Bryant Holsenbeck, Chris Krueger, Martha Stancill, Terry Vance, Bob Williams, Bob Vaillancourt, Sydney Cruze, Ben Finholt, Dianitia Hutcheson: *merci royalement.*

This book is for you, sent off as another year begins, with my eye set on the horizon we share.

Durham—Paris
December 2025 / January 2026

Notes

Prologue: Calendar

1. Nicole Oresme, *Le Traictié de l'Espere* (1365–68), Paris, BnF, f. fr. 565, fols. 1–22, ed. Terrence J. McGovern, Catholic University Press, 1974; *Livre du ciel et du monde* (1375), Paris, BnF, f. fr. 565, fols. 23–171, ed. Albert D. Menut, trans. Alexander J. Denomy and Albert D. Menut (University of Wisconsin Press, 1968), 478–79. I give references to manuscripts and to editions in print. Violaine Giacometto-Charra and Sylvie Nony, *La Terre plate. Généalogie d'une idée fausse* (Folio, 2023), 114.

2. *Livre du ciel et du monde*, Paris, BnF, f. fr. 1082, fol. 157; *Du sphere*, Vatican City, Biblioteca Apostolica Vaticana, ms. Reg. lat. 1337, fols. 40v–41; Ken Mondschein, *On Time. A History of Western Timekeeping* (Johns Hopkins University Press, 2020), 68.

3. Max Lejbowicz, "Nicole Oresme et les voyages circumterrestres ou un poème entre la science et la religion," *Archives d'histoire doctrinale et littéraire du Moyen Âge* 55 (1988): 99–142.

4. Matthew S. Champion, *The Fullness of Time: Temporalities of the Fifteenth-century Low Countries* (University of Chicago Press, 2017). On Baghdad, center of astronomical science, Antoine Borrut, "Court Astrologers and Historical Writing in Early Abbasid Baghdad," in *The Place to Go: Contexts of Learning in Baghdad, 750–1000 CE*, ed. J. Scheiner and D. Janos (Darwin Press, 2014), 455–501.

5. Claudia Kren, "The Rolling Device of Naṣir āl-Dīn al-Ṭūsī in the *De Sphera* of Nicole Oresme?" *Isis* 62, no. 4 (winter 1971): 490–98. Oresme cites the work of astronomer al-Bāttāni (c. 900 CE) in his *De Commensurabilite*, Paris, Arsenal, ms. 522, fols. 110–21 (dated c. 1395–98); Paris, BnF, f. fr. lat. 7281, fols. 259–73; ed. Edward Grant, *Nicole Oresme and the Kinematics of Circular Motion* (University of Wisconsin Press, 1971), 284–85. Seyyed Mohammed Mozaffari and George Zotti, "The Observational Instruments at the Maragha Observatory after AD 1300," *Suhayl: International Journal for the History of the Exact and Natural Sciences in Islamic Civilisation* 12 (2013): 45–179; and *Journal of American Oriental Society* 132 (2012). George Saliba gives a defining overview in *Islamic Science and the Making of the European Renaissance* (MIT Press, 2007).

6. Some hundred years earlier than Oresme, around 1303, artists working with Gossuin de Metz on his *Image du monde* rendered a similar image with two men standing on both poles; it does not represent the idea of the time lag created by a round earth in rotation: Rennes, Bibliothèque municipale, ms. 593, fol. 63v. See Michael Evans on this design: "The Geometry of the Mind," *The Architectural Association Quarterly* 12, no. 4 (1980): 35, 47. An excellent overview is Jeffrey F. Hamburger, "Mindmapping: The Diagram Paradigm in Medieval Art and Beyond," in *The Visualization of Knowledge in the Medieval and Early Modern Period*, ed. Marcia Kupfer, Adam S. Cohen, and J. H. Chajes (Brepols, 2020), 61–86.

7. Among various works, Michel Foucault, "What Is an Author?" in *Language, Counter-memory, Practice: Selected Essays and Interviews by Michel Foucault*, ed. and trans. Donald F. Bouchard and Sherry Simon (Cornell University Press, 1982), 134–36 ("Qu'est-ce-qu'un auteur?" 1969).

8. *Compost et Kalendrier des bergiers*, Angers, Bibliothèque mun., Rés. SA 3390, fol. 64v–65.

9. *Compost et Kalendrier des bergiers*, Angers, Bibliothèque mun., Rés. SA 3390; Paris BnF, Réserve livres rares, vélin-518 (Paris: Guy Marchant, 1493); ed. Max Engammare (Fondation Martin Bodmer, 2008). Denis Hüe, "*Le Calendrier et compost des bergers*. Un vade-mecum populaire," in *Lire, choisir, écrire. La vulgarisation des savoirs du Moyen Âge et de la Renaissance*, ed. Violaine Ghiacomotto-Charra and Cristine Silvi (École nationale des chartes, 2014), 71–96; *Les Calendriers. Leurs enjeux dans l'espace et dans le temps*, ed. Jacques Le Goff, Jean Lefort, and Perrine Mane (Hermann, 2016), 17–22, 249–58.

10. "Almanach pour toujours," Cambridge, Gonville and Caius College, ms. 187/220; Jean Molinet, *Les Pronostications joyeuses*, ed. Jelle Koopmans and Paul Verhuyk (Droz, 1998); François Rabelais, "Pronostications et almanachs" and "Almanach pour l'An 1533, 1535, 1541," in *Œuvres complètes*, ed. Mireille Huchon (Gallimard, 1994), 936–57.

11. "Le Nouveau calendrier," Jean Molinet, *Pronostications joyeuses*, ll. 43–44, 57. All translations throughout the book are mine unless otherwise noted.

12. Blaise Cendrars, *Œuvres autobiographiques complètes*, ed. Claude Leroy with Michèle Touret (Gallimard, 2013), 29–144; Eric Robertson, *Blaise Cendrars: The Invention of Life* (Reaktion Books, 2022); Miriam Cendrars, *Blaise Cendrars* (Baland, 1984). Clément Marot's *Œuvres de Françoys Villon de Paris reveues et remises en leur entier* (1533) is the updated Villon that Cendrars first encounters.

13. Letter written to editor Paul Lafitte, August 1938, in "Sous le signe de Francois Villon," in *Œuvres autobiographiques complètes*, 6; published first in *La Table ronde* 49 (January 1952), 48. Bern, BN Suisse, Archives littéraires suisses, Fonds Blaise Cendrars, P 79–82.

14. Zrinka Stahuljak, *Médiéval contemporain. Pour une littérature connectée* (Éditions Macula, 2020).

15. Carolyn Dinshaw, "All Kinds of Time," *Studies in the Age of Chaucer* 35 (2013): 4–6; *How Soon Is Now? Medieval Texts, Amateur Readers, and the Queerness of Time* (Duke University Press, 2012), 5–12; "Touching on the Past," *Getting Medieval: Sexualities and Communities, Pre- and Postmodern* (Duke University Press, 1999).

16. *Le Robert Dictionnaire historique de la langue française*, ed. Alain Rey (2004), 306.

17. *Œuvres autobiographiques complètes*, 5. Le Quellec Cottier and the Pléiade editors establish the sequence of Cendrars's writing about prochrony and Villon from the 1930s to 1952. Jacqueline Cerquiglini Toulet reproduces Cendrars's prefatory letter to his first editor, Paul Lafitte, in her edition: François Villon, *Œuvres complètes* (Gallimard, 2014).

18. "The Concept of Anachronism and the Historian's Truth," trans. Tim Stott and Noel Fitzpatrick, *InPrint* 3, no. 1 (2015): 21–52; "Le Concept d'anachronisme et la vérité de l'historien," *L'Inactuel. Psychanalyse et culture* 6 (Autumn 1996): 53–68. In the visual arts, see Alexander Nagel and Christopher S. Wood, *Anachronic Renaissance* (Zone Books, 2020).

19. Rancière, trans. Stott and Fitzpatrick, "The Concept of Anachronism," 47.

20. Political theorist Samuel Chambers draws a notion of literarity out of Rancière's work, one with an unpredictable, disruptive relation to chronological time. Chapter 3 in *The Lessons of Rancière* (Oxford University Press, 2015). See also Todd May, *Contemporary Political Movements and the Thought of Jacques Rancière: Equality in Action* (Edinburgh University Press, 2010); Kristin Ross, "Historicizing Untimeliness," in *Jacques Rancière: History, Politics, Aesthetics*, ed. Gabriel Rockhill and Philip Watts (Duke University Press, 2009), 15–29, especially 16.

21. Bruce Holsinger, *The Premodern Condition: Medievalism and the Making of Theory* (University of Chicago Press, 2005); Roland Betancourt, co-editor with Karla Mallette of the centenary issue, *Speculum* 100, no. 1 (2025).

22. Algernon Charles Swinburne, *Poems and Ballads, Second Series* (1866), in *The Poems of Algernon Charles Swinburne in Six Volumes*, vol. 3 (Chatto & Windus, 1904); Dante Gabriel Rosetti, *Poems* (F. S. Ellis, 1870).

23. Nathalie Koble and Amandine Mussou, eds., *Ut musica poesis. Poésie visuelle et sonore au Moyen Âge et aujourd'hui* (Éditions Macula, 2024), 33.

24. Aby Warburg, *Der Bilder Atlas: Mnemosyne* (1924–29), in *Gesammelte Schriften* II, 1, ed. Martin Warke and Claudia Brinke (Akademie Verlag, 2008). The English and French translators of his unfinished *Memory Atlas* (1924–29) followed suit. Christopher D. Johnson, *Mnemosyne: Meanderings through Aby Warburg's Atlas* (Cornell University Library with the Warburg Institute, 2013–24); *L'Atlas Mnémnosyne*, trans. Sacha Silberfarb (L'Écarquillé, 2012). See David Freedberg and Claudia Wedepohl, eds., *Aby Warburg 150: Work, Legacy, Promise* (de Gruyter, 2024), especially the contribution by Ulrich Raulff, "*Nachleben*," followed by a "Letter from Georges Didi-Huberman," 64. Elizabeth Sears is at work on her collective biography, "Warburg Circles: Towards a Cultural Historical History of Art, 1929–1964." On uses of the term in this century: Davide Sisto, *Online Afterlives*, trans. Bonnie McClennan-Broussard (MIT Press, 2020); Ann Rigney, *The Afterlives of Walter Scott: Memory on the Move* (Oxford University Press, 2012); Kristin Ross, *May '68 and Its Afterlives* (University of Chicago Press, 2002).

25. Oxford, Bodleian Library, Oriental ms. 133, attributed erroneously, Warburg underscores, to Abû Ma'shar; Warburg, *L'Atlas Mnémosyne*; Al-Qazwînî, *Merveilles des choses créées et les curiosités des choses existantes*; Alfonso X of Castile, *Libro de ajedrez, dados et tablas*; Matfre Ermengaud, *Breviari d'Amor*; Christine de Pizan, *Épître d'Othéa*.

26. Georges Didi-Huberman, *The Surviving Image: Phantoms of Time and the Time of Phantoms: Aby Warburg's History of Art*, trans. Harvey L. Mendelsohn (Pennsylvania State University Press, 2017) (*L'Image survivante*, 2002).

27. "Poetrie est science qui aprent a fainre et a faire fictions fondees en raison" (Book II, chap. 25). Jacques Legrand, *Archiloge Sophie*, Paris, BnF, f. fr. 24232, fol. 61v; ed. Evencio Beltran (Slatkine, 1986), 149. Jonathan Morton, "Textual Experiments: Thinking with Fiction," in *Medieval Thought Experiments: Poetry, Hypothesis, and Experience in the European Middle Ages*, ed. Philip Knox, Jonathan Morton, and Daniel Reeve (Brepols, 2018), 1–20.

28. Jacques Rancière, *The Edges of Fiction*, trans. Steven Corcoran (Polity Press, 2021), introduction (*Les Bords de la fiction*, 2017); "Fictions of Time," in *Rancière and Literature*, ed. Grace Hellyer and Julien Murphet (Edinburgh University Press, 2016), 25.

29. On al-Fārābī: Deborah Black, in *The Routledge History of Islamic Philosophy*, ed. Seyyed Hossein Nasr and Oliver Leaman (Routledge, 1996), 1:178–97; "Alfarabi (Al-Fārābī)," in *A Companion to Philosophy in the Middle Ages*, ed. J. J. E. Gracia and Timothy B. Noone (Blackwell, 2003), 109–17.

30. "it is known, in general, that the name of poetry should be taken for any fiction. That is to say, for any narration or introduction that signifies a meaning that is apparent, it signifies another one or several others in hidden ways, so much so that to say it properly, poetry is that fiction whose aim is truth"; "si est assavoir que comme en general le nom de poesie soit pris pour fiction quelconque, c'est a dire pour toute narracion ou introduction apparaument signifiant un senz, et occultement en segnifie un aultre ou plusieurs, combien que plus proprement dire celle soit poesie dont la fin est verite." Christine de Pizan, Paris, BnF, f. fr. 10153, fol. 103; *Fais et bonnes mœurs du sage roy Charles V*, ed. Suzanne Solente (Champion, 1940), 2:176.

31. "De renardie et fiction," *Prologue du Dit de la Queue de Renart*, Paris, BnF, f. fr. 12483, fol. 240; *Due dits del XIV secolo. Dit de la queue de Renart. Dit de Fauvain*, ed. Marguerita Lecco (Edizioni dell'Orso, 2009).

32. *Le romant des Fables Ovide le Grant, ou les Métamorphoses d'Ovide moralisées en vers français par Chrestien Legouais de Sainte-More près Troyes*, Paris, Arsenal, ms. 5069, fols. 1–245v.

33. Estelle Doudet, *Poétique de George Chastelain (1415–1475). Un cristal mucié en un coffre* (Champion, 2005); Jean-Claude Mühlethaler, "Un manifeste poétique de 1463. Les 'Enseignes' des Douze Dames de Rhétorique," in *Grands Rhétoriqueurs. Actes du Ve Colloque international sur le moyen français* (Università Catholica del Sacro Cuore, 1985) 1:83–101.

34. Cambridge, Cambridge University Library, ms. Nn. 3. 2, fol. 43v; Georges Chastelain, Jean Robertet, and Jean de Montferrant, *Les Douze Dames de Rhétorique*, ed. David Cowling (Droz, 2002), 168.

35. Mühlethaler sees Boethian Philosophy in this figure of Science ("Un manifeste poétique"). Cynthia J. Brown, "A Late Medieval Cultural Artifact: The Twelve Ladies of Rhetoric (Les douze dames de rhétorique)," *Allegorica: A Journal of Medieval and Renaissance Literature* 16 (1995): 73–105; Rebecca Dixon and Finn E. Sinclair, eds., *Poetry, Knowledge, and Community in Late Medieval France* (Boydell & Brewer, 2017); Adrian Armstrong and Sarah Kay, *Knowing Poetry* (Cornell University Press, 2011).

36. "Je monte au ciel, je descens es enfers, Je plonge en mer, je parvole les aers." Cambridge, Cambridge University Library, ms. Nn. 3. 2, fol. 26v, *Les Douze Dames*, 138.

37. Cambridge, Cambridge University Library, ms. Nn. 3. 2, fol. 34v; *Les Douze Dames*, 151.

38. Jacques Roubaud, introd., and Albert-Marie Schmidt, ed., *L'Amour noir* (Slatkine, 1982; 1st edition, 1959). Schmidt, one of the founders, creates the name Ouvroir from language around 1400; *Panorama des XIVe–XVe siècles français* (Éditions Seghers, 1964). Nathalie Koble and Mireille Séguy, eds., *Jacques Roubaud, médiéviste* (Champion, 2017); Pierre Bayard, *Le Plagiat par anticipation* (Éditions de Minuit, 2008); Nathalie Koble and Mireille Séguy, *Mémoire du moyen âge* (Champion, 2012).

39. Paris, BnF, f. fr. 810 and 811; Michael Hanly, ed., *Medieval Muslims, Christians and Jews in Dialogue: The Apparicion Maistre Jehan de Meun of Honorat de Bovet* (Arizona Center for Medieval and Renaissance Studies, 2005); Boston Public Library, ms. 1528; Brussels, KBR ms. 10973; Paris, BnF, f. fr. 452; Christine de Pizan, *Le Livre des Trois Vertus*, ed. Charity Cannon Willard (Champion, 1989).

40. Jean Boivin, *Apologie d'Homère et le bouclier d'Achille* (Paris: chez François Jouenne, 1715); Édith Thomas, Paris, Archives nationales [AN] 318 AP.

41. Paris, BnF, f.fr. 20041, Stockholm, KB, ms. Vu. 22, *Le grand Testament, Codicille, Ballades, Petit Testament* (Paris: Pierre Levet, 1489); *Œuvres complètes*, ed. Jacqueline Cerquiglini-Toulet (Gallimard, 2014). The translation of poet Galway Kinnell, *The Poems of François Villon* (University of New England Press, 1982 [Houghton Mifflin, 1977]).

42. Victor Hugo, *Le Dernier jour d'un condamné*, ed. Roger Borderie (Gallimard, 2000); Langston Hughes, *Collected Poems of Langston Hughes* (Knopf, 1994); George Faludy, *Selected Poems, 1933–1980*, ed. Robin Skelton (University of Georgia Press, 1985); Édouard Glissant, *La Terre, le feu, l'eau et les vents. Une anthologie de la poésie du tout-monde* (Éditions Galaade, 2010).

43. Paris, BnF, f. fr. 815, 816, 15064; Chantilly, Musée Condé, 614; *Le Mystère de la Passion d'Arnoul Gréban*, ed. Omer Jodogne (Palais des Académies, 1965–83); *Le Mystère du Vieil Testament* (Pierre Le Dru pour Jean Petit, vers 1500), ed. Émile Picot and Baron James de Rothschild (Firmin Didot, 1878); Wolfenbüttel, Herzog August Bibliothek, 9 Blankenberg; *Les Mystères de la Procession de Lille*, ed. Alan E. Knight (Droz, 2001–11); Paris, BnF, f. fr. 24332; *Le Mystère de Saint Martin*, ed. André Duplat (Droz, 1979); Chantilly, Musée Condé, ms. 615; *Le Mystère de la Résurrection*, ed. Pierre Servet (Droz, 1993); *Le Recueil de Florence. 53 farces imprimées à Paris en 1515*, ed. Jelle Koopmans (Éditions Paradigme, 2011); Paris, BnF, f. fr. 24366; *Le Garçon et l'aveugle*, ed. Carol Symes, "The Boy and the Blindman: A Medieval Play and Its Editors," in *The Book Unbound: Editing and Reading Medieval Manuscripts and Texts*, ed. Siân Echard and Stephen Partridge (University of Toronto Press, 2004), 128–41.

44. Paris, BnF, Département Arts du spectacle, fonds Charles Dullin Simone Jollivet 40 COL 42; Simone de Beauvoir, *Les Bouches inutiles* (Gallimard, 1945), trans. Margaret A. Simons and Marybeth Timmermann, *"The Useless Mouths" and Other Literary Writings* (University of Illinois Press, 2011), 33–87; Samuel Beckett, *Fragment de théâtre I* in *Pas* (Éditions de Minuit, 1978), 21–34, trans., *Rough for Theater I* in *Collected Shorter Plays* (Grove Press, 1984), 65–74.

45. Two plays, "The Drowning Eye" (*L'Œil se noie*) and "Parallel Hands" (*Les Mains parallèles*), in Frantz Fanon, *Écrits sur l'aliénation et la liberté* (Éditions de la Découverte, 2018), 79–109.

46. Dario Fo, *Mistero Buffo*, trans. Ed Emery, in *Plays: One* (Methuen,1993), 1–122; *Mystère Bouffe*, adapted by Ginette Herry (Dramaturgie, 1984); Bernard-Marie Koltès, *In the Solitude of Cotton Fields*, ed. David Bradby, trans. Jeffrey Wainwright (Methuen Drama, 1997), 2:187–215; *Dans la solitude des champs de coton* (Éditions de Minuit, 1986).

47. Bruce Holsinger, *On Parchment: Animals, Archives, and the Making of Culture from Herodotus to the Digital Age* (Yale University Press, 2023).

48. *Dictionnaire historique de la langue française*, 2452; Avinoam Shalem, *The Oliphant: Islamic Objects in Historical Context* (Brill, 2004); Philippe Cordez, "Objets, images, et trésors d'église," in *Les images dans l'Occident médiéval*, ed. Jérôme Baschet and Pierre-Olivier Dittmar (Brepols, 2015), 125–27; Rita Costa-Gomes, "In and Out of Africa: Iberian Courts and the Afro-Portuguese Olifant of the Late 1400s," in *Contact and Exchange in Late Medieval Europe: Essays in Honor of Malcolm Vale*, ed. Hannah Skoda et al. (Boydell, 2012), 167–89.

49. Roland's fictional horn has been associated with one in Toulouse; Musée des Arts Précieux Paul-Dupuy, #18038. Similar horns from the same period: the Olifant de la Chartreuse des Portes at the BnF, and one at the Boston Museum of Fine Arts.

50. Sarah M. Guérin, *French Gothic Ivories: Material Theologies and the Sculptor's Craft* (Cambridge University Press, 2022).

51. My focus: belongings of the Inuit community of Ikpiarjuk/Arctic Bay, Nunavut, with Matthew Betts and Janet Young, "Nuvumiutaq: The Arctic Bay Kayaker," Gatineau, Canadian Museum of History, exhibit installed 2017; Matthew Betts and Janet Young, "Repatriation Tells Remarkable Story," museum blog, August 24 and 30, 2017; Amy Phillips-Chan, ed. and comp., *Our Stories Etched in Ivory: Qulip'yugut Iksiaqtuumaruat: Tuugaami: The Smithsonian Collections of Engraved Drill Bows with Stories from the Arctic* (Smithsonian, 2021); Cécile Pelaudeix, *Art Inuit. Formes de l'âme et représentations de l'être. Histoire de l'art et anthropologie* (Éditions de Pise, 2007). See also the work of the previous generation of archaeologists, Herbert Maschner, Owen Mason, and Robert McGhee, eds., *The Northern World, 900–1400* (University of Utah Press, 2009); Robert McGhee, *Ancient People of the Arctic* (University of British Columbia Press, 1996).

52. Sean P. A. Desjardins, Natasha Lyons, and Mari Kleist, "Inuit Voices: Community-based Archaeology across the North American Arctic," *Études Inuit Studies* 46, no. 2 (2022); Mari Kleist, "Making Inuit Archaeology Matter in Kalaallit Nunaat," in *Working As Indigenous Archaeologists: Reckoning New Paths between Past and Present Lives*, ed. George Nicolas and Joe Watkins (Routledge, 2024), 228–38.

53. Hans Christian Gulløv, ed., *Grønlands Forhistorie* (Gyldendal, 2005); James H. Barrett, ed., *Contact, Continuity, and Collapse: Norse Colonization of the North Atlantic* (Brepols, 2003). See Gerald McMaster on Inuit Thule figurine, dated 1250–1300, that may represent a Norseman: "Indigenizing the Museum," *Medieval Art Matters*, podcast, August 2022; Jill Caskey, Adam S. Cohen, and Linda Safran, *Art and Architecture of the Middle Ages: Exploring a Connected World* (Cornell University Press, 2022).

54. Daniel Weetaluktuk, "Canadian Inuit and Archaeology," Canadian Archaeological Association (1978); "Archéologie du Nunavik et du Labrador. Hommage à Patrick Plumet," *Études Inuit Studies* 39, no. 2 (2015); Sergei Arutiunov, *Ancient Cultures of the Asiatic Eskimos* (National Park Service, 2006).

55. Alain Rey, *Le Voyage des mots. De l'Orient arabe et persan vers la langue française*

(Guy Trédaniel, 2014), 36–39; Daniel Martin Varisco, *Seasonal Knowledge and the Almanac Tradition in the Arab Gulf* (Palgrave Macmillan, 2022), 1, 26–27. See also Varisco's study of a thirteenth-century work in *Medieval Agriculture and Islamic Science: The Almanac of a Yemeni Sultan* (University of Washington Press, 1994).

56. A. Tunç Şen outlines the tabular form of fifteenth-century *takvîms*, or annual almanachs with astrological prognostications, as well as their "hodge-podge of contents"; he situates the *takvîm* in the Chester Beatty Library among sixteen from c. 1421–1575, "The Science and Politics of Chronology in Late Medieval and Early Ottoman Almanacs," in *Osmanli'da ilm-I Tarih*, ed. Zahit Atçil, Ercüment Asil, and Cemal Atabaş (Isar Yayinian, 2023), 49–50, 59. Many of the earliest Arabo-Muslim works of astronomical knowledge were not called *al-manâkh*; a cross-check of dictionary entries reveals that the Arabic etymology is given for the term in Romance languages and in English and German, while Turkish gives the Latin one. *Deutsches Fremdwörterbuch* (de Gruyter, 1995); *Büyuk Luga Ansiklopedï* (Meydan Yayinevi, 1980).

57. Paris, BnF, ms. f. héb. 1064; f. lat. 7272. The term appearing in "Le canon sus l'almenach au juif," in an ensemble including "tables astronomiques" and "kalendrier," and the *Image du monde* of Gossuin de Metz; Rennes, Bibliothèque municipale, ms. 593, fol. 41; Sophie Cassagnes-Brouquet, *L'image du monde. Un trésor enluminé de la Bibliothèque de Rennes* (PUR, 2003). On Judah Ibn Tibbon, chap. 9 in Ram Ben Shalom, *The Jews of Provence and Languedoc*, trans. Schmuel Sermoneta-Gertel (Liverpool University Press, 2024).

58. The expression *almanach perpetuum* appears in Oresme's treatise, *De commensurabilitate vel incommensurabilitate motuum celi*, Paris, BnF, ms. lat. 7281, fols. 259–73; Arsenal, ms. lat. 522, fols. 110–21; ed. and trans. Edward Grant, in *Nicole Oresme and the Kinematics of Circular Motion*, 278–79, 286–87, 320–21.

59. *Türkenkalendar*, Munich, BSB, P.O. germ. 1697/18; Eckehard Simon, *The Türkenkalendar (1454) Attributed to Gutenberg and the Strasbourg Lunation Tracts* (Medieval Academy of America, 1988); Yves Perrousseaux, *Histoire de l'écriture typographique* (Atelier Perrousseaux, 2005), 51. Printer Hans Folz, *Parodistischer Almanack*, 1480. See Kristina Richardson, "A New Narrative of Afro-Eurasian Printing," in *Roma and the Medieval Islamic World: Literacy, Culture, and Migration* (I. B. Tauris, 2021), 105.

60. Hilmi Kaçar and Jan Dumolyn, "The Battle of Nicopolis (1396), Burgundian Catastrophe and Ottoman Fait Divers," *Revue belge de philologie et d'histoire* 91, no. 4 (2013): 905–34. For the religious ideology of this long political antagonism: Noel Malcolm, *Useful Enemies: Islam and the Ottoman Empire in Western Political Thought 1450–1750 (*Oxford University Press, 2019); Mohammed Arkoun, ed., *Histoire de l'Islam et des Musulmans en France* (Albin Michel, 2006).

61. Current debates over categorizing the span of 1200–1500 name it "early" instead. This may free cultures from familiar stigmas, but it introduces other chronological ambiguities. Finbarr Barry Flood and Beate Fricke, *Tales Things Tell: Material Histories of Early Globalisms* (Princeton University Press, 2024), 17–18. A parallel choice to renew the historiography: *Nouvelle histoire du Moyen Âge*, ed. Florian Mazel et. al. (Seuil, 2021).

62. Edmund Spenser, *Shepheard's Calender*, 1579, p. iii; ed. Kenneth Borris (Manchester University Press, 2022).

63. *Almanach de Québec de 1789 pour l'année bissextile, avec compost ecclésiastique*, and *Almanach de 1805, Nouvelle Orléans, avec comput ecclésiastique*.

64. Claire Gaspard, "Les Almanachs de l'an II. Quoi de neuf hors le calendrier?" *Annales historiques de la Révolution française* 264 (April–June 1986): 141–59; Geneviève Bollème, *Les Almanachs populaires aux XVIIe et XVIIIe siècles. Essai d'histoire sociale* (de Gruyter, 1969), 11–21; Phoebe Jensen, *Astrology, Almanacs, and the Early Modern English Calendar* (Routledge, 2021). Avant-garde artists took to its malleable, time-specific form: Jean Dubuffet et al., *Almanach de l'art brut*, ed. Sarah Lombardi and Baptiste Brun (5 Continents Editions, 2016).

65. *The Poor Richard Almanack for the Year 1732*, written by Richard Saunders (place of printing unidentified).

Entry 1: Free and Safe Passage

1. Paris, BnF, f. fr. 810 and 811, two manuscripts overseen by Bovet; the excellent edition of Michael Hanly, *Medieval Muslims, Christians and Jews in Dialogue: The Apparicion Maistre Jehan de Meun of Honorat Bovet* (Arizona Center for Medieval and Renaissance Studies, 2005).

2. Hilmi Kaçar and Jan Dumolyn, "The Battle of Nicopolis (1396)," *Revue belge de philologie et d'histoire* 91 (2013): 914–16, 922. On Bovet criticism: Helen Solterer, "Another Land's End of Literature: Honorat Bovet and the Timbuktu Effect," in *Founding Feminisms in Medieval Studies* (Boydell & Brewer, 2016), 153–68; Hélène Biu, "Honorat Bovet," *Histoire littéraire de la France* 43, no. 1 (2005): 95; Hélène Millet and Michael Hanly, "Les Batailles d'Honorat Bovet. Essai de biographie," *Romania* 114 (1996): 144; Zeynep Kocabiyikoglu Çeçen, "Praising the Turk after Nicopolis: French Sources," *Tarih İncelemeleri Dergisi* 36, no. 1 (2021): 187–207 (DOI 10.18513/egetid.974606).

3. Judith Schlanger, *Présences des œuvres perdues* (Hermann, 2010), 12–13.

4. Kristina Richardson, "The Boundaries and Geographies of Medieval Blackness," in *Islam on the Margins: Studies in Memory of Michael Bonner*, ed. Robert Haug and Steven Judd (Brill, 2023), 221, 227, 231; Roland Betancourt and Ambereen Dadabhoy, "Geographies of Race: Constructions of Constantinople/Istanbul in the Western European Imaginary," in *Race before Race: Visual Culture and the Racial Matrix in the Premodern World*, ed. Noémie Ndiaye and Lia Markey (ACMRS Press, 2023), 84; Rachel N. Schine, *Black Knights: Arabic Epic and the Making of Medieval Race* (University of Chicago Press, 2024), 7–10.

5. On these energetic debates: *Digital Philology* 15, no. 1 (January 2026), special issue, ed. Sarah Ifft Decker, especially Marcel Elias, "'Resistance Within': Honorat Bovet on Expansionism and Race"; Cord. J. Whitaker, Nahir I. Otaño Gracia, and François-Xavier Fauvelle, "Race, Race-Thinking and the Global Middle Ages," *Speculum* 99, no. 2 (April 2024), especially on an Arabic geographical dictionary, c. 1220, pp. 324–26. Lynn Ramey on black figures in works from French-speaking regions: *Black Legacies: Race and the European Middle Ages* (University of Florida Press, 2018); Cord J. Whitaker on Chaucer, Mandeville, and other works of the so-called English Middle Ages: *Black Metaphors: How Modern Racism Emerged from Medieval Race-based Thinking* (University of Pennsylvania Press, 2021). Other significant contributions: Geraldine Heng, *The Invention of Race in the European Middle Ages* (Cambridge University Press, 2018); and

Maaike van der Lugt, "La peau noire dans la science médiévale," *Micrologus* 13 (2005): 439–75.

6. Thierry Hentsch, *L'Orient imaginaire. La vision politique occidentale de l'Est méditérranéen* (Éditions de Minuit, 1988), 79–80; Hišām Gu'ayt [Hichem Djaït], *L'Europe et Islam* (Seuil, 1978).

7. Noel Malcolm, *Useful Enemies: Islam and the Ottoman Empire in Western Political Thought 1450–1750* (Oxford University Press, 2019), chaps. 1–2, pp. 1–56.

8. On the European continent in the south, Hussein Fancy, *The Mercenary Mediterranean: Sovereignty, Religion, and Violence in the Medieval Crown of Aragon* (University of Chicago Press, 2016), 94–99; Robert I. Burns, "The Guidaticum Safe-conduct in Medieval Arago-Catalonia: A Mini-institution for Muslims, Christians and Jews," *Medieval Encounters* 1 (1995): 68–78; Daniel Nordman, "Sauf-conduits et passeports à la Renaissance," in *Voyager à la Renaissance*, ed. Jean Céard, J.-C. Margolin; and Daniel Nordman, *Frontières de France* (Gallimard, 1998). In the ancient Roman Mediterranean, Luca Scholz, *Borders: Freedom of Movement in the Holy Roman Empire* (Oxford University Press, 2020). In fiction in French, safe passage is represented both on southern frontiers, in zones of conflicts with Muslims, in the *Chanson de Roland*, as on the Channel coast, during the Hundred Years' War, in the ballads of Eustache Deschamps, "A gens qui sont a maladie," "Proclamation d'un Tournoi à Paris," in *Œuvres complètes*, ed. Marquis de Queux de Saint-Hilaire (Firmin Didot, 1877) 2: 89–91.

9. Paris, BnF, ms. espagnol 30. See the In Transit collective, "Arts of Migration," in *Migrants Shaping Europe: Multilingual Literatures, Arts and Cultures*, ed. Helen Solterer and Vincent Joos (Manchester University Press, 2022), 251–53.

10. On his legal Latin commentaries, Geneviève Hasenohr, "Discours vernaculaire et autorités latines," in *Mise en page et mise en texte du livre manuscrit* (Éditions du Cercle de la Librairie–Promodis, 1990), 315. On the multilingual practices pioneered by James I of Aragon, in French, Catalan, Castilian, and Latin: Antonio Zaldivar, "James I and the Rise of Codeswitching Diplomacy in Thirteenth-century Catalonia," *Viator* 47, no. 3 (2016): 207.

11. Christiane Marchello-Nizia, "La Rhétorique des songes et le songe comme rhétorique dans la littérature française médiévale," in *I Sogni nel Medioevo*, ed. Tullio Gregory (Edizioni dell'Ateneo, 1985), 256–58; Toufy Fahd, "The Dream in Medieval Islamic Society," in *The Dream and Human Societies*, ed. G. E. von Grunebaum and Roger Caillois (University of California Press, 1966), 351–63. Ṭāriq ibn Ziyād's dream about the conquest of the Iberian peninsula is a defining example.

12. Map of Paris, called the Tapestry Map, Paris BnF, Estampes, VA-419, c. 1540. La Tournelle is the eastern gate on the Seine's southern bank, known as the Left Bank.

13. The *Testament* of Jean de Meun, claiming to gather all the poet's wisdom, the *Livre de l'estat du monde*, paired with the *Rose*: Paris, BnF, f. fr. 1565, fol. 169v, dated 1352; *Testament Maistre Jehan de Meun. Un caso letterario*, ed. Silvia Buzzetti Gallarati (Edizioni dell'Orso, 1989).

14. Jean-Bertrand Pontalis, *Le dormeur éveillé* (Mercure de France, 2004), 8–12; Piero della Francesca, *The Dream of Constantine*, San Francesco, Arezzo, 1464.

15. Philippe de Mézières, *Songe du viel pelerin*, ed. Joël Blanchard, 2 vols. (Droz, 2015); *The Dream of Bernat Metge Del Somni d'en Bernat Metge*, trans. Antonio Cortijo

Ocaña and Elizabeth Lagrese (John Benjamins, 2013); *El Sueño*, trans. Martin de Riquer (Planeta, 1985); Jean-Claude Mühlethaler, *L'écrivain face aux puissants au Moyen Âge, de la satire à l'engagement* (Champion, 2019), 282–84.

16. *Le Songe du vergier, édité d'après le manuscrit Royal 19 C IV de la British Library*, ed. Marion Schnerb-Lièvre (Éditions du CNRS, 1982).

17. Ryan Szpiech, ed., *Medieval Exegesis and Religious Difference: Commentary, Conflict and Community in the Premodern Mediterranean* (Fordham University Press, 2015); Alex J. Novikoff, *The Medieval Culture of Disputatio: Pedagogy, Practice, and Performance* (University of Pennsylvania Press, 2013).

18. Judah Halevi, c. 1130, *The Kuzari in Defense of the Despised Religion*, trans. N. Daniel Korobkin (Jason Aronson, 1998); Mohammed Shahrastani, c. 1130, *Book of Religions and Philosophical Sects*, ed. William Cureton (Gorgias Press, 2002).

19. Joëlle Rollo-Koster, *Avignon and Its Papacy, 1309–1417: Popes, Institutions, and Society* (Rowman & Littefield, 2015); Bénédicte Sère, *Les Débats d'opinion à l'heure du grand Schisme. Ecclésiologie et politique* (Brepols, 2016). On Aragon, Carlos Laliena and Philippe Sénac, *Musulmans et Chrétiens dans le haut Moyen Âge. Aux origines de la reconquête aragonèse* (Minerve, 1991).

20. *Selected Works of Ramón Lull (1232–1316)*, ed. and trans. Anthony Bonner (Princeton University Press, 1985), vol. 1; Paris, BnF, f. fr. 22933, fols. 60v–119. See also Dominique de Courcelles's French translation of Lull's Catalan, *Le Livre du Gentil et des trois sages* (Éditions de l'Éclat, 1992); and William E. Burgwinkle, "The Translator As Interpretant: Passing with the Work of Ramon Llull," in *Rethinking Medieval Translation: Ethics, Politics, Theory*, ed. Emma Campbell and Robert Mills (D. S. Brewer, 2012), 184–203. Lull admits the difficulty of his *modus loquendi arabicus* at the University of Paris, c. 1310. *A Contemporary Life*, ed. and trans. Anthony Bonner (Barcino, 2010), 46–47, n36.

21. BnF, f. fr. 810, fol. 12, ed. Hanly, *Medieval Muslims*, ll. 366–71, p. 86.

22. BnF, f. fr. 810, fol. 10v, ed. Hanly, *Medieval Muslims*, ll. 1236–43, p. 130.

23. Ram Ben-Shalom, "Southern France," in *The Cambridge History of Judaism*, ed. Robert Chazan (Cambridge University Press, 2018), 6:204, 212; Gilbert Dahan, ed., *L'Expulsion des juifs de France, 1394* (Éditions du Cerf, 2004), 177–87.

24. Joëlle Rollo-Koster, *The People of Curial Avignon: A Critical Edition of the Liber Divisionis and the Matriculae of Notre Dame la Majour* (Edwin Mellen Press, 2009).

25. BnF, f. fr. 810, fol. 7v, ed. Hanly, *Medieval Muslims*, l. 185, p. 73.

26. BnF, f. fr. 810, fol. 10v–11, ed. Hanly, *Medieval Muslims*, ll. 303–10, p. 82.

27. E. Nathalie Rothman, *Dragoman Renaissance: Diplomatic Interpreters and the Routes of Orientalism* (Cornell University Press, 2021), 3–6; Zrinka Stahuljak, *Fixers: Agency, Translation, and the Early Global History of Literature* (University of Chicago Press, 2024), 3–6 (*Les Fixeurs au Moyen Âge. Histoire et littérature connectées*, 2020); Stahuljak, "Medieval Fixers: Politics of Interpreting in Western Historiography," in *Rethinking Medieval Translation*, 148–49; Laura Minervini, "Les Emprunts arabes et grecs dans le lexique français d'Orient (XIIIe–XIVe siècles)," *Revue de linguistique romane* 76 (2012) : 27–28. In manuscript, Paris, BnF, f. fr. 811, fol. 11, a later hand adds "truchement." Sharon Kinoshita, "Beyond Philology: Cross-cultural Engagement in Literary History and Beyond," in *A Sea of Languages: Rethinking the Arabic Role in Medieval*

Literary History, ed. Suzanne Conklin Akbari and Karla Mallette (University of Toronto Press, 2013), 33.

28. BnF, f. fr. 810, fol. 18, ed. Hanly, *Medieval Muslims*, ll. 732–34, p. 104.

29. Houari Touati, *Islam and Travel in the Middle Ages* (University of Chicago Press, 2010) (*Islam et le voyage au Moyen Âge*, 2000); Émilie Picherot, *La Langue arabe dans l'Europe humaniste, 1500–1550* (Classiques Garnier, 2023), 38–57. Picherot and I worked together on Bovet's writing, 2016–22.

30. Ibn Khaldûn, *Muqaddimah: An Introduction to History*, trans. Franz Rosenthal (Princeton University Press, 2005), 30; Ibn Khaldoûn, *Les Textes sociologiques et économiques de la Mouqaddima, 1375–1379*, trans. and ed. G.-H. Bousquet (Éditions Marcel Rivière, 1965), 19; Ramzi Rouighi, *The Making of a Mediterranean Emirate: Ifrīquiyā and Its Andalusis, 1200–1400* (University of Pennsylvania Press, 2011), 132.

31. "For you, I am valuable there as an interpreter because I understand Latin well, and I speak both 'Saracen' [Arabic] and Turkish." ["Je vous y vail un drugeman / Pour ce que j'entends bien latin / Et que je parle sarrasin et turquien."] In *Miracle de Nostre Dame par personnages*, BnF, f. fr. 819–20, fol. 231, ed. Gaston Paris and Ulysse Robert (Firmin Didot, 1876), 5:328, ll. 2123–26; Jean Froissart, *Chroniques*, London, Harley ms. 4379–80, fol. 20, ed. Peter Ainsworth, and Godfried Croenen in *Online Froissart*, book 4, chap. 15.

32. Paris, Arsenal, ms. 5070, fols. 379v–386v; Boccaccio, *Décaméron*, trans. Laurent Premierfait, ed. Giuseppe di Stefano (Éditions de CERES, 1998), Day 10, Story 44, 1188–1212; Sharon Kinoshita, "Noi Siamo Mercatanti Cypriani: How to Do Things with the Medieval Mediterranean," in *Philippe de Mézières and His Age: Piety and Politics in the 14th Century*, ed. R. Blumenfeld-Kosinski and Kiril Petlov (Brill, 2011), 41–60.

33. Shirin A. Khanmohamadi, *In Light of Another's Word: European Ethnography in the Middle Ages* (University of Pennsylvania Press, 2015), 3.

34. Coluccio Salutati, letter to the Margrave of Moravia, August 20, 1397, in *Epistolario di Coluccio Salutati*, ed. Francesco Novati (Istituto estorico italiano, 1896), 3:208–9.

35. Jean Batany, "Un Usbek au XIVe siècle. Le Sarrasin juge des Français dans *L'Apparicion Jehan de Meun*," in *Images et signes de l'Orient dans l'Occident médiéval. Littérature et civilisation*, ed. Jean Arrouye, *Senéfiance* 11 (1982): 43. Michael Hanly calls the *Sarrazin* "the *Prieur* in black-face": "Et prendre nom de Sarrazin: Islam as the Symptom of Western Iniquity in Honorat Bovet's *L'Apparicion maistre Jehan de Meun*," *multilingua* 18, no. 2–3 (1999): 232.

36. "Et se je fusse com jadiz, / Je deisse bien mon adviz / Au monde plain d'iniquité . . . De dire le vray sans mentir / Quer vecy tres perilleux temps" (fol. 4v, ll. 21–27, p. 64).

37. Bovet addresses specifically Louis, duc d'Orléans, the brother of Charles VI, and the soldier Jean de Montaigu; Paris, BnF, f. fr. 810, fol. 1r–v.

38. BnF, f. fr. 810, fol. 11, ed. Hanly, *Medieval Muslims*, ll. 323–26, p. 82.

39. Fancy, *The Mercenary Mediterranean*, 52, 151; Robin Vose, *Dominicans, Muslims and Jews in the Medieval Crown of Aragon* (Cambridge University Press, 2009). The overview of Robert I. Burns is still useful: "The Significance of the Frontier in the Middle Ages," in *Medieval Frontier Societies* ed. Robert Bartlett and Angus McKay (Oxford University Press, 1992), 319–29.

40. Honoré Bovet, *L'arbre des Batailles*, ed. Reinhilt Richter-Bergmeier (Droz, 2017); *La traduction occitane de L'arbre des Batailles d'Honorat Bovet*, ed. Hélène Biu (École nationale des chartes, 2001); *Arból de batailIas*, Castilian translation by Antonio Contreras Martín (Ministerio de defensa, 2008).

41. "Je di que en cestui cas de bonne equite permissive de droit tous Crestiens, mais qu'il ne venist en tel puissance avec gens d'arme dont il peust grever lez Crestiens" (487). In the Brussels manuscript for Philip the Good of Burgundy, Liédet does not paint "Saracens."

42. BnF f.fr. 810, fol. 17v, ed. Hanly, *Medieval Muslims*, l. 710, p. 104.

43. Fancy, *The Mercenary Mediterranean*, 99; Burns, "The Guidaticum Safe-conduct in Medieval Arago-Catalonia," 76; Hassan S. Khalilieh, *Islamic Law of the Sea: Freedom of Navigation and Passage Rights in Islamic Thought* (Cambridge University Press, 2019).

44. Timothy Hampton, *Fictions of Embassy: Literature and Diplomacy in Early Modern Europe* (Cornell University Press, 2009), 18.

45. "De qualitate et moribus ambaxiatorum," *Ambaxiator Brevilogus*, BnF, lat. 6020, fol. 46v–47v. Composed by Bernard de Rosier, a Toulouse jurist and Bovet's near contemporary in 1436. On Rosier, see Patrick Gilli, "Bernard de Rosier et les débuts de la réflexion théorique sur les missions d'ambassade," in *De l'ambassadeur*, ed. Stefano Andretta, Stéphane Péquignot, and Jean-Claude Waquet (École française de Rome, 2015); P. Arabeyre, "Un prélat languedocien au milieu du XVe siècle. Bernard de Rosier, archevêque de Toulouse (1400–1475)," *Journal des savants* 34 (1990): 291–326; as well as Arabeyre, "La France et son gouvernement au milieu du XVe siècle d'après Bernard de Rosier," *Bibliothèque de l'École des Chartes* 150 (1992): 245–85.

46. "cellui qui suy hors de mon pays, et pour la guerre que maistre Remond Rogier a faitte tant longuement en Prouvence." (fol. 32, ll. 161–62 p. 148).

47. BnF, f. fr. 810, fol. 33v, ed. Hanly, *Medieval Muslims*, ll. 213–18, p. 152.

48. To Johannes Messina is attributed the *Speculum sapientiae*, a collection of some ninety prose fables assembled around 1340. On Messina (the Sicilian port), see Sarah Davis-Secord, *Where Three Worlds Met: Sicily in the Early Medieval Mediterranean* (Cornell University Press, 2017), 237–40.

49. Nāsir-i Khusraw, Divan 20, ed. and trans. Alice C. Hunsberger, *Pearls of Persia: The Philosophical Poetry of Nāsir-i Khusraw* (I. B. Tauris, 2012); *Nāsir E Khusraw, A Portrait of the Islamic Poet, Traveler and Philosopher* (Islamic Publications Ltd., Institute of Ismaili Studies, 2000, 2003), 2; "La platane et la courge" (fable), trans. Henri Massé, in *Anthologie persane, XI–XIXe* siècle (Éditions Payot, 1997 [1950]), 86–87. Annemarie Schimmel's translation is still standard: *Make a Shield from Wisdom, Selected Verse from Nāsir-i Khusraw's Dīwān* (I. B. Tauris, 2001), 38–39. Schimmel identified a plane tree (*chinār*) as having branches resembling hands reaching up in prayer, as according to the Koran. This is the *plantanus orientalis*, reputed for its longevity, that appears in Pliny's *Natural History*, Book 16, 88.

50. Cleric Ulrich von Pottenstein transposed the story for German-speaking audiences: "Chiurbis & Palm," in *Das buch der Natürlichen weißheit* (*The Book of Natural Wisdom*), c. 1415: Munich, Bavarian State Library, Cgm 9602, fol 73. It was printed quickly in German towns that had printers, and generated an emblem appearing in Augsburg; André Alciat, *Emblemata* (1531).

51. Andrew Griebeler, *Botanical Icons: Critical Practices of Illustration in the Premodern Mediterranean* (University of Chicago Press, 2024), 24–25; Lisa Reilly, *Invention of Norman Visual Culture: Art, Politics, Dynastic Ambitions* (Cambridge University Press, 2020), 178–83.

52. Baltimore, Walters Art Museum, W. 659, Ottoman Turkish version of *Wonders of Creation*, *Aja'ib al-makhluqat*, Zakariya al-Qazwini, c. 1290; and Avignon, Palace of the Popes, Matteo Giovannetti, *Room of the Deer*, c. 1343. A ninth-century Byzantine image for the tree of life: *Cosmas Indicopleustes*, Vatican City, Biblioteca Apostolica Vaticana, Greek ms. 699.

53. On the *sermo humilis*, Erich Auerbach, *Literary Language and Its Public in Late Latin Antiquity and in the Middle Ages*, trans. Ralph Mannheim (Princeton University Press, 1965), 60, 65.

54. His Latin gloss: *non sum ausus plane loqui*, Paris, BnF f. fr. 811, fol. 18; Hanly, ed. *Medieval Muslims*, 207.

55. Paris, BnF, f. fr. 5594, fol. 4, c. 1488–1500; see also Édith Garnier, *L'alliance impie. Soleiman le magnifique et François Ier (1529–47)* (Félin, 2008).

56. Patrick Boucheron, "Fictions politiques," seminar, Collège de France, January–March 2017; *Political Fictions from the Middle Ages to the "Post-Truth" Present*, trans. Willard Wood (Other Press, 2025), 33.

57. London, British Museum, drawing, 1479–81.

58. Two later versions show little sign of extended debate around exchange with the Ottomans: London, BM, Lansdowne 214; Vatican City, Biblioteca Apostolica Vaticana, Reg. lat. 1683; Hanly, ed., *Medieval Muslims*, 27–29.

59. Avicenne, *La Logique*, trans. Pierre Vattier (Paris, 1658–59); *L'Élegie du Tograï, le tout nouvellement traduit de l'arabe par P. Vattier* (R. Soubret, 1660); *L'onirocrite mussulman. Ou la doctrine et l'interprétation des songes selon les Arabes par Gabdorrhachaman fils de Nasar*, trans. Pierre Varriter (T. Jolly, 1664).

60. Jean Boivin, "Le Datillier et la courge," in *Apologie d'Homère et le bouclier d'Achille* (chez François Jouenne, 1715), 254–58. Bovet's dream had made a cameo appearance in Claude Fauchet, *Recueil de l'origine de la langue et la poésie française* (Mamert Patisson, 1581), 201.

61. Fredric Jameson qualifies the debate in terms of an absolute present, and of chronological time: *The Ancients and the Postmoderns: On the Historicity of Forms* (Verso, 2017), 19.

62. Montesquieu, *Mes Pensées* (1721), trans. Henry C. Clark (Liberty Fund, 2012). "In the last debates over the Ancients and the Moderns . . . Boivin was merely a scholar" (*Pensée* 894, p. 258).

63. "On peut comparer les empires à un arbre dont les branches trop étendues ôtent tout le suc du trônc, et ne servent qu'à faire de l'ombrage. De Paris, le 18 de la lune de Rhamazan 1718." *Lettres persanes* (chez Pierre Brunel, 1721), 2:194. (First edition printed anonymously; letter 121 in 1828 edition.)

Entry 2: Equitable Labor

1. The papers of Édith Thomas cover her journalistic writing, her political activism, and much unpublished work: Paris, Archives nationales [AN] 318 AP; Dorothy

Kaufmann, *Édith Thomas: A Passion for Resistance* (Cornell University Press, 2004). Critic Isabelle Tournier and archivists Denise Ogilvie and Odile Welfelé are pursuing the editing of different works of Thomas's voluminous writings, as has Chloé Le Prince, *Les Pétroleuses* (Gallimard, 2021); *The Women Incendiaries*, trans. James and Starr Atkinson (Haymarket Books, 1963).

2. Édith Thomas, "Les Archives nationales," *Lettres françaises*, May 1, 1946; Paris, AN 318 AP/4, folder 1. In her personal diary, she writes on October 8, 1941: "Today I went to the General Committee against Unemployment to register as an 'unemployed intellectual'" (AN 318 AP/13, folder 8).

3. Édith Thomas, "Christine de Pisan," *Domaine Français, Messages, 1943* (Éditions des Trois Collines, 1943), 263–71.

4. *Le Livre de l'advision Cristine*, BnF, f. fr. 1176, Part 3, chap. 10, fol. 62; ed. Christine Reno and Liliane Dulac (Champion, 2001), 111; Andrea Tarnowski, "Introduction," in *Approaches to Teaching the Works of Christine de Pizan* (MLA Publications, 2018), 31.

5. *Le Livre des fais d'armes et de chevalerie*, Brussels, KBR, ms. 9009–11, fol. 181v; ed. Lucien Dugaz (Classiques Garnier, 2021), 373. A High Alemanic translation: *Das Bouch von dem vechten und von der ritterschaft*, c. 1450, Berlin, SBB, ms. germ. fol. 1705, fol. 115v; ed. Earl Jeffrey Richards and Danielle Buschinger (De Gruyter, 2022), 333; and William Caxton's English version in print, *The Book of Fayttes of Armes and of Chyvalry*, 1489, London, BL, Royal 15 E VI.

6. Joëlle Ducos and Hélène Biu, eds., *Émergence d'une littérature militaire (XIIe–XVe siècle)* (Champion, 2022). On the relation between Bovet and Christine de Pizan, see Hélène Biu, "Aux sources d'une (ré)écriture. L'Arbre des batailles lu par Christine de Pizan," *Le Moyen Âge* 125 (2020): 93–110; "Et la gist la Maistrie." De *L'Arbre des Batailles* au *Livre des faits d'armes et de chevalerie*," in *Une femme et la guerre à la fin du Moyen Âge*, ed. Dominique Demartini, Claire Le Ninan, Anne Paupert, and Michelle Szkilnik (Champion, 2016), 151.

7. *Le Livre de la Cité des Dames*, Paris, BnF, f. fr. 607; London, BM, Harley 4431, fols. 290–374, of some twenty-seven handmade books; ed. Claire Le Ninan, Anne Paupert (Champion, 2023). *Le Livre des Trois Vertus*, Boston, Public Library, f. med. 101, of some twenty-two manuscripts; ed. Charity Cannon Willard and Eric Hicks (Champion, 2016 [1989]). Paris, BnF, f. fr. 1177 and Brussels, BR 9235–37 contain both works. Sarah Delale, *Diamant obscur. Interpréter les manuscrits de Christine de Pizan* (Droz, 2021), 101–2, 609.

8. On the ample criticism, see Andrea Valentini, "La tradition manuscrite de la *Cité des Dames*. Genèse et évolution d'un texte majeur du XVe siècle," *Romania* 137, no. 3–4 (2019): 394–445; *Album Christine de Pizan*, ed. Gilbert Ouy, Christine Reno, and Inès Villela-Petit (Brepols, 2012), 178, 287–92, 333–43, 517–57, 609–25.

9. A translation by Laurent de Premierfait of Boccaccio, *De claribus mulieribus*, in 1401: Jean Boccace, *Des cleres et nobles femmes*, Paris, BnF, f. fr. 12420, fols. 3–167v; anonymous translation, *Livre des femmes nobles et renommées*, Paris, BnF, f. fr. 598, fols. 3–161, ed. Jeanne Baroin and Josiane Haffen (Belles Lettres, 1993–95).

10. "Je qui femme sui," in *Le Livre des épîtres du débat sur le Roman de la Rose*, London, BL, Harley 4431, fol. 240, ed. Andrea Valentini (Classiques Garnier, 2016), 163. Versions of this phrase are found in many of her works.

11. "Je, comme personne traveillie de si gran labour avoir accompli . . . mes membres et mon corps lasséz pour cause du long et continuel excercite." Boston 101, fol. 3; Brussels 10973, fol. 4; Yale Beinecke 427, fol. 1; BnF, f. fr. 452, fol. 3v, ed. Willard, 8.

12. Giacomo Todeschini, *Les Marchands et le temple. La Société chrétienne et le cercle vertueux de la richesse du Moyen Âge*, trans. Ida Giordano (Albin Michel, 2017) (*I mercanti e i tempio*, 2002); Mathieu Arnoux, *Le Temps des laboureurs* (Albin Michel, 2012), 339–42; Hubert Faes, *Peiner, œuvrer, travailler. Sur le travail et la condition humaine* (Harmattan, 2003); *Travail et travailleurs en Europe au Moyen Âge et au début des temps modernes*, ed. Claire Dolan (PIMS, 1991). For Jacques Le Goff's baseline on labor in this social hierarchy, see "Le travail dans les systèmes de valeur de l'Occident médiéval," in *Le Travail au Moyen Âge. Une approche interdisciplinaire*, ed. Jacqueline Hamesse and Colette Muraille-Samaran (Publ. de l'Institut d'études médiévales de l'Université catholique de Louvain, 1990), 7–21.

13. On *otium/negotium*, see Frank La Brasca and Christian Trottman, eds., *Vie active et vie contemplative au Moyen Âge et au seuil de la Renaissance* (École française de Rome, 2009); Lori J. Walters, "Autobiographie et humanisme. La réception de Pétrarque par Christine de Pizan," in *Dynamique d'une expansion culturelle. Pétrarche en Europe, XVe–XXe siècle*, ed. Pierre Blanc (Champion, 2001), 184.

14. "So it is with labor and work, just as with women who go through labor forget the pain once they hear the cry of their child, so you'll forget the pain of this labor hearing the voice of your volumes." ["Non obstant le labour et traveil, lequel tout ainsi comme la femme qui a enfanté si tost que elle ot le cry de son enfant oublie son mal, oublieras le traveil du labour oyant la voix de tes volumes."] *Le Livre de l'advision Cristine*, Book 3, 10; Paris, BnF, f. fr. 1176, fol. 61v; ed. Reno-Dulac, 110.

15. In his commentary on servitude, Nicole Oresme distinguishes the type of caretaker who gives us a sense of the hierarchy of those laboring in domestic service. *Le Livre d'Yconomiques*, Book I, 5; Rouen, Bibl. mun., ms. 697, fols. 431–32v; Avranches, Bibl. mun., ms. 223, fols. 335–37; ed. A. D. Menut, *Maistre Nicolas Oresme: Le Livre d'Yconomiques, Transactions of the American Philosophical Society* 47, no. 5 (1957): 817–21. See also Sandrine Victor, *Les Fils de Canaan. L'esclavage au Moyen Âge* (Vendémiaire, 2019).

16. Nicole Oresme, *Le Livre d'Ethiques*, book 5, chaps. 19 and 21; Brussels, BR 2902, fols. 108–9, 110–12; Paris, BnF, f. fr. 541; ed. Albert D. Menut (G. E. Stechert, 1940), 319, 323–25. See my first discussion: "Flaming Words: Fiction, Free Speech, and the "Querelle des femmes," *Romanic Review* 86, no. 2 (March 1995): 375.

17. *Le Livre des Trois Vertus*, André Vérard, 1497; Michel Le Noir, 1503. Cynthia J. Brown, "The Reconstruction of an Author in Print: Christine de Pizan in the Fifteenth and Sixteenth Centuries," in *Christine de Pizan: Categories of Difference*, ed. Marilynn Desmond (University of Minnesota Press, 1998), 215–35.

18. Christine's work was translated within two generations into English and Flemish, for noble and bourgeois households in England and Burgundian territories where French letters were part of life. *Het Bouc van De Stede der Vrauwen*, London, BL, Add. 20698, 1475; ed. Orlanda Soei Han Lie, Mark Aussems, Martine Meuwese, and Hermina Joldersma, *Christine de Pizan in Bruges: The Flemish Codex of* Le Livre de la Cité Des Dames (Verloren Publishers, 2015). A diplomatic transcription of the middle Dutch or

Flemish variant text is available online. Scot McKendrick and Lieve De Kesel, "French Literary Culture in the Burgundian Netherlands," in *Colard Mansion, Incunabula, Prints and Manuscripts in Medieval Bruges*, ed. Evelien Hauwaerts, Evelien de Wilde, and Ludo Vandamme (Musea Brugge Snoeck, 2018), 141; *The Boke of the Cyte of Ladyes*, trans. Brian Ansley (1551); Anne E. B. Coldiron, *The 'Miroer" and "Maistresse" of "Intelligence": Christine de Pizan's Translated Authority in Early English Print* (Routledge, 2009).

19. Édith Thomas, "Vers un humanisme féminin," AN 318 AP/ 3, unpublished ms., 1948.

20. Joël Blanchard and Michel Quereuil, *Lexique de Christine de Pizan* (Klincksieck, 1999), s.v. "labeur," 235; Helen Solterer, "States of Siege: Gender, Violence, and Place, Paris around 1400," *New Medieval Literatures* 2 (1997): 101.

21. Deborah McGrady, *The Writer's Gift or the Patron's Pleasure?* (University of Toronto Press, 2019), 194, 204, 237.

22. In Bovet's presentation to patron Louis d'Orléans, he makes this critical commentary in reference to another patron: "he [Bernabo of Milan] put more of his learning into gold than knowledge." ["il avoit son estude plus en or qu'en science."] Bovet, *Apparition*; BnF, f. fr. 810, fol. 2; ed. Hanly, 60.

23. "La royne Cerés, qui trouva l'art de labourer les terres et maintes autres ars" (I, 35); BnF, f. fr. 1178, fol. 49; ed. Le Ninan, Paupert, 370; ed. Curnow, 2:743.

24. London, BL, Add. 20698, fol. 84.

25. "Et ainsi par ceste dame fu ramené le siècle de bestialité a vie humaine et raisonnable" (I, 35); BnF, f. fr. 1178, fol. 49v; ed. Le Ninan, Paupert, 372; ed. Curnow 2:744.

26. I, 33; BnF, f. fr. 1178, fol. 46; ed. Le Ninan, Paupert, 360; ed. Curnow, 2:735.

27. Jacqueline Cerquiglini-Toulet, "Christine de Pizan et les arts," 207.

28. "Simples femes de labour et es villages . . . Il est necessite que le monde soit secouru qui en labeur . . . qui est la sustenacion et nourissement de toute creature humaine" (III, 12). Boston 101, fol. 95v; ed. Willard, 219.

29. III, 9; Boston 101, fol. 90; ed. Willard, 207.

30. III, xiii; Boston 101, fol. 97v; ed. Willard, 224.

31. BnF, f. fr. 604, fols. 112–17; f. fr. 835, fols. 97–103; *Le Livre des épîtres du débat sur le Roman de la Rose*, ed. Valentini; *The Debate on the Romance of the Rose*, ed. and trans. David F. Hult (University of Chicago Press, 2010); Helen Solterer, "Fiction versus Defamation: The Quarrel over the *Romance of the Rose*," *Medieval History Journal* 2, no. 1 (1999): 111–41.

32. III, "fin et conclusion"; Boston 101, fol. 97v; ed. Willard, 225.

33. *Album Christine de Pizan*, ed. Ouy, Reno, and Villela-Petit, 516, 589, 614.

34. "entray en lit de repos, traveillable," I, i; BnF, f. fr. 1176, fol. 1; ed. Reno-Dulac, 11.

35. II, iii; BnF, f. fr. 1176, fol. 26v–27; ed. Reno-Dulac, 54. Claire Le Ninan, "Écrire avec Boccace, écrire contre Boccace. Le traitement du mythe de l'âge d'or," in "Actes du XIe Colloque Christine de Pizan," *Le Moyen français*, forthcoming,.

36. Susan Dudash, "Christine de Pizan and the "Menu peuple," *Speculum* 78, no. 3 (July 2003), 817.

37. III, iii; BnF, f. fr. 1176, fol. 53; ed. Reno-Dulac, 96.

38. "tout ainsi comme l'ouvrier" III, xi; BnF, f. fr. 1176, fol. 62 ; ed. Reno-Dulac, 111.

39. Jacqueline Cerquiglini-Toulet, *La Couleur de la mélancholie. La fréquentation des livres, 1300–1415* (Hatier, 1993).

40. "Mais, Dieu merci, toute plaine de blé, Ont les Anglés le feu bouté dedens." Eustache Deschamps, "Je fu jadiz de terre vertueuse," Ballade 120, BnF, f. fr. 840, fol. 217b, ed. Clotilde Dauphant, *Anthologie* (Lettres gothiques, 2014), 416–19; Helen Solterer, "Calais Enclave: Fictions for Locking In and Opening Up, 2018–1346," in *Migrants Shaping Europe, Past and Present: Multilingual Literatures, Arts, and Cultures*, ed. Helen Solterer and Vincent Joos (Manchester University Press, 2022), 171–96.

41. "à vostre povre peuple vueilliez donner en temps de tribulacion une piecete de la parole et du labour de votre hautesse et puissance," 257; *Epistre a la Reine*, Paris, BnF, f. fr. 580, fols. 53–54v, ed. Angus J. Kennedy, *Revue des langues romanes* 92, no. 2 (1988): 253–64.

42. Paris, BnF, f. fr. 607, fol. 2r, Duc de Berry, vol. 5 of collected works, c. 1408. A. E. B. Coldiron, "Feminist Hermeneutic Tools: Visual Metaphors of Christine de Pizan's Literary Labor," *Digital Philology* 11, no. 1 (spring 2022): 121–41.

43. Giacomo Todeschini, "Servitude et travail à la fin du Moyen Âge. La dévalorisation des salariés et les pauvres peu méritants," *Annales E.S.C.* 70, no. 1 (2015): 81–89. This essay responds to Thomas Piketty and his defining argument about economic inequality.

44. Thomas Piketty, *Capital in the Twenty-first Century*, trans. Arthur Goldhammer (Harvard University Press, 2014) (*Le capital au XXIe siècle*, 2013).

45. Cary Nederman, *Lineages of European Political Thought* (Catholic University Press, 2009), 248.

46. Deborah McGrady, *The Writer's Gift or the Patron's Pleasure*, 194, 204, 237, 240.

47. II, xxii, BnF, f. fr. 1176, fol. 49v; ed. Reno-Dulac, 89.

48. bird-catcher/*oiseleur*: *Cité des dames*, III, 19, BnF, f. fr. 607, fol 79; ed. Le Ninan, Paupert, 808; *Trois Vertus* I, 1, Boston 101, fol. 3; ed. Willard, 7; waffle maker /*a faire gauffres*: *L'Advision*, I, ii; BnF, f. fr. 1176, fol. 1v, ed. Reno-Dulac, 13.

49. "Tout instant de l'histoire est à la fois point d'arrivée et point de départ." "Vers un humanisme féminin," 1; AN 318 AP/ 3.

50. William Morris, foreword to Thomas More's *Utopia* (Kelmscott Press, 1893), 4.

51. Édith Thomas, Curriculum, lists CNE [Comité national des écrivains], 1942; AN 318 AP/13. Dorothy Kaufmann, "L'humanisme féminin," in *Intellectuelles. Du genre en histoire des intellectuelles*, ed. Nicole Racine and Michel Trebitsch (Complexe, 2004), 177; Gisèle Sapiro, *The French Writers' War, 1940–53*, trans. Vanessa Doriott Anderson and Dorrit Cohen (Duke University Press, 2014), chap. 7, p. 69 (*La Guerre des écrivains: 1940–1953* [Fayard, 1999]).

52. Letter to Louis Aragon, October 21, 1946, Cahier 7, AN 318 AP/13. "Cher Louis, Je trouve des plus regrettables la façon dont on a rendu compte de la vérité du C.N.E. Tout se passe comme si il n'y avait que Elsa Triolet, Toi, et à peine? Quelques exceptions que tu ne peux vraiment passer sous silence"; her article, "Critique et Autocritique," *Combat* 16–17 December 1949.

53. Entries for September–October 1941, Diary # 6, June 1940-December 1941, AN 318 AP /13; Thomas, "Christine de Pisan," *Domaine Français*, 264, 266–67.

54. "Vers un humanisme féminin," 6, AN 318 AP/ 3, p. 2.

55. "Here, I've brought together some texts that show the development of the consciousness of woman when facing problems society poses for her. They constitute in themselves a 'history' that is not worth commenting on. I've limited myself to situating them, as well as their authors, in time." ["J'ai réuni ici des textes qui montrent le développement de la conscience de la femme devant les problèmes que lui pose la société. Ils constituent en eux-mêmes une 'histoire' qu'il était inutile de commenter. Je me suis bornée à les situer, dans le temps, ainsi que leurs auteurs."] "Vers un humanisme féminin," 21, AN 318 AP/ 3.

56. *Collection des meilleurs ouvrages françois composés par des femmes, dediées aux femmes françaises* (Paris, chez l'auteur, 1787–89), 2:109–467; 3:1–132. See also J.-M.-L. Coupé, "Anecdotes sur Christine de Pizan," in *Ses romans et ses principaux ouvrages, Bibliothèque universelle des romans* 2 (October 1779): 117–73. On Kéralio, see Sarah Delale, *Diamant obscur*, 235–36; Claire Le Brun-Gouanvic, "Mlle de Kéralio commentatrice de Christine de Pizan au XVIIIe siècle, ou la rencontre de 2 femmes savantes," in *Christine de Pizan. Une femme de science, une femme de lettres*, ed. Juliette Dor and Marie-Elizabeth Henneau (Champion, 2008), 325–41; Carla Hesse, *The Other Enlightenment: How French Women Became Modern* (Princeton University Press, 2001), 52; E. J. Richard, "Medieval "femme auteur" As a Provocation to Literary History: 18th-century Readers of Christine de Pizan," in *Reception of Christine de Pizan from the XVth through the XIXth Centuries: Visitors to the City*, ed. Glenda K. McLeod (Edwin Mellen Press, 1991), 105.

57. *Le Livre des Trois Vertus*, in *Collection des meilleurs ouvrages françois composés par des femmes*, 2:416; *La Vision de Christine de Pizan*, 3:1–21; *La Cité des Dames*, 22–50.

58. Kéralio, *Collection des meilleurs ouvrages françois composés par des femmes*, 2:132. Thomas writes, "Voila donc une femme seule au XVe siecle obligée de gagner sa vie et celle de sa famille. Il lui fallait tout inventer. On la voit tenir tête dans ce temps puis pour défendre un unique héritage." Untitled handwritten piece, AN 318 AP / 4, I, 13. This second version differs from "Christine de Pisan," in *Domaine Français, Messages, 1943*.

59. First-wave American feminist critics seem to have launched the view of Christine's dream vision as a utopia: Judith Kellogg, "*Le Livre de la Cité des Dames*: Feminist Myth and Community," *Essays in Arts and Sciences* 18 (1989): 1–15; more recently, Kate Robin, "Du nulle part au partout. L'utopie de Wittig pour changer le présent et l'avenir," *Temporalités* 12 (2010): 21.

60. "Towards a Feminized Humanism," 2. On posthumanism, see Jean-Michel Besnier, *L'avenir du posthumanisme ou les limites du humain* (l'Institut Diderot, 2023); Besnier, *Demain, les post-humains* (Fayard, 2012); *Post-human Glossary*, ed. Rosi Braidotti and Maria Hlavajova (Bloomsbury, 2018).

61. Kaufmann,"L'humanisme féminin," 177–79.

62. Kaufmann,"L'humanisme féminin," 177–97.

63. ". . . cet humanisme féminin qui, en France, a commencé au XVe siècle avec Christine de Pizan . . . contribuera peut-être, un jour, à jeter des bases du véritable humanisme." Thomas, review of Claire Malraux, *La Lutte inégale* (Julliard, 1958), in *Évidence* (November–December 1958); AN 318 AP/4, folder 1949–1969.

64. "et il n'est rien qui tant aprengne creature raisonnable que fait l'exercite et expe-

rience de plusieurs choses et diverses." I, 27, BnF, f. fr. 1178, fol. 41v; ed. Le Ninan, Paupert, 342; ed. Curnow, 2: 722.

65. Rosalind Brown-Grant tracks such a sex-neutral term substituting for the more ambiguous "men." "Christine de Pizan: Feminist Linguist avant la lettre," in *Christine de Pizan 2000: Studies on Christine de Pizan in Honour of Angus J. Kennedy*, ed. John Campbell and Nadia Margolis (Brill, 2000), 76.

66. Natalie Zemon Davis, preface to Christine de Pizan, *The Book of the City of Ladies*, trans. Earl Jeffrey Richards (Persea, 1998), xx.

67. Geneviève Fraisse addresses this: *Service ou servitude. Essai sur les femmes toutes mains* (Seuil, 2021 [1979]).

68. *City*, II, 13; BnF, f. fr. 1178, fol. 76v; ed. Le Ninan, Paupert, 480.

69. "qui des debas de mariaige vouldroit faire informacion pour en faire nouvel livre selonc le vrai, on trouveroit autres nouvelles." *City*, II, 13; BnF, f. fr. 1178, fol. 76v; ed. Le Ninan, Paupert, 480.

70. Julie Singer, "Christine de Pizan's "doulce nourriture," in *Out of the Mouths of Babes: Infant Voices in Medieval French Literature* (University of Chicago Press, 2025), 126–36; Tracy Adams, *Christine de Pizan and the Fight for France* (Pennsylvania State University Press, 2014), 157; Adams, "*Moyennerresse de traictié de paix*: Christine de Pizan's Mediators," in *Healing the Body Politic: The Political Thought of Christine de Pizan* (Brepols, 2005): 177–200; Lori J. Walters, "Christine de Pizan as Translator and Voice of the Body Politic," in *Christine de Pizan: A Casebook*, ed. Barbara K. Altman and Deborah McGrady (Routledge, 2003; rpt., 2020), 25–41.

71. "que ceste guerre puist estre eschivee, et en ce se vouldra traveillier et labourer saigement en appellant Dieu a son aide et par bon conseil." *Three Virtues*, I, x; ed. Willard, 34; see also I, ix; ed. Willard, 35.

72. *Livro das tres verdudes*, Madrid, Biblioteca nacional de España, ms. 11515; Ana Luisa Sonsino, "*Le Livre de Trois Vertus* in Portugal: Translation, Tradition . . . Treason?" in *Genèses et filiations dans l'œuvre de Christine de Pizan*, ed. Dominique De Martini and Claire Le Ninan (Classiques Garnier, 2021), 185–200; *The Boke of the Cyte of Ladyes*, trans. Brian Ansley, 1561; in modernized English, ed. Christine Reno (Iter Press, 2024).

73. Rose Rigaud, *Les idées féministes de Christine de Pisan* (Frères Attinger, 1911), 120; Eric Hicks, "Political Significance of Christine de Pizan," in *Politics, Gender, Genre: Political Thought of Christine de Pizan*, ed. Margaret Brabant (Westview Press, 1992), 12. Nadia Margolis traces another pattern in "'Each . . . according . . . to his intention': Three Phases of Christine de Pizan's Literary Influence through the Ages," *Florilegium* 18, no. 1 (2001): 97–121.

74. Joséphine Pencalet, a communist elected in Brittany, was stripped of her right to take office because the right to vote was not yet codified in law.

75. Susan Groag Bell, "Christine de Pizan (1364–1430): Humanism and the Problem of the Studious Woman," *Feminist Studies* 3, no. 3–4 (1976): 173–84; Roberta Krueger, "Towards Feminism: Christine de Pizan, Female Advocacy, and Women's Textual Communities in the Middle Ages and Beyond," in *The Oxford Handbook of Women and Gender in Medieval Europe*, ed. Judith Bennett and Ruth Mazo Karras (Oxford University Press, 2013), 591–606.

Entry 3: Equality in Dying

1. Édouard Glissant, *La Terre, le feu, l'eau et les vents. Une anthologie de la poésie du tout-monde* (Éditions Galaade, 2010), 21–31. Drafts of the anthology in manuscript: Paris, BnF, ms. n.a.f. 28894, folder 4.

2. For Glissant's notion of "relation" in medieval fiction, see the dialogue with his colleague: Édouard Glissant with Alexandre Leupin, *Les Entretiens de Baton Rouge* (Gallimard, 2008), 102; *The Baton Rouge Interviews*, trans. Kate Cooper (Liverpool University Press, 2020), 54. On the poet's interest in such poetry, see especially Alexandre Leupin, *Édouard Glissant. Héraclite et Hegel dans le Tout-Monde* (Éditions Hermann, 2016); trans. Andrew Brown, *Édouard Glissant: Heraclitus and Hegel in the Whole-World* (New York State University Press, 2021); Jean-Pascal Pouzet,"Le Moyen Âge d'Édouard Glissant. Codicologie, philologie et Relation," Valérie Loichet, ed., "Entours d'Édouard Glissant," *Revue des sciences humaines* 309 (January–March 2013): 17–36.

3. Abel Meeropol, "Strange Fruit" (1939).

4. Glissant, *La Terre*, 21.

5. Paris, BnF, f. fr. 20041, fol. 107v; ed. Cerquiglini-Toulet, *Villon*, XI, 214–15; the defining literary translation in American English, Galway Kinnell, *The Poems of François Villon* (Houghton Mifflin, 1977), 208–9.

6. Ida B. Wells-Barnett, *On Lynchings*, ed. Patricia Hill Collins (Rowman & Littlefield, 2002 [1892, 1895, 1900]). In 1892, eighteen lynchings in Louisiana, the third highest figure among sixteen southern states. Elijah Gaddis, *Gruesome Looking Objects: A New History of Lynching and Everyday Things* (Cambridge University Press, 2023), 140; Michael Pfeiffer, "Lynching and Criminal Justice in South Louisiana, 1878–1930," *Louisiana History* 40, no. 2 (spring 1999): 155–77.

7. Glissant, *La Terre*, 19.

8. Jacques Rancière, "The Concept of Anachronism and the Historian's Truth," trans. Tim Stott and Noel Fitzpatrick, *InPrint* 3, no. 1 (2015): 21–52, at 47.

9. *Entretiens de Baton Rouge*, 60–61; *Baton Rouge Interviews*, 1.

10. Paris, BnF, f. fr. 20041, ed. Cerquiglini-Toulet, *Villon*,"Double Ballade," 75; fol. 125, XXII, 41; fol. 116, LXX, 77, fol. 126; Kinnell, 67, 37, 70. Since our knowledge of Villon's poetry has grown over the decades, there are some discrepancies between the verse in French, and Galway Kinnell's translation. I still choose this translation because it is poetry of a major poet. David Georgi offers a good, recent scholarly translation, *Poems* (Northwestern University Press, 2013).

11. Kateb Yacine, "La Langue, la création du peuple," Entretien, 1978, in *Le Poète comme boxeur. Entretiens 1958–1989* (Seuil, 1994), 80. On the outstanding criticism of this Villon over generations, see especially Laetitia Tabard, "Je, Françoys Villon, escollier. Portrait du poète en étudiant," in *Villon à la lettre*, ed. Nathalie Koble et al. (Publications de la SILC, 2023); Nancy Freeman Regalado, *L'art poétique de François Villon, l'effet de réel* (Éditions Paradigme, 2018); Helen Swift, *Representing the Dead: Epitaph Fictions in Late-Medieval France* (D. S. Brewer, 2016); Jane Taylor, *The Poetry of François Villon, Text and Context* (Oxford University Press, 2001); Jean-Claude Mühlethaler, *Poétique du quinzième siècle, François Villon et Michault Taillevent* (A.-G. Nizet, 1983).

12. "Quoy que pense riche paillart, / Tous sommes soubz mortel coustel." Paris, BnF, f. fr. 20041, fol. 120v; ed. Cerquiglini-Toulet, *Villon*, XLIII, ll. 422–23, p. 57; Kinnell, 53.

13. Undated "Dark Testament" typescript, 2, section 2, Pauli Murray Papers, Schlesinger Library, Radcliffe Institute for Advanced Study at Harvard University, Box 80. This passage excised from the poem in Pauli Murray, *Dark Testament and Other Poems* (Silvermine, 1970), the base for the most recently published edition, *Dark Testament and Other Poems* (W. W. Norton, 2018), 16.

14. "fremir, pallir . . . Le corps moslir, Joinctes, oz, nerfz croistre et estendre." Paris, BnF, f. fr. 20041, fol. 118v; ed. Cerquiglini-Toulet, *Villon*, XLI, ll. 321–27, p. 51; Kinnell, 47.

15. "la les vois . . . ensemble en ung tas, pesle-mesle." Paris, BnF, f. fr. 20041, fol. 146v; ed. Cerquiglini-Toulet, *Villon*, CLXIII, ll. 1757–58, pp. 148–49; Kinnell, 137.

16. Paris, BnF, f. fr. 20041, fol. 146; ed. Cerquiglini-Toulet, *Villon*, CLIX, ll. 1726–27, p. 147; Kinnell, 135.

17. "What's worse, as he died, sorely / The spur of love pricked into him" ["Qui plus en mourant, mallement / L'espoingoit d'Amours l'esguillon."] Paris, BnF, f. fr. 20041, fol. 151v; ed. Cerquiglini-Toulet, *Villon*, ll. 2014–15, p. 167; Kinnell, 154–55.

18. "Les Contredits de Franc Gontier," Paris, BnF, f. fr. 20041, fol. 141; ed. Cerquiglini-Toulet, *Villon*, CLIX, ll. 1478–79, 1482, p. 131; Kinnell, 118–20.

19. "Retournez cy, quant vous serez en ruyt / En ce bordeau ou tenons nostre etat." Paris, BnF, f. fr. 20041, fol. 143v; ed. Cerquiglini-Toulet, *Villon*, ll. 1599–1600, p. 139; Kinnell, 126–27.

20. "Tout aux tavernes et aux filles." "A vous parle, compains de galle . . . soyez tous recors: / Une foyz viendra que mourrez." Paris, BnF, f. fr. 20041, fol. 145v–146; ed. Cerquiglini-Toulet, *Villon*, Ballade, l. 1699, p. 145; Kinnell, 133. CLIX, l. 1727, p. 147; Kinnell, 135.

21. *Œuvres de François Villon avec les remarques de diverses personnes*, 3 parts, ed. Jean-Antoine Du Cerceau (A. Moetjens, 1742).

22. Du Cerceau, *Œuvres de François Villon*, 18.

23. Du Cerceau, *Œuvres de François Villon*, part 3, 65.

24. Théophile Gautier, *Les Grotesques* (Michel Lévy, 1873 [1844]), 21, 28. Jelle Koopmans, "François Villon: Character Within or Without His Own Poetry?" in *The Author as Character: Representing Historical Authors in Western Literature*, ed. Paul Franssen and Ton Hoenselaars (Associated University Presses, 1999), 72.

25. Gautier, *Les Grotesques*, 28; *La Comédie de la mort* (Desessart, 1838).

26. "les dernières pensées d'un misérable." Hugo, *Dernier Jour*, ed. Borderie, preface of 1829, 17; "C'était toujours fête dans mon imagination. Je pouvais penser à ce que je voulais; j'étais libre." (39).

27. "L'argot, qu'on y consente ou non, a sa syntaxe, sa poésie. C'est une langue . . . on reconnaît que Villon l'a parlée." Victor Hugo, *Les Misérables* (Gallimard, 2012 [1862]), 322.

28. Hugo, *Dernier Jour*, *1832* preface, 143–44.

29. "toutes manieres de farsseurs . . . tous gens d'estrange nassion." *Le Recueil des repues franches de maistre François Villon et de ses compagnons*, ed. Jelle Koopmans and

Paul Verhuyck (Droz, 1995), 53–62; Christopher Lucken, "Un livre contre la faim. Les Repues franches de Maistre François Villon et de ses compagnons," in *Écrits et discours culinaires. Quand les mots se mettent à table*, ed. Anne Parizot and Kilien Stengel (L'Harmattan, 2016), 71–85. Variants of lines appearing in the printed editions of the *Repues franches*, Paris, BnF, Ye 260, fol. 24, dated 1497–98; Ye 248, fol. 24, dated 1493.

30. "Maistre François Villon sus ses vieux jours se retira à S. Maixent en Poictou, soubs la faveur d'un home de bien, abbé du dict lieu. Là pour donner passetemps au peuple entreprint faire jouer la passion en gestes et languaige Poictevin." *Le Quart Livre des faicts et dits heroiques du bon Pantagruel*, chap. 13, "Comment à l'exemple de Maistre François Villon, le seigneur de Basché loue ses gens." See also chap. 67. Rabelais, *Œuvres complètes*, ed. Mireille Huchon (Gallimard, 1994), 568, 699.

31. Umberto Eco, "On Some Functions of Literature," trans. Martin McLaughlin, *Yale Review* 92, no. 4 (2004): 7.

32. Paul Verlaine, *Les Poètes maudits* (L. Vanier, 1884), 5.

33. "Et s'aucun me vouloit reprendre / Et dire que je le mauldiz . . . Veci tout le mal que j'en dis." Paris, BnF, f. fr. 20041, fol. 113; ed. Cerquiglini-Toulet, *Villon*, III, ll. 17–18, 21, pp. 29, 31; Kinnell, 27.

34. "Mais être lui, comment donc faire?" Paul Verlaine, "Triolets," *La Revue parisienne* (1893); Cerquiglini-Toulet, *Villon*, 563.

35. Marcel Schwob, "d'estre pendu et estranglé, *finaliter* . . . et eu regard à la mauvaise vie dudit Villon, le bannist jusqu'a dix ans de la ville." "Date de la condamnation à mort de Villon," Académie des Inscriptions, session of February 24, 1899, reprinted in *François Villon* (Éditions Alia, 2008), 75.

36. "Quant a ceste paine arbitraire / On me juga par tricherie." Paris, BnF, f. fr. 20041, fol. 112v; ed. Cerquiglini-Toulet, *Villon*, L'Appel de Villon, XV, ll. 6–7, p. 239; Kinnell, 217.

37. Marcel Schwob, "il fut petit, faible, lâche . . . si il fut subtil par perversité, c'est de sa perversité même que sont nés ses plus beaux vers." "François Villon d'après des documents nouveaux," *Revue des deux mondes* 112 (1892): 412.

38. Marcel Schwob, *Vies imaginaires* (G. Charpentier, 1896), 20–21; Alexandre Gefen, *Inventer une vie. La fabrique littéraire de l'individu* (Brussels: Impressions nouvelles, 2015).

39. Ezra Pound, *The Spirit of Romance* (New Directions, 1968 [1910]), 178.

40. Daniel Heller-Roazen, *Dark Tongues: The Art of Rogues and Riddlers* (Zone Books, 2013), 19 and following. On Schwob's jargon poetry inspired by language of the Coquillard gang of thieves, see Bruno Fabre, "L'Art de la biographie," in *Vies imaginaires de Marcel Schwob* (Champion, 2010), 21.

41. Robert Louis Stevenson, "François Villon: Student, Poet, Housebreaker," in *Familiar Studies of Men and Books* (Scribner's, 1895), 217.

42. c. 1895–97. In Germain Viatte, *Jacques Villon né Gaston Duchamp (1875–1963)* (Expressions contemporaines, 2011), 14, 212.

43. *Le Grand Testament* (H. Jonquières, 1963).

44. Pascale Casanova, *La Langue mondiale, traduction et domination* (Seuil, 2015), 127–28.

45. See also the lesser known *Poems of Master Francis Villon of Paris; now first done*

into English verse in the original forms, trans. John Payne (printed for the Villon Society, for private distribution, 1878). Algernon Swinburne, *Poems and Ballads, Second Series, The Poems of Algernon Charles Swinburne in Six Volumes*, vol. 3 (Chatto & Windus, 1904).

46. Letter, February 5, 1876, in *Swinburne Letters*, ed. Cecil Y. Lang (Yale University Press, 1960), 3:132.

47. Susan Stewart, *Crimes of Writing: Problems in the Containment of Writing* (Oxford University Press, 1991), chap. 4, "Scandals of the Ballad," 102–31.

48. The refrain from Swinburne's "A Ballad of François Villon, Prince of All Ballad-Makers," in *Poems and Ballads, Second Series*, 3:88–89.

49. Claire Pascolini-Campbell, *François Villon in English Poetry: Translation and Influence* (D. S. Brewer, 2018).

50. Pascale Casanova, *The World Republic of Letters*, trans. M. B. DeBevoise (Harvard University Press, 2004) [*La République mondiale des lettres*, 1999].

51. This is part of Dutch critic Willem Bijvanck's portrait of Schwob in *Un Hollandais à Paris en 1891. Sensations de littérature et d'art* (Perrin, 1892), 221.

52. Akutagawa Ryūnosuke, *A Fool's Life*, trans. Anthony Barnett and Toraiwa Naoko (Penguin, 2007), 54.

53. Klaus Kinski, *Vermächtnis, Autobiographisches, Erzählungen, Briefe, Photographien, Zeichnungen, Listen, Privates*, ed. Peter Geyer and Oliver-A. Krimmel (Edel Germany, 2011), 41–67; *Kinski spricht Werke der Welt-Literatur*, sound recording (Berlin Universal Music, 2003 [1960]).

54. Andrew McCann, "Kinski Speaks Villon: Literary Media and the *Poète maudit*, 1952–1962," *Modernism/Modernity* Print Plus, vol. 3, cycle 3, October 2018.

55. "Ballad in which MacHeath Begs All Men Forgiveness," in Bertolt Brecht, *Poems and Songs from the Plays*, ed. and mainly trans. John Willett (Methuen, 1990), 59–60; in *The Threepenny Opera*, trans. Ralph Manheim and John Willett (Penguin, 2007), 79–80. Brecht gave first form to his affection for Villon's ballads in his "Sonnet on the New Edition of François Villon," in *The Collected Poems of Bertolt Brecht*, trans. Tom Kuhn and David Constantine (Liveright, 2019), 398–99. See Philip Thomson, "The Poet in Dark Times: Messages in Exile," in *The Poetry of Brecht: Seven Studies* (University of North Carolina Press, 1989), 96–118.

56. *François Villon Balladái* (Magyar Vilâg, 1937); Ottó Süpek, "Villon en Hongrie," in *Villon hier et aujourd'hui*, ed. Jean Dérens et al. (Bibliothèque historique de la ville de Paris, 1993), 249–59; *Selected Poems, 1933–1980*, trans. Robin Skelton (University of Georgia Press, 1985); George Faludy, *Learn This Poem of Mine by Heart* (Hounslow Press, 1983), 1–2.

57. Arnold Rampersad, *The Life of Langston Hughes, 1914–1967* (Oxford University Press, 2002), 1:52–54; Langston Hughes, "Ships, Seas, and Africa: Random Impressions of a Sailor on His First Trip down the West Coast of Africa," *Crisis* 26 (December 1923): 69–71; "The Fascination of Cities," *Crisis* 31, no. 3 (January 1926): 138; *Collected Poems of Langston Hughes* (Knopf, 1994).

58. Hughes, "Cities," 128.

59. Langston Hughes, "Lynching Song," in *A New Song* (International Workers Order, 1938), 30; *Collected Poems*, 214.

60. Undated "Dark Testament" typescript, p. 2, section 2, PM Papers, Box 80. Pro-

nouns are one sign of Murray's struggle over gender identity; during a long life, she worked through the constraining norm of feminine ones as a person identifying as a man. The choices of pronoun that were not available publicly to Murray are more and more in use in 2026; I introduce "s/he," used currently by the Pauli Murray Center, Durham, North Carolina. Between the two sets lies Murray's difficult, intrepid experience.

61. PM Papers, Box 4, 83v; Box 80. Rosalind Rosenberg, *Jane Crow, The Life of Pauli Murray* (Oxford University Press, 2017), 28, 39, 47, 130, 143.

62. In Murray's scrapbook, a section called "Vagabondia." PM Papers, Box 4, 83v; Box 80.

63. "Dark Testament," typescript annotated by Langston Hughes, April 21, 1944; PM Papers, Box 1394, 1395.

64. Rancière, "The Concept of Anachronism," 47.

65. Rosenberg, *Jane Crow*, 95, 300, 387; Patricia Bell-Scott, *The Firebrand and the First Lady: Portrait of a Friendship, Pauli Murray, Eleanor Roosevelt and the Struggle for Social Justice* (Alfred Knopf, 2016), 276–77, 281.

66. Rampersad, *The Life of Langston Hughes*, 51.

67. Glissant, *Entretiens*, 60; *The Baton Rouge Interviews*, 31.

68. Bob Dylan, "The Times They are a-Changin'" (1963); Timothy Hampton, *Bob Dylan's Poetics: How the Songs Work* (Zone Books, 2019).

69. Freeman Vines, with Zoe van Buren, *Hanging Tree Guitars* (Piedmont Press in association with the Music Maker Fondation, 2020).

Entry 4: Dependence

1. Fonds Dario Fo, Paris, BnF, Arts du spectacle, 4-SW-8140; Dario Fo, *Mistero Buffo. Giullerata popolare* (Einaudi, 1969, 1973, 1977). Fo first released the work in Paduan, then "translating" it into standard Italian in subsequent scripts; Franca Rame's edition is the last (Einaudi, 2003). In French, *Mystère Bouffe*, adapt. Ginette Herry (Dramaturgie, 1984). In English, "Mistero Buffo or Comic Mysteries," trans. Ed Emery, in *Plays*, vol. 1 (Methuen Drama, 1992). See also translation by Ron Jenkins, reviewed by Rame, in *Collected Plays of Dario Fo* (Theater Communications group, 2006), vol. 2.

2. *Cahiers du Cinéma* 250 (May 1974), a special issue devoted to Fo's work in Paris in 1973. Paris, BnF, Arts du spectacle, 4-SW-8140; 4-SW-9997.

3. Katell Lavéant dates the ms. of the *Mystère d'Arras* to 1450–80, and is prudent about attributing the text performed to Marcadé; see *Un théâtre des frontières. La culture dramatique dans les provinces du Nord aux XVe et XVIe siècles* (Paradigme, 2011), 297, 430–31.

4. Victor Turner, "Social Drama and the Stories about them," *Critical Inquiry* 7, no. 1 (autumn 1980), 158; Turner, *Dramas, Fields and Metaphors: Symbolic Action in Human Society* (Cornell University Press, 1974), chap. 2 on collective medieval performances.

5. The pair is also linked to the almanach, for example, "The Blind and the Lame" engraving of Nicolas Constant Dorgez in *L'esprit du siècle* (1790). See John Grand-Carteret, *Les Almanachs français, bibliographie-iconographie, 1600–1883* (Slatkine Reprints, 1968 [1896]), 252.

6. Jody Enders continues her excellent American English translations of the plays: *Trial by Farce* (University of Michigan Press, 2023); *Immaculate Deception and Further Ribaldries* (University of Pennsylvania Press, 2022); *Holy Deadlock and Further Ribaldries* (University of Pennsylvania Press, 2018); *The Farce of the Fart* (University of Pennsylvania Press, 2011). See also Jody Enders, ed., *A Cultural History of Theatre in the Middle Ages*, vol. 2 (Bloomsbury, 2017); Noah Guynn, *Pure Filth: Ethics, Politics and Religion in Early French Farce* (University of Pennsylvania Press, 2020).

7. Nicole Oresme, *Le Livre d'Ethiques*, Rouen, Bibl. mun., ms. 927, book 1, chap. 7, fol. 6v; ed. A. D. Menut, 116.

8. "Et de serf et pouvre dient aucun en manière de proverbe laisez vivre ce pauvre homme et sa beste," book 1, i: Avranches, Bibl. mun. 223, fol. 5v; Rouen, Bibl. mun. 927, fol. 188v; *Maistre Nicole Oresme Le Livre de politiques d'Aristote*, ed. and trans. A. D. Menut, *Transactions of the American Philosophical Society* 60, no. 6 (1970), 47. The Avranches ms., dated c. 1377, a working handbook of Oresme; the Rouen ms., dated c. 1452, commissioned by the Norman town council.

9. "Table des mots," in *Livre de politiques d'Aristote*; Avranches, Bibl. mun. 223, "Serf, Servile," fol. 324; Rouen, Bibl. mun. 927, "Serf, Servile, Servitude," fol. 410v. Catherine Malabou, *Il n' y a pas eu de Révolution. Réflexions sur la propriété privée, le pouvoir et la condition servile en France* (Bibliothèque Rivages, 2024), 16–17.

10. Helen Solterer, Véronique Dominguez, and Olivier Halévy, "Fortune scéniques au XXe siècle," in *Le Théâtre du Moyen Âge et de la Renaissance*, ed. Darwin Smith, Gabriella Parussa, and Olivier Halévy (Éditions Avant-scène Théâtre, 2014), 87–88.

11. Jean-Paul Sartre, "Forgers of Myth: The Young Playwrights in France," *Theatre Arts* 30, no. 6 (June 1946): 324–25; Simone de Beauvoir, *La Force de l'âge* (Gallimard, 1960), 63–76; Hannah Simpson, *Samuel Beckett and the Theatre of Witness* (Oxford University Press, 2022), 7–13.

12. Fonds Charles Dullin et Simone Jollivet, Paris, BnF, Arts du spectacle, 40 COL 42.

13. Simone de Beauvoir, *Les Bouches inutiles* (Gallimard, 1945), trans. Margaret A. Simons and Marybeth Timmermann, "*The Useless Mouths" and Other Literary Writings* (University of Illinois Press, 2011), 3–87.

14. Samuel Beckett, *Fragment de théâtre I* in *Pas* (Éditions de Minuit, 1978), 21–34, trans. as *Rough for Theater I* in *Collected Shorter Plays* (Grove Press, 1984), 65–74.

15. Fanon, "L'Oeil qui se noie," in *Écrits sur l'aliénation et la liberté* (Éditions de la Découverte, 2018), 79–109.

16. Koltès, *Dans la solitude des champs de coton (*Éditions de Minuit, 1986), trans. Jeffrey Wainwright, *In the Solitude of Cotton Fields, Plays*, ed. David Bradby (Methuen Drama, 1997), 2: 187–215.

17. Jelle Koopmans, "Arras, where burghers and jongleurs meet, play, and develop forms—afterwards seen as theatre . . ." in *Routledge Research Companion to Early Drama and Performance*, ed. Pamela M. King (Routledge, 2016), 30–42. Lavéant establishes a list of performances in these regions: *Un Théâtre des frontières*, 417–84.

18. Jan Dumolyn and Jelle Haemers, *Communes and Conflict: Urban Rebellion in Late Medieval Flanders*, ed. Andrew Murray and Johannes van den Maagdenberg (Brill, 2023).

19. *Justice et Miséricorde. Discours et pratiques dans l'Occident médiéval*, compiled by Catherine Vincent (Presses de l'Université de Limoges, 2015); Agnès Le Bouteiller, "Le Procès du Paradis du Pèlerinage de Jésus Christ. Un débat allégorique, théologique et juridique porté au seuil de la dramatisation," in *Guillaume de Digulleville. Les Pèlerinages allégoriques*, ed. Frédéric Duval and Fabienne Pomel (PUR, 2008), 131–42; Jody Enders, *Rhetoric and Origins of Medieval Drama* (Cornell University Press, 1992), 169–204.

20. Avraham Grossman, *Rashi*, trans. Joel Linsider (Oxford University Press, 2012), 238; Rebecca Moore, "Jewish Influence on Christian Biblical Interpretation: Hugh of Saint Victor and the Four Daughters of God," in *Of Scribes and Sages: Early Jewish Interpretation and Transmission of Scripture*, vol. 2, ed. Craig A. Evans (T & T Clark International, 2004), 149 and following.

21. Arras, Bibliothèque/Médiathèque municipale 625 (formerly 697), fols. 2–13v; ed. Jules-Marie Richard, *Le Mystère de la Passion: texte du manuscrit de la Bibliothèque d'Arras* (Imprimerie de la Société de Pas-de-Calais, 1891 [Slatkine Reprints, 1976]), 2–12. Laura Weigert, "Illuminating the Arras Mystery Play," in *Excavating the Medieval Image*, ed. David S. Aveford and Nina A. Rowe (Ashgate, 2004), 81–106.

22. The *Castle of Perseverance* script describes dress of characters. Washington, DC, Folger Library, ms. V.a. 354.

23. "Quoi que j'attende je feray / Tant se que je puis devers mon pere / Et aulcuns moyen je trouveray / Pour oster lhomme hors son misère." Arras, Bib. mun. 625, fol. 2; Day 1, ll. 120–23, ed. Richard, *Le Mystère de la Passion*, 2.

24. "Que le roy celestre . . . Qu'il vosist homme devenir / Et la jus au monde morir / Pour rachater humain lignaige / Que pechié a mis en serviage." Arras, Bib. mun. 625, fol. 5v; Day 1, ll. 330–34, ed. Richard, *Le Mystère de la Passion*, 4. I use the overarching term of "servitude" for "servage" or "serfdom" in French of the period since serfdom is one chief form of it, slavery being the other; Nicolas Carrier, "De l'esclavage au servage. Pour une étude des dynamiques de la servitude," *Médiévales* 81 (2022): 191.

25. Paris, BnF, f. fr. 816, fols. 17–25; ed. Omer Jodogne, *Le Mystère de la Passion d'Arnoul Gréban* (Académie royale de Belgique, 1965), prologue de la première journée, 37–50. *Le Livre de Conduite du Régisseur et le Compte des Dépenses du Mystère de la Passion joué à Mons, 1501*, ed. Gustave Cohen (Librairie Istra, 1925), 37–46; Darwin Smith, "Arnoul Gréban et l'expérience théâtrale ou l'universitaire naissance des mystères," in *Vers une poétique du discours dramatique au Moyen Âge*, ed. Xavier Leroux (Champion, 2011), 185–224. Véronique Dominguez does not treat the "Trial in Paradise" scene, but her analysis of Arnoul Gréban's script is still pertinent: *La Scène et la croix. Le jeu de l'acteur dans les Passions dramatiques françaises XIVe–XVe siècles* (Brepols, 2007).

26. "Entendez bien mes argumens, je conclurray, par lois actives, et par raisons demonstratives." Paris, BnF, f. fr. 816, fol. 17v–18; ed. Jodogne, *Le Mystère de la Passion*, ll. 2230–32, pp. 37–38. Gréban's figure looks akin to the Justice that painter Ambrogio Lorenzetti had created for the fresco on Good and Bad Government in the town hall of the city-state of Siena a hundred years earlier. Patrick Boucheron, *The Power of Images: Siena, 1338*, trans. Andrew Brown (Polity Press, 2018), 85–88 [*Conjurer la peur*, 2013].

27. "a le delivrer de servage." Paris, BnF, f. fr. 816, fol. 22; ed. Jodogne, *Mystère*, l. 2797, p.44; "en cause civile," fol. 23, l. 2912, p. 46.

28. Humankind/Humain Lignaige: "Everyone who comes by here, consider me a

stranger." ["Toutes gens qui par ci passez / Voeullies moy comme estrangier prendre."] *Le Livre de Conduite du Régisseur*, 39.

29. Mons, Bibiothèque publique, ms. 535 R1/B 1086, fol. 37v; the dramaturge's account book, *Le Livre de Conduite du Régisseur*, 563.

30. *Pratiques sociales et politiques judiciaires dans les villes de l'Occident à la fin du Moyen Âge*, ed. Jacques Chiffoleau, Claude Gauvard, and Andrea Zorzi (École française de Rome, 2007); Hélène Servant, *Artistes et gens de lettres à Valenciennes à la fin du Moyen Âge* (Éditions Klincksieck, 1998), 237–38; Sébastien Hamel, *La Justice dans une ville du Nord du royaume de France. Étude sur la pratique judiciaire à Saint Quentin* (Brepols, 2012).

31. *The Art of Law: Artistic Representations and Iconography of Law and Justice in Context from the Middle Ages to the First World War*, ed. Georges Martyn, Vanessa Paumen, and Stefan Huygebaert (Springer, 2018), 319–36.

32. Dumolyn and Haemers, *Communes and Conflict*; Jan Dumolyn, "Flanders Was the Epicenter of Class Conflict in Medieval Europe," *Jacobin*, July 10, 2023; Jelle Haemers and Vincent Challet, "La révolte médiévale en image," in *Images et Révoltes dans le livre et l'estampe (XIVe-milieu du XVIIIe siècle)*, ed. Yann Sordet (Éditions du Cendre, 2016), 53–77.

33. *Les Faicts et Dictz de Jean Molinet*, ed. Noël Dupire, 3 vols. (SATF, 1936); Adrian Armstrong, "Molinet imprimé. Perspectives éditoriales," in *Les premiers imprimés français et la littérature de Bourgogne (1470–1550)*, ed. Jean Devaux, Matthieu Marchal, and Alexandra Velissariou (Champion, 2021), 77–87; *Jean Molinet et son temps*, ed. Jean Devaux, Estelle Doudet, and Élodie Lecuppre-Desjardin (Brepols, 2013). Armstrong is preparing a new edition.

34. *Ressource du petit peuple* (Valenciennes: Jean de Liège, 1481). Manuscripts: Brussels, KB 6978 (dated 1482), fols. 125–38; Brussels, KB 21551 (late 15th century to early 16th), fols. 170–77v; Paris, BnF, f. fr. 1716 (first quarter 16th century), fols. 77v–85; Paris, BnF, Rothschild 471 (second quarter 16th century), fols. 57–67; ed. Noël Dupire, *Les Faicts et Dictz de Jean Molinet*, 1:137–61.

35. "la miserable violence dont Justice estoit oppressee." *Ressource*, Valenciennes, feuillet lvii v. I punctuate quotations to make them easier to read.

36. His figure also resembles an overburdened, indignant worker devised by writer Alain Chartier to represent the strife dividing French society: Alain Chartier, *Le Quadrilogue invectif*, Paris, BnF, f. fr. 126, fol. 191; 200v–201v; ed. Florence Bouchet (Champion, 2011), 26; *Fifteenth-century Translations of Alain Chartier's Le Traité de l'Esperance and Le Quadrilogue Invectif*, ed. Margaret S. Blayney (Oxford University Press, 1974), 164–75.

37. Adrian Armstrong, "Molinet imprimé. Perspectives éditoriales," in *Les premiers imprimés français et la littérature de Bourgogne*, ed. Jean Devaux et al. (Champion, 2021), 77–87; Armstrong, "Manuscript Reception of Jean Molinet's *Trosne d'Honneur*," *Medium Aevum* 74, no. 2 (2005): 319. Armstrong tracks the "protean" quality of this verse-and-prose work in twelve manuscripts that makes Justice's lament more or less linked to the Burgundian and/or French destructive face-off in politics: "The Practice of Textual Transmission: Jean Molinet's *Ressource du petit peuple*," *Forum for Modern Language Studies* 33, no. 3 (1997): 275–76; Jean Devaux, *Jean Molinet indiciaire Bourguignon* (Champion, 1996), 192–93.

38. Hélène Servant, *Artistes et gens de lettres à Valenciennes*, 269–77.

39. Sebastien Brant, *Das Narrenschiff* (Basel: Johann Bergmann, 1494); ed. Joachim Knape (Stuttgart: Reclam, 2005); Jennifer Oliver, "Du Navire au livre. Des Nefs publiés en France, 1497–1507," *Réforme, Humanisme, Renaissance* 96, no.1 (2023): 9–36; Jan-Dirk Müller, "Literarischer Text und kultureller Text in der Frühen Neuzeit am Beispiel des 'Narrenschiffs' von Sebastian Brant," in *Zwischen den Disziplinen: Perspektiven der Frühneuzeitforschung*, ed. Helmut Puff and Christopher Wild (Wallstein, 2003), 81–101; Dennis E. Curtis and Judith Resnik, "Images of Justice," *Yale Law Journal* 96 (1987): 1743–45. On lawyers and comedy, Marie Bouhaïk-Gironès, *Les clercs de la Basoche et le théâtre comique. Paris, 1420–1550* (Champion, 2007); *Le Mystère de Romans: 1509, une cité en spectacle* (Éditions EHESS, 2023).

40. "There is another [people] who wish to do their duty by using traps and attractive art, corrupting the guardians of justice and law with big money." ["Et lautre veut faire devoir / User de cautele et art gent / De corrompre par grant argent / Des gardeurs de justice et droit."] *La Nef des Folz du monde* (Paris: Geoffroy de Marnef, Johann Philippi de Cruzenach, Magnus Steyner, 1497), fol. 63v.

41. Martin Jay, "Must Justice Be Blind? The Challenge of Images to the Law," *Filozofski vestnik* 17 (1996): 65–81.

42. Estelle Doudet, "Dame Justice et ses suppôts, un personnel sur la scène des moralités et des sotties, XVe et XVIe siècles," in *La Permission et la sanction. Théories légales et pratiques du théâtre (XIVe–XVIIe siècle)*, ed. Marie Bouhaïk-Gironès, Jelle Koopmans, and Katell Lavéant (Classiques Garnier, 2017), 305; Joel Blanchard, "La Moralité du bien public (1468), Musée Condé, ms. 685," *Bibliothèque d'humanisme et Renaissance* 70, no 3 (2008): 615–61.

43. Paris, BnF, f. fr. 24366, fols. 242–45; Carol Symes's diplomatic edition of this single surviving copy, "The Boy and the Blindman: A Medieval Play and Its Editors," in *The Book Unbound: Editing and Reading Medieval Manuscripts and Texts*, ed. Siân Echard and Stephen Partridge (University of Toronto Press, 2004), 128–41. *Le Garçon et l'aveugle*, ed. Mario Roques, trans. Jean Dufournet (Champion, 1989). *Medieval French Plays*, trans. Richard Axton and John Stevens (Blackwell, 1971), 197–206. It transmits meager signs of being put into play; allusions to Tournai nearby place it in the heartland of this northern theatrical culture.

44. Jonathan Hsy, Tory V. Pearman and Jonathan R. Eyler, eds., *The Cultural History of Disability in the Middle Ages* (Bloomsbury, 2022), especially chap. 4; "Disability and the Social Body," ed. Julie Singer, *postmedieval*, Summer 3, no. 2 (2012); Edward Wheatley, *Stumbling Blocks before the Blind: Medieval Constructions of a Disability* (University of Michigan Press, 2010).

45. Julie Singer, "Able-bodied Fragility," *Digital Philology* 9, no. 1 (Spring 2020): 50, 60; Carol Symes, *A Common Stage: Theater and Public Life in Medieval Arras* (Cornell University Press, 2018), 132–33; Michel Rousse, *La Scène et les tréteaux. Le théâtre de la farce au Moyen Âge* (Paradigme, 2004), 51–69.

46. Paris, BnF, f. fr. 24366, fol. 242; Symes,"The Boy," appendix.

47. "tu prieras ie canterai sarons asses argent et pain." Paris, BnF, f. fr. 24366, fol. 242; Symes,"The Boy," appendix.

48. "Seignor ai je bien mis apoint ce la weule qui na point argent ne de houce ausi." Paris, BnF, f. fr. 24366, fol. 245; Symes,"The Boy," appendix.

49. Arras, Bibliothèque mun., ms. 625, fol. 107v–8, ll. 8431–46.

50. Arnold of Liège, "Caecus," exemplus 140, *Alphabetum narrationum*; Paris, BnF, n.a. lat. 730, fol. 35; ed. Elisa Brilli, with Jacques Berlioz and Marie Anne Polo de Beaulieu (Brepols, 2015), 82–83.

51. Paris, BnF, f. fr. 24332, fols. 204–10v; "La Moralité de l'aveugle et du boiteux," ed. Estelle Doudet, in *Recueil général de moralité d'expression française* (Classiques Garnier, 2012), 2:532–35.

52. Guynn, *Pure Filth*, 6.

53. "Je ne vouldroye poinct aller droit . . . Mieulx j'aimeroye / Que grant maleurté me fust dehue . . . Que se qu'on m'eust rendu la veue!" Paris, BnF, f. fr. 24332, fols. 237v–40v, ed. Doudet, ll. 141–43, 150–53, p. 543–44.

54. "Je feray bien de la personne / Playne de desolation . . . Dirai ge, 'voyez ce povre homme, / Lequel, par grant extorcion, est tourmenté, vous voyez comme!'" Paris, BnF, f. fr. 24332, fol. 240v, ed. Doudet ll. 250–55, p. 551.

55. On the commedia dell'arte character Zanni and Molière's Scapin/Scapino, see Judith Chaffee and Olly Crick, eds., *The Routledge Companion to Commedia dell'Arte* (Routledge, 2015), 57, 118, 211; Kenneth and Laura Richards, *The Commedia dell'Arte: A Documentary History* (Basil Blackwell, 1990).

56. Paris, BnF, f. fr. 24332, fol. 234, ed. Doudet ll. 17–20, p. 534.

57. Nicolas Oresme, *Le Livre de politiques*, book 1, chaps. 1, 4, 5; book 7, chaps. 18, 29, 32; Avranches, Bibl. mun. 223, fols. 4v, 10–12v, 264, 280–81v, 284–86; Rouen, Bibl. mun. 927, fols. 188, 191v–193, 370–74, 384–85v, 388v–389; ed. Menut, 46, 52–55, 306, 323, 328. *Le Livre d'Yconomiques*, book 1, chap. 5; Avranches, Bibl. mun. 223, fol. 335–37; Rouen, Bibl. mun. 697, fol. 431–32v; ed. A. D. Menut, *Maistre Nicolas Oresme*: *Le Livre d'Yconomiques, Transactions of the American Philosophical Society* 47, no. 5 (1957): 817–21.

58. "Il entend des servs en servitude par violence ou contre leur volonté ou leur nature. Ceste paour ou criente est appellee servile: Timor servilis." Oresme, *Yconomiques*, book 2, 5; Rouen, Bibl. mun. 697, fol. 439; Paris, BnF, f. fr. 204, fol. 342v; ed. Menut, 839. On the serf in the late medieval imaginary: Daisy Delogu's ongoing work, Paris, Collège de France, May, 2024.

59. Jacques Dalarun, *To Govern Is to Serve: An Essay on Medieval Democracy*, trans. Sean L. Field (Cornell University Press, 2023), [*Gouverner, c'est servir*, 2012], 3.

60. *Le Mystère de la Résurrection Angers (1456)*, Chantilly, Bibl. Condé, ms. 615, fols. 67–69, 74v–81v, 220–28v, 238–43v, 259–61; ed. Pierre Servet (Droz, 1993), ll. 4314–4408, pp. 254–59; ll. 4753–5174, 275–95; 1ère Journée; ll. 14087–14550, 663–86; 2ème Journée; ll. 15170–16576, 710–70; 3ème Journée.

61. "Je suis joyeulx de ce marchié / Vous avez bien a point marchier. / Pour recouvrer une telle aventure, / Car je suys je le vous assure bien propice pour vous mener." Chantilly, Bibl. Condé, ms. 615, fol. 68v; ed. Servet, *Résurrection*, ll. 4398–4403.

62. "Certainement il me convient / De vostre chançon acheter / Plusieurs coppies pour porter / Avecques moi et les revendre." Chantilly, Bibl. Condé, ms. 615, fol. 78; ed. Servet, *Résurrection*, ll. 4961–4964.

63. Chantilly, Bibl. Condé, ms. 615, fol. 79v–80; ed. Servet, *Résurrection*, ll. 5069–5072, 5077–5089.

64. "Venez amy . . . vous me semblez homme de bien." Chantilly, Bibl. Condé, ms. 615, fol. 223; ed. Servet, *Résurrection*, ll. 14267–14269.

65. Chantilly, Bibl. Condé, ms. 615, fol. 226v–27; ed. Servet, *Résurrection*, ll. 14449–14454, 14473–14479.

66. Jean-Louis Roch, "Le Jeu de l'aumône au Moyen Âge," *Annales E.S.C.* 44, no. 3 (April–May 1989): 505–27.

67. McGrady, *The Writer's Gift or the Patron's Pleasure* (University of Toronto Press, 2019), 252–53.

68. Well-known examples are Guillaume Machaut's wall-eyed lover, and Rutebeuf suffering from cataracts. Jacqueline Cerquiglini Toulet, "Sur les bègues, les borgnes, et les boîteux dans la littérature et dans l'iconographie médiévale," presentation, Fondation Martin Bodner, June 2023. On the character Molinet appearing in a comic sketch in a mystery play, see Jacques Lemaire, "Un témoignage curieux sur Molinet en 1500," *Romania* 101 (1980): 105–15.

69. Nicole Oresme, *Le Livre d'Ethiques*, Rouen, Bibl. mun., ms. 927, book 1, chap. 7, fol. 6v; ed. Menut, 116.

70. Albert Memmi, *Dependence: A Sketch for a Portrait of the Dependent*, trans. Philip A. Facey (Beacon Press, 1994), [*La Dépendance*, 1979], 185. I provide another translation for this phrase.

71. Fanon on "The So-called Dependency Complex in the Colonized," chap. 4 of *Black Skin, White Masks*, trans. Richard Philcox (Grove Press, 1967) [*Peau noire, masques blancs*, 1952]; both Fanon and Memmi were critiquing Octave Mannoni's *Psychologie de la décolonisation* (Seuil, 1950) in which he used the Shakespearean personae Prospero and Caliban for analyzing this psychology (their names in title of second edition). Aimé Césaire also refuted this view powerfully with his play *The Tempest / La Tempête* (1969).

72. Memmi, *Dependence*, 47; I provide another translation for this key term.

73. Yann Robert, *Dramatic Justice: Trial by Theater in the Age of the French Revolution* (University of Pennsylvania Press, 2019); Paul Friedland, *Political Actors: Representative Bodies and Theatricality in the Age of the French Revolution* (Cornell University Press, 2002).

74. Ingrid Galster, *Beauvoir dans tous ses états* (Tallandier, 2007), 111–49; Beauvoir, "Une Foire au Moyen Âge," Radio Vichy script, January 17, 1944, pp. 114–16; Paris, BnF, Arts du spectacle, 40 YA 3553, Radio.

75. *Le Mystère du Siège d'Orléans*, ed. Gérard Grois (Livre de poche, 2002); ed. Vicky L. Hamblin (Droz, 2002).

76. "Il ne s'agit ni de vous, ni de nous. Il s'agit de notre commune et de l'avenir du monde tout entier." Beauvoir, *Les Bouches inutiles*, 81; *The Useless Mouths*, 59.

77. Beauvoir, *Les Bouches inutiles*, 94; *The Useless Mouths*, 69.

78. Jean-Paul Sartre, "Forgers of Myth: The Young Playwrights in France," *Theatre Arts* 30, no. 6 (June 1946): 324–25; *Bariona*, typescript, Paris BnF, n.a.f. 28405 (6); Helen Solterer, *Medieval Roles for Modern Times: Theater and the Battle for the French Republic* (Pennsylvania State University Press, 2010), 128–30.

79. "Les Cours de l'École d'Art dramatique du Théâtre de la Cité," BnF, Arts du spectacle, fonds Charles Dullin et Simone Jollivet, 40 COL 42/176 (4).

80. Solterer, *Medieval Roles for Modern Times*, 61–92.

81. *The Bet [Le Pari]* in "Connaissance de Sartre, textes de présentation de Colette

Audry," *Cahiers de la Compagnie Madeleine Renaid Jean-Louis Barrault* 13 (October 1955): 5–59.

82. "Le rideau se lève sur un couple misérable de personnes déplacées . . . tout à coup: coup de tonnerre, effet fantastique à la manière du théâtre moyenâgeux." Sartre, *The Bet*, 54–55.

83. Robert Misrahi, *Sartre ou le premier chemin de la liberté (L'Être et le Néant)* (Le Bord de l'Eau, 2017).

84. "Grâce à son apport personnel, à son choix, et à son sens de la liberté, il métamorphose cette vie atroce en une vie sublime." Sartre, *The Bet*, 56.

85. John Ireland,"Freedom As Passion: Sartre's Mystery Plays," *Theatre Journal* 50, no. 3 (1998): 335–48.

86. Étienne de la Boétie, *Discours de la servitude volontaire* (Paris, 1576).

87. Beckett, *Fragment de théâtre I*, 21–22; *Rough for Theater I*, 65–66.

88. "Non, non c'est trop injuste. Nous ne nous mendierons pas leur pitié." Beauvoir, *Les Bouches inutiles*, 82; *The Useless Mouths*, 59.

89. Program, November 1, 1945, Paris, BnF, Arts du spectacle, fonds Jacques Lemarchand. His review in *Combat* 10 (November 1945). All reviews in Paris, BnF, Arts du spectacle, 8-RSUPP-1707. See also Jacques Lemarchand, *Journal 1944–1952* (Éditions Claire Paulhan, 2016), 181; and Simone de Beauvoir's reaction to Lemarchand, in *Force de l'âge*, 1:78.

90. "Car si l'on commence à traiter certains hommes comme des choses, c'est l'homme même qui apparaît n'etre plus qu'une chose; la justice, la liberté étant niées seule la force commande." Program, November 1, 1945, Paris, BnF, Arts du spectacle, Lemarchand Papers.

91. Joby Fanon, *Frantz Fanon, My Brother: Doctor, Playwright, Revolutionary*, trans. Daniel Nethery (Lexington Books, 2014), chap. 12, pp. 57–62 [*Frantz Fanon*, 2004]; Robert J. C. Young, Introduction to Frantz Fanon, *Écrits sur l'aliénation, et la liberté* (Éditions de la Découverte, 2018), 18. Adam Shatz touches on Fanon's theater as a "rehearsal for life as a writer, even if a necessary detour." See *The Rebel's Clinic: The Revolutionary Lives of Frantz Fanon* (Farrar, Straus & Giroux, 2024), 51–52.

92. Fanon, *Écrits sur l'aliénation et la liberté*, 79.

93. "Prendre les mots du clochard et en rénover la dentition." Joby Fanon, trans. Nethery, *Frantz Fanon*, 58; quoted in Robert J. C. Young's introduction to Fanon, *Écrits sur l'aliénation*, 26.

94. On an argument linking Beckett's wartime with his theater, see Pierre and Valentin Temkine, *Godot dans l'histoire* (Circé, 2023); on the common understanding of the alphabet of plots, see Arnold of Liège, *Alphabetum narrationum*, in note 50 above.

95. Beckett, *Fragment de théâtre I*, 27; *Rough for Theater I*, 64.

96. Beckett, *Fragment de théâtre I*, 27, 30; *Rough for Theater I*, 65.

97. Fo, *Mistero Buffo*, 331–62.

98. Herry, *Mystère Bouffe*, 62, my translation.

99. Herry, *Mystère Bouffe*, 69–70, my translation.

100. Vladimir Mayakovsky, *Mystery-Bouffe: An Heroic, Epic, and Satiric Portrayal of Our Epoch*, trans. Dorian Rottenberg, in Mayakovsky, *Selected Works*, vol. 3 (Raduga Publishers, 1987).

101. Dario Fo, "Contra Jogulatores Obloquentes," Nobel Lecture, December, 1997; Erminia Artese, *Dario Fo parla di Dario Fo* (Edizioni di Lerica, 1977), 18. His practice of debating each sketch with the audience in a critical Brechtian vein confirms it.

102. Serge July, "Dario Fo est arrivé!" *Libération*, January 8, 1974; Fonds Dario Fo, Paris, BnF, Donald Reid, *Opening the Gates: The Lip Affair, 1968–1981* (Verso, 2018). Reid does not cite Fo's agit-prop performance during this strike, but touches on the links between this exemplary workers' movement and theater (456–57).

103. The Nobel Committee cited Fo as a leading figure in modern political theater "who emulates the jesters of the Middle Ages in scourging authority and upholding the dignity of the downtrodden."

104. "Entretien avec Bernard-Marie Koltès," *Bleu Sud*, March–April 1987, 17–18. Paris, BnF, Arts du spectacle, Fonds Bernard-Marie Koltès, 40 SW 10870. Patrick Chéreau, who worked with Koltès closely on producing all his plays, called him, after Koltès died in 1989, his "theatrical director of conscience." François Koltès, *Chéreau/ Koltès. Une rencontre*, documentary film, 1995; Arnaud Maïsetti, *Dans la solitude des champs de coton de Bernard-Marie Koltès, ou, le théâtre au corps à corps* (Champion, 2023).

105. Koltès, *Dans la solitude*, trans. Wainwright, *In the Solitude.*

106. "Car si la vraie injustice de ce monde est celle du hasard de la naissance d'un homme du lieu et de l'heure." (Koltès, *Dans la solitude*, 58). Brandon Jacobs Jenkins's rendition of a mystery play, *Everybody* (2017), turns on chance, too, with characters chosen for each performance by lottery.

107. Bernard-Marie Koltès, "On se parle ou on se tue" (Propos recueillis, Colette Godard, *Le Monde*, January 12, 1987; Paris, BnF, Arts du spectacle, 4 SW10870; Marion Scali, "La Solitude à deux," *Libération*, November 23, 1987; Paris, BnF, Arts du spectacle, 4 SW. 10871 (3); Arnaud Maïsetti, *Bernard-Marie Koltès* (Éditions de Minuit, 2018), 298–99.

108. "They passed the red empty crossroads with deep red gulches on either side, and rotten grey shacks set in the lonesome cotton fields." Carson McCullers, *The Member of the Wedding, A Play* (New Directions, 1951), 174.

109. *Dans la solitude*, 58, my translation.

110. "Soyons 2 zéros bien ronds impénétrables." (Koltès, *Dans la solitude*, 52).

111. "l'injustice aveugle de l'ami" (Koltès, *Dans la solitude*, 49). Koltès muses on the provisional advantage of the word "brother" for characterizing human relations: "Home" in *Prologue* (Éditions de Minuit, 1991), 121.

112. François Koltès, *Chéreau/Koltès.*

113. The town is known for its own *Mystère de saint Clément de Metz*, ed. Frédéric Duval (Droz, 2011), 69. Maïsetti, *Bernard-Marie Koltès*, 21–23. Jean Mambrino, the Jesuit and poet, was a mentor for Koltès, starting in his high school classes at the Collège de Saint-Clément.

114. Bernard-Marie Koltès, *Lettres* (Éditions de Minuit, 1986), letter describing his trip to Bahia, Brazil, December 22, 1985, 501; Maïsetti, *Bernard-Marie Koltès*, 263. During the same years, critic Paul Zumthor also began thinking with *capoeira.*

115. Bill Irwin, *On Beckett, In Screen* (2020). *Rough* is a current favorite, what avant-garde directors Peter Brook and Marie-Hélène Estienne call "existential slapstick"; *Fragments*, program notes, Paris, Bouffes du Nord, 2007.

116. "Nahel Sans Justice ni paix," *Mediapart*, July 5, 2023; "Protests Swell as George Floyd Is Mourned near His Birthplace," *New York Times*, June 7, 2020; "*'Pas de justice, pas de paix'*: à Beaumont-sur-Oise, un défilé en mémoire d'Adama Traoré," *Le Monde*, July 22, 2017.

Entry 5: Living Together in the Animal World

1. Sarah Guérin analyzes this major case in *French Gothic Ivories*. Michel Pastoureau tracks ivory moving along routes in Norway, Sweden, and Denmark, in the indigenous and Norman domains in Scotland and Ireland that supplied artisans working on the continent. "Preface" to Pierre Bureau, *Les Matrices de sceau en ivoire de morse. Histoire symbolique d'un objet d'exception (Xe–XVe siècle)* (Léopard d'or, 2022), 12–15.

2. "Li quens Rollant par peine et par ahans, par grant dulor, sunet sun olifan." Oxford, Bodleian, ms. Digby 23, part 2, fols. 1–72; *Chanson de Roland*, laisse 84, ll. 1785–1787; ed. Ian Short (Livre de poche, 1990), 134–37. In contrast, the *Pèlerinage de Charlemagne*, c. 1190, describes a horn of white ivory: "un cor d'ivoire blanc," l. 351; ed. Glyn S. Burgess (Garland, 1988). The manuscript, London, BL, Royal 16.E. VIII, last seen c. 1879. See Christopher Lucken, "De la *chanson* de Roland à l'*histoire* de Charlemagne d'après le pseudo-Turpin. Chanter ou écrire la guerre?" *Le Moyen Âge* 125, no. 1 (2019): 53–73.

3. Jean Fouquet, *Grandes Chroniques de France*, Paris, BnF, f. fr. 6465, fol. 113; Simon Marmion, *Grandes Chroniques de France*, c. 1455, Saint Petersburg, Russian National Library, Hermitage, ms. fr. 88, fol. 154v.

4. Philippe Cordez, "Objets, images, et trésors d'église," in *Les Images dans l'Occident médiéval*, ed. Jérôme Baschet and Pierre-Olivier Dittmar (Brepols, 2015), 123–26.

5. *Le Roman de la Rose*, Paris, BnF, f. fr. 19156, fol. 134 (dated 1325–50), ed. Armand Strubel (Livre de poche, 1992), ll. 20817–20826; Guérin, *French Gothic Ivories*, 47–48, 210; Peggy McCracken, "Animate Ivory: Animality, Materiality, and Pygmalion's Statue," Oxford Medieval Studies Lecture, 2020; also her ongoing work.

6. This creator was akin to those who had created a feminized body out of mammoth teeth nearly thirty millennia ago: The Venus of Lespugue, dated c. 25,000 years before present, Paris, Musée de l'Homme. Poet Christine de Pizan protects the inestimable knowledge of Philosophy behind a small ivory door that she imagines in her *L'advision Cristine*, Paris, BnF, f. fr. 1176, fol. 50v; part III, I; ed. Reno-Dulac, 92.

7. Toronto, the Thomson collection at the Art Gallery of Ontario; ivory gravoir or hair parter, c. 1300–1350, Limerick, Hunt Museum, MG 018.

8. Guérin, *French Gothic Ivories*, 18; New York, Metropolitan Museum, ivory cataloguing project of major collection.

9. A section devoted to the Arctic, under the direction of André Leroi-Gourhan, was established in April 1934: André Delpuech et al., eds., *Les Années folles de l'ethnographie: Trocadéro 28–37* (Musée national d'histoire naturelle, 2017), 910–11; Alice L. Conklin, *In the Museum of Man: Race, Anthropology and Empire, 1850–1950* (Cornell University Press, 2013), 35–36; Benoît l'Estoile, *Le Goût des autres. De l'Exposition coloniale aux arts premiers* (Flammarion, 2007), 135. Gwénaëlle Guigon surveys Inuit ivories that collectors had removed from Inuit lands and brought to France earlier: "Taitsumainialuk. Les collections de l'Arctique canadien et du Groënland dans les musées français au XIXe siècle," *Études Inuit Studies* 30, no. 2 (2006): 87–115.

10. *Early Inuit Studies: Themes and Transitions, 1850s–1980s*, ed. Igor Krupnik (Smithsonian Institution Scholarly Press, 2016). Among French anthropologists in the first years of academic fieldwork: Marcel Mauss and Henri Beuchat, "L'essai sur les variations saisonnières des sociétés eskimos. Étude de morphologie sociale," *L'Année sociologique* 9 (1906): 39–132. See *Études Inuit Studies* 30, no. 2 (2006) examining Mauss's work, especially Bernard Saladin d'Anglure, "L'influence de Marcel Mauss sur l'anthropologie des Inuit," pp. 26–31. André Leroi-Gourhan, "L'Écriture des Eskimos," *La Nature* 65 (1937): 219–24. On his work on the soundscape of Inuit song, see Delpuech, *Les Années folles*, 817.

11. *Inuit*, in the series *The Indigenous Peoples Atlas of Canada* (Ottawa: Canadian Geographic, 2018), section 6, "Early History." A major overview from Inuit perspective, available in English. For a detailed account of ivory, Claire Houmard, "Exploitations des ivoires marins dans les sociétés arctiques de l'Amérique nord-est (~2500BC–1900 AD)," *Anthropologie* 122 (2018): 546–78.

12. The Greenlandic National Museum and Archives, Nuuk, holds and exhibits the largest collection in the circumpolar regions. On current-day methods, see Mari Kleist, "Making Inuit Archaeology Matter in Kalaallit Nunaat," in *Working as Indigenous Archaeologists: Reckoning New Paths between Past and Present Lives*, ed. George Nicolas and Joe Watkins (Routledge, 2024), 228–38.

13. Davide Zori, *Age of Wolf and Wind: Voyages through the Viking World* (Oxford University Press, 2024), 367–72; Martin Appelt and Hans-Christian Gulløv, "Tunit, Norsemen and Inuit in Northwestern Greenland—Dorset between the Devil and Deep Blue Sea," in *The Northern World, 900–1400 AD*, ed. Herbert Maschner (University of Utah Press, 2009), 300–320; and in the same volume, Patricia D. Sutherland, "The Question of Contact between Dorset Paleo Eskimos and Early Europeans in the Eastern Arctic," 279–99. For encounters in the early twentieth century, William Barr, "Arctic Voyages of Louis-Philippe-Robert, Duc d'Orléans, 1905," *Polar Record* 46, no. 1 (2010): 21–43.

14. Bjarne Grønnow and Einar Lund Jensen, "Utimut: Repatriation and Collaboration between Denmark and Greenland," in *Utimut, Past Heritage, Future Partnerships: Discussions on Repatriation in the 21st Century*, ed. Mille Gabriel and Jens Dahl (International Working Group for Indigenous Affairs, Greenland National Museum and Archives, 2008), 180–91; "The Repatriation of Greenlandic Cultural Heritage from Denmark," in *Sharing Knowledge and Cultural Heritage: First Nations of the Americas: Studies in Collaboration with Indigenous Peoples in Greenland, North and South America*, ed. Laura Van Brookhoeven, Cunera Buijs, and Pieter Hoevens (Sidestone Press, 2011). Gerald McMaster, a major curator, starting with his exhibit at the Canadian Museum of Civilization in 1992; "Indigena, A Native Curator's Perspective," *The Art Journal* 51, no. 3 (1992): 66–73.

15. Pia Arke, *Stories from Scoresbysund: Photography, Colonisation, and Mapping* (Pia Arke Selskabet and Kuratorisk Aktion, 2010), 58–60; Robert Gessain, *Inuit. Images d'Ammassalik, Groenland, 1934–36* (Éditions La Martinière, 2007). The little known account of a Breton seaman, a precedent for Victor's venture: Yves-Joseph Kerguelen-Trémarec, *La Relation d'un voyage dans la mer du Nord, aux côtes d'Islande, de Gröenland, de Ferro, de Schettland, des Orcades, et de Norvège* (Paris: Prault, 1771).

16. Jean-Baptiste Charcot, *Dans la mer du Groenland. Les croisières de Pourquoi pas?* (Librairie Granger, 1937); Serge Kahn, *Jean-Baptiste Charcot, navigateur des mers, explorateur des pôles* (Grénat, 2006).

17. One example of a narwhal tooth identified as a unicorn horn in Dieppe, a port for transatlantic trade, Château Musée, Cat. O. 1; *La licorne et le bézouard. Une histoire des cabinets de curiosité*, ed. Myriam Marrache-Gouraud et al. (Gourcuff Gradenigo, 2013), 10; F. Dupuis, *Jean Ango. Navigation et Renaissance à Dieppe / Inventaire général des richesses artistiques de la France. Commission régionale Haute Normandie* (Connaissance du patrimoine de Haute-Normandie, 1992).

18. Sean P. A. Desjardins, Natasha Lyons, and Mari Kleist, "Inuit Voices: Community-based Archeology across the North American Arctic," *Études Inuit Studies* 46, no. 2 (2022): 9–16; Matthew Betts, *The Archaeology of the Atlantic Northeast* (University of Toronto Press, 2021), 5–6; "Inuit," in *The Indigenous Peoples Atlas of Canada*, section 6.

19. Amy Phillips-Chan, ed. and comp., *Our Stories Etched in Ivory: Qulip'yugut Iksiaqtuumaruat. Tuugaami: The Smithsonian Collections of Engraved Drill Bows with Stories from the Arctic* (Smithsonian, 2021), 30.

20. Dorothy Jean Ray, *Artists of the Tundra and the Sea* (University of Washington Press, 1961), 160–61.

21. H. Kapel, N. Kromann, F. Mikkelson, and E. Loytved Rosenløv, "Tattooing," in *The Greenland Mummies*, ed. Jens Peder Hart Hansen et al. (McGill-Queen's University Press, 1991), 111–12 [1st Greenlandic, Danish edition, 1985]; Niels Lynnerup, "The Thule Inuit Mummies in Greenland," *The Anatomical Record* 298 (May 2015): 1001–6.

22. Knud Rasmussen collection, Copenhagen, National Museum of Denmark.

23. Guy Mary-Rousselière, *Les jeux de ficelle d'Arviligjuarmiut* (Imprimeur de la reine, 1969).

24. Painter Jean-Paul Riopelle has done just that with his work depicting such forms in string, "Riopelle. À la rencontre des territoires nordiques et des cultures autochtones," Montréal, Musée des Beaux Arts, 2020.

25. Manasie Akpaliapik, "Univers inuit," Montréal, Musée McCord Stewart, 2024–25.

26. *Immram Brain: Bran's Journey to the Land of Women*, ed. S. MacMathúna (Niemyer, 1985), Dublin, Royal Irish Academy 1229, olim 23 E 25, fols. 121–24. Another *imramma*, Brendan's tale, has multiple translations in Celtic, Scandanavian, English, and Romance languages. *Le Voyage de Saint Brendan*, ed. I. Short and B. Merrilees (Champion, 2006); ms. de saint braindain, Paris, Arsenal 3516, fols. 96–100 (c. 1201–1300); *Navigatio Sancti Brendani Abbati*, ed. C. Selmer (Notre Dame University Press, 1959); Paris, BnF, f. lat. 2333A; bestiaries such as Paris, BnF, f. fr. 249513, fol. 46; London, BM, Harley 4751, fol. 69; on Brendan's whale, Michel Pastoureau, *La Baleine* (Seuil, 2022), 53–56.

27. Bernardus Sylvestris, *Cosmographia*, I, Megacosmos, 3, in *Poetic Works*, trans. Winthrop Wetherbee (Harvard University Press, 2015), 58–59.

28. Albert the Great, *On Animals: A Medieval Summa Zoologica*, trans. Kenneth F. Kitchell Jr. and Irven Michael Resnick (Johns Hopkins University Press, 1999). *De animalibus*, Paris, BnF, ms. lat. 16169 (elephant, fol. 49).

29. One school of archaeologists hypothesizes that Inuit and Norse seafarers likely first had dealings with one another along the coastline of today's Labrador, around 1200; Patricia D. Sutherland, "The Norse and Native North Americans," 247.

30. Povl Skårup and Raymond Arveiller, "Le Mot français narwal," *Revue romane* 1 (1975): 281–92. Around 1350, *La Dame à la licorne et le beau chevalier* transmits images of the animal that become iconic; trans. Nathalie Koble (Phebus, 2022).

31. The small scale of the graphics complements other tiny objects or amulets of walrus, bird, whale, and seal; Inuit Thule collections, Nuuk, Greenland National Museum and Archives; *Art Inuit. La collection Brousseau* (Musée national des beaux arts du Québec, 2016).

32. Louis-Jacques Dorais, *Language of the Inuit* (McGill University Press, 2014), 146; John MacDonald, *The Arctic Sky: Inuit Astronomy, Star Lore, and Legend* (ROM, 1998), 192–208; Finn Gad, *History of Greenland: From Earliest Times to 1700*, trans. Ernst Dupont (McGill University Press, 1971) [*Grønlands historie*, 1967]; Raymond C. Gagné, "Towards a Canadian Eskimo Orthography and Literature," *Canadian Journal of Linguistics* 7 (1962): 95–107; 8 (1962): 33–39.

33. Evelyn Edson and Emilie Savage-Smith, eds., *Medieval Views of the Cosmos* (Bodleian Library, 2004).

34. The longest day, *ullutusiit*, and longest night, *ullukitutt*. Louis-Jacques Dorais, *Words of the Inuit: A Semantic Stroll through a Northern Culture* (University of Manitoba Press, 2020), 21–22, 25–27; the story of the siblings moon and sun, Aningaaq and Maliina, Greenland National Museum exhibit; "The Canadian Inuit and Their Language," in Dirmid R. F. Collis, *Arctic Languages: An Awakening* (UNESCO, 1990), 185–289; Bernard Saladin d'Anglure, "L'organisation sociale traditionnelle des esquimaux de Kangirsujuaaq" (PhD diss., Université Laval, Québec, 1967), 10.

35. No. 27, "The Moon, Kanaginak Pootoogook," in *The Inuit World: An Annotated Block Print Illustrating Wildlife, Weapons, Tools and Objects of Everyday Life* (Kinngait Press, 1977). Frédéric Laugrand, Francis Levesque, "Spotlight on Arctic Animals: Introduction to the Inuit Bestiary," *Études Inuit Studies* 41, no. 1–2 (2017): 17–28.

36. "Inuit," in *The Indigenous Peoples Atlas of Canada*, section 6; l'Estoile, *Le Goût des autres*,192; Saladin d'Anglure, *Être et renaître inuit, homme, femme ou chamane* (Gallimard 2006), 61; B. Trigger, *Natives and Newcomers* (McGill University Press, 1986), chap. 2, "Before History"; Jørgen Meldgaard, *Eskimo Sculpture*, trans. Jytte Lynner and Peter Wait (Methuen, 1960), 10 [*Eskimo Skulptur*, 1959]. On prehistory in Western historiography, Stefanos Geroulanos, *The Invention of Prehistory: Empire, Violence, and Our Obsession with Human Origins* (Liveright, 2024), 345; Anne Lehoërff, *Dictionnaire amoureux de l'archéologie* (Plon, 2021), 408–11; Daniel Lord Smail and Andrew Shryock, "History and the 'Pre,'" *American Historical Review* 118, no. 4 (2013): 709–37.

37. *The Search for the Origins of the Inuit and Ultima Thule*, case study of the Arctic Cultures project, Cambridge University, European Research Council, 2017–; Peter R. Martin, "The 'Deer-men' and the 'Bowhead-men': The Colonial Co-optation of Arctic Indigenous Knowledge within the 'Origins of the Inuit' Debates," *Transactions of British Institute of Geography* 49, no. 1 (2023).

38. l'Estoile, *Le Goût des autres*, 113–14, 135.

39. Margaret W. Conkey, "Images without Words: The Construction of Prehistoric

Imaginaries for Definitions of 'Us,'" *Journal of Visual Cultures* 9, no. 3 (December 2010): 272–83; Ingo Hessel, *Inuit Art: An Introduction* (Douglas & MacIntyre, 1998), 10; Saladin d'Anglure, *L'organisation sociale traditionnelle*, 61.

40. Heather Igloliorte, "Forever Hooked on Primitive Peoples: James Houston and the Transformation of 'Eskimo Handcrafts' to Inuit Art," in *Mapping Modernisms: Art, Indigeneity, Colonialism*, ed. Elizabeth Harney and Ruth Phillips (Duke University Press, 2019), 79. See an early formulation by the radical geographer E. Reclus, *Les Primitifs. Études d'ethnologie comparée* (G. Chamerot, 1885).

41. *Franz Boas among the Inuit of Baffin Island, 1883–1884, Journal and Letters*, ed. Lüdger Müller-Wille (University of Toronto Press, 1998); *Journal of the Eskimos of Baffin Land and Hudson Bay* (American Museum of Natural History, 1901); L. Oschinsky, *The Most Ancient Eskimos* (Canadian Research Centre for Anthropology, 1964). See the critical assessments of Vincent Debaene: *Far Afield: French Anthropology between Science and Literature*, trans. Justin Izzo (University of Chicago Press, 2014); and Daniel J. Sherman, *French Primitivism and the Ends of Empire, 1945–1975* (University of Chicago Press, 2011).

42. Matisse's lithographs appear in Georges Duthuit, *Une Fête en Cimmérie* (Tériade, 1963). See also F. Duchemin-Pelletier, "Surréalisme et art inuit. La fascination du Grand Nord," *Journal of Surrealism and the Americas* 2, no. 1 (2008): 74–80. For the history of the modern rediscovery in France, G. Guigon, "Histoire des collections inuit (Arctique canadien et Groenland) du département d'archaéologie du Musée des antiquités nationales, Saint-Germain-en-Laye," *Société des Amis du Musée des Antiquités nationales* 36 (2004).

43. Peter Whitbridge, "Classic Thule [Classic Precontact Inuit Culture]," in *The Oxford Handbook of the Prehistoric Arctic*, ed. Max Friesen and Owen Mason (Oxford University Press, 2016), 827–50.

44. Robert McGhee, *The Last Imaginary Place. A Human History of the Arctic World* (Oxford University Press, 2005), 22.

45. Knud Rasmussen with Therkel Mathiassen, *Report of the Fifth Thule Expedition: The Danish Expedition to Arctic North America* (Gyldendal, 1927–52). On the Inuk woman participant key to Rasmusssen's Fifth Expedition, see Pauline Knudsen, *Arnarulunnguaq* (Iperaq, 2024), 22–47. The collection published on the centenary of Rasmussen's expedition, *Alaska Journal of Anthropology* 19, no. 1–2 (2021), includes many reassessments of its research; see especially Mari Kleist, "The Fifth Thule Expedition and the Indigenous Participants Who Made It Possible," 37–55; Mikhail Bronshtein, "Five Engraved Walrus Tusks from Chucotka," 150–60; Martin Appelt et al., "Inuit Pencil Drawings and Co-creation: Discovering the Artwork Made during the Fifth Thule Expedition," 212–28; William W. Fitzhugh, "Epilogue: Reflection on the Fifth Thule Centennial," 264–69.

46. Kapel et al., *The Greenland Mummies*, 15.

47. Jean Malaurie's first such essay, *Les Derniers rois de Thulé* (Plon, 1955); the most recent, *Ultima Thulé, les Inuit nord-groenlandais face aux conquérants polaires* (Bordas, 1990).

48. Kirsten Hastrup, *Thule på tidens rand* (Lindhardt og Ringhof, 2015).

49. Whitbridge, "Classic Thule [Classic Precontact Inuit Culture]," 828.

50. Mark Rothko, "Indigenous Art," in *The Artist's Reality: Philosophies of Art*, 2d ed. (Yale University Press, 2023), 117. "Even the art of the Eskimo, were it completely incorporated into our art, would be more acceptable than an influence from France. France in particular seems to be in disfavor as a foreign influence. Its art is at once branded as alien and as a violation of the native trend. . . . Why is it that the traditions of Bruges, London, and Venice, or the return to the Renaissance, are acceptable as the basis of an indigenous art, while the schools of Paris or thirteenth-century Florence are not? Why the Eskimo is considered closer to our current lives than the African Negro or the Australian aborigine is difficult to say." The essay, written in 1940–41, xvii.

51. Étienne Anheim, "Les 'primitifs.' L'invention de la peinture médiévale dans l'histoire de l'art et la critique (XVIIIe–XIXe s.)," in the seminar, "Espaces-temps historiographiques. Le Moyen Âge, ses lieux et ses autres," Paris, EHESS, March–April 2024.

52. *Les Primitifs flamands et l'art ancien* [Primitive Flemish Painters], a major exhibition in Bruges (1902) that launched this art from around 1400 back into the public eye and spurred critical attention. Followed by *Exposition des primitifs français* (Paris, 1904). Andrée Hayum, "The 1902 Exhibition, Les Primitifs Flamands: Scholarly Fallout and Art Historical Reflections," *Journal of Art Historiography* 11 (2014):1–20.

53. These critical steps go with the ongoing work of archaeology proceeding as collaborations with Indigenous community members. Mari Kleist, "The Future of Archaeological Partnerships in Avanersuaq," *Études Inuit Studies* 46, no. 2 (2022): 17–34.

54. Dorais, *Language of the Inuit*, 162–65, *Words of the Inuit*, 93.

55. Pauloosie Kasukluak, "Nothing Marvelous," in *Port Harrison / Inoucdjouac*, ed. Jean Blodgett (Winnipeg Art Gallery, 1977), 15; in Inuktitut, *sananguaq*, which Inuit translators rendered roughly as "a little likeness-reality that we have achieved." George Swinton, *Sculpture of the Eskimo* (McClelland & Stewart, 1972), 130.

56. Manasie Akpaliapik, "Univers inuit."

57. William Fitzhugh and Bernadette Driscoll Englestad, "Inuguat: Prehistoric Human Figures in the North American Arctic," in *The Oxford Handbook of Prehistoric Figurines* (Oxford University Press, 2017), 382. In today's Inuit art world, an Inukjuak cultural committee in cooperation with Québécois curators coined the term *Takuminartut*, designating works "that are beautiful and of great emotional appeal that draw the eye again and again." "L'art inuit contemporain et actuel de 1948 à nos jours," Montréal, Musée des Beaux arts, December, 2023.

58. Philadelphia, Penn Museum, story knife from Baffin Island, object #94-26-12; *Inua, Spirit World of the Bering Sea Eskimo*, ed. William Fitzhugh, Susan A. Kaplan, and Henry B. Collins (Smithsonian Institution Press, 1982), 158–59; Dorothy Jean Ray, *Graphic Arts of the Alaskan Eskimo* (Indian Arts and Crafts Board, 1969), 9–10; Charles A. Martijn, "Eskimo Carving in Historical Perspective," *Anthropos* 54, no. 3–4 (1964): 546–96; synopsis in *Eskimo of Canadian Arctic*, ed. Victor F. Valentine and Frank. G. Vallee (McGill University Press, 1978), 67–75; Hans Himmelheber, *Eskimo Artists: Fieldwork from Alaska, June 1936 until April 1937* (University of Alaska Press, 1993), 28 and following [*Eskimokünstler*, 1938].

59. On Inuit spatio-temporal rhythms of community life, *The Inuit World*, No. 21, "Ulluriaq the Star"; its changing position told time during months when there is no

dawn. Peter Whitbridge, "Landscapes, Houses, Bodies, Things: 'Place' and the Archaeology of Inuit Imaginaries," *Journal of Archaeological Method and Theory* 11 (2004), 233; Tim Ingold, "The Temporality of the Landscape," *World Archaeology* 25, no. 2 (1993): 253.

60. A reproduction can currently be viewed in the exhibit, "Nuvumiutaq, the Arctic Bay Kayaker," curated by Janet Young and Matthew Betts, Gatineau, Canadian Museum of History (CMH).

61. Whitbridge, "Landscapes, Houses, Bodies, Things," 223; Moreau S. Maxwell, "A Contemporsary Ethnography from the Thule Period," *Arctic Anthropology* 20, no. 1 (1983): 79–87; Robert McGhee, *Canadian Arctic Prehistory* (Van Nostrand Reinhold, 1978), plate 12; Hessel, *An Introduction*, 17. See also Whitbridge's extensive comparative analysis of such graphics: "Manufacturing Reality: Inuit Harvesting Depictions and the Human Animal Relations, in *Re-Imagining Human Animal Relations in the Circumpolar North*, ed. Erica Hill and Peter Whitbridge (Routledge, 2023), 47–49, 58–59.

62. Matthew Betts and Janet Young, "Repatriation Project Tells Remarkable Story," parts 1 and 2, August 24 and 30, 2017, CMH.

63. Phillips-Chan, ed., *Our Stories Etched in Ivory* , 27–29. *Niiortuut* is the Greenlandic term for the same implement.

64. Incised ivory fishing lure, c. 1400–1500, Ottawa, Canadian Museum of History, IC-2256.

65. Betts and Young, "Repatriation Project Tells Remarkable Story," parts 1 and 2; discussion with Janet Young, Gatineau, CMH, December 5, 2023.

66. "Nuvumiutaq," CMH.

67. "Nuvumiutaq," CMH.

68. The Ikpiarjuk-CMH team puts forth a hypothesis explaining how and why this piece is so intricate and complex. The ivory bowdrill was found next to an Inuk's skeleton bearing signs of a major injury that would have immobilized this person for long periods, and thus would have allowed the time for incising ivory. That is, the human bones show something of what the bowdrill's lines represent.

69. Claudio Aporta, "The Trail as Home: Inuit and Their Pan-Arctic Routes As Home," *Human Ecology* 37 (2006): 144.

70. L3 7331, Nuuk, Greenlandic National Museum. *Trap Kalaallit Nunaat*, ed. Niels Elers Koch (Gads Forlag, 2023), 111. The first description: Eric Holtved, "Archaeological Investigation of the Thule District," in *Meddelelser om Gronland* 141, no.1 (1944): 277–78. See also *Grønlands Forhistorie*, ed. Hans Christian Gulløv (Gyldendal, 2005).

71. Mikkel Myrup's photography of the Inuit Thule house, National Greenlandic Museum.

72. The first description: Therkel Mathiassen, "Archaeology of the Central Eskimos," in *Report of the 5th Thule Expedition, 1921–24*, vol. 4, part 1, p. 185; Whitbridge, "Manufacturing Reality," 49.

73. *Arktische Waljäger vor 3000 Jahren. Unbekannte sibirische Kunst*, ed. A. M. Leskov and H. Müller-Beck (Hase & Koehler Verlag, 1993); those dated are c. 100–400 CE (138–39). Jeannine Veisse, "Les Défenses de morse du Musée Eskimau de Churchill," *Vie des arts* 22, no. 89 (Winter 1977–78): 60–99; "Tumisuit Collection," Copenhagen, National Museum of Denmark; Amundsen's Gjoa Haven Collection, Oslo, Museum

of Cultural History, University of Oslo; Inuit collection, Saint Petersburg, Peter the Great Museum of Anthropology and Ethnography; Chukotka, Russia, Centre Heritage Museum; Upopoy, Japan, National Ainu Museum; London, British Museum; Vancouver, Museum of Anthropology, University of British Columbia; Berlin Ethnologisches Museum. Krupnik is spearheading several projects with French and Polish colleagues; see Daria Chevoli, Igor Krupnik, and Virginie Vaté, "The Nicholas Goddatti Collection," *Arctic Studies Newsletter* 32 (2025). Current geopolitical confrontations between NATO members are making some of these investigations difficult.

74. Christopher P. Heuer, "Arctic Matters in Early America," in *Scale*, ed. Jennifer Roberts (Terra Foundation, 2016), 180–214; Elizabeth Hutchinson, "Bow Drills: Messages across Time and Space, Inupiat Drawings from the 1890s at Columbia University," exhibition, New York, Columbia University, 2015.

75. Phillips-Chan, ed., *Our Stories Etched in Ivory*, 19–62. See Whitbridge, "Manufacturing Reality," 64 and following; Jean Ray, *Artists of the Tundra and the Sea: Graphic Arts of the Alaskan Eskimo* (1969); "Reflections in Ivory," in *Inua*, ed. Fitzhugh and Kaplan, 254–67.

76. See Phillips-Chan's description of four graphic narratives on this bow photographed in its entirety. Phillips-Chan, ed., *Our Stories Etched in Ivory*, 131.

77. Phillips-Chan, ed., *Our Stories Etched in Ivory*, 28. See view of carver Henry Koonook, p. 76.

78. Betts and Young, "Repatriation Project Tells Remarkable Story," parts 1 and 2 (Gatineau, CMH); Washington, DC, Smithsonian Institution, Archives, Lawrence Oschinsky Papers, boxes 7–18.

79. Gatineau, CMH, report, photos, April 1962; Smithsonian Institution, Oschinsky Papers, boxes 7–18; Guy Mary-Rousselière, "A Remarkable Specimen of Eskimo Art," *Eskimo* 54 (1960): 10–14; G. Mary-Rousselière, "The Thule Culture on North Baffin Island: Early Thule Characteristics and the Survival of the Thule Tradition," in *Thule Eskimo Culture: An Anthropological Retrospective*, ed. Allen P. McCartney, *National Museum of Man. Mercury Series. Archaeological Survey of Canada* 88 (1979): 54–75; Guy Mary-Rousselière, *Qillarsuaq*: *Beretningen om en arktisk folkevandring* [*Qillarsuaq: The Story of an Arctic Migration*], ed. Hans Engelund Kristiansen (Nuuk: Forlaget Atuagkat, 2002); Maxwell, "A Contemporary Ethnography from the Thule Period," 79.

80. Mari Kleist, "The Expedition Would Not Have Succeeded without Them," *Arctic Studies Newsletter* 29 (May 2022), 9–15. This was the view of Eric Holtved.

81. This is also the case for other early ivories that Mary-Rousselière, a Jesuit priest who militated for Inuit cultures in his missionary work, took to Paris in 1949; they were placed in the anthropological Musée de l'Homme, now part of Musée Quai Branly collections. See Claire Houmard, *La collection Guy Mary-Rousselière du musée du quai Branly remise dans le contexte de l'archéologie de l'Arctique canadien* (Paris: Musée du quai Branly, 2015).

82. Alice Conklin, *In the Museum of Man*, 152.

83. Janet Young, "Responsive Repatriation: Human Remains Management at a Canadian National Museum," *Anthropology News* (March 2010): 9, 12.

84. Repatriation of Inuit belongings to their communities is happening across Inuit lands. Harvard University restored the Inuit Thule mummies of Qilakitsoq to Green-

land following the initiative of the National Museum in 2024; they had been taken in 1929 by an ethnography researcher named Martin Luther. Ernest A. Hooten, "Finns, Lapps, Eskimos, and Martin Luther," *Harvard Alumni Bulletin* 19 (1930–32): 545–53.

85. Germaine Arnaktauyok and Gyu Oh, *My Name Is Arnaktauyok. The Life and Art of Germaine Arnaktauyok* (Inhabit Media, 2015), 3. She also spells her name "Arnattaujuq."

86. Arnaktauyok and Oh, *My Name Is Arnaktauyok*, 23, 49, 57. On today's ivory tool makers, see Keggutet Enret Tugkaraat-Ilu, "Teeth, Bone, and Ivory," in *Yuungnaqpiallerput. The Way We Genuinely Live: Masterworks of Yup'ik Science and Survival*, text by Anne Fienup-Riordan (University of Washington Press, 2007), 69–73.

87. Germaine Arnaktauyok, *Combs*, etching (2007).

88. "Radical Remembrance: The Sculpture of David Ruben Piqtoukun / Mémoire fondamentale. Les Sculptures de David Ruben Piqtoukun," exhibition, Toronto, Art Gallery of Ontario (AGO), 2023.

89. Pat Fehely, discussion, Toronto, May 18, 2023. Kenojuak Ashevak and Tim Pitsiulak, *Tunirrusiangit*, curated by Koomuatuk Curley, Taqralik Partridge, Jocelyn Piirainen, and Laakkuluk Williamson Bathory (AGO, 2018), 95 and following.

90. Walrus (*Odobenus Rosmarus*) was last assessed by the International Union of Conservation of Nature as "vulnerable" on its Red List (2016). Archaeologists James Barrett, Sanne Boesekool, Catherine J. Kneale, Tamsin C. O'Connell, and Bastiann Staar examine the threat to walrus in history: "Ecological Globalisation, Serial Depletion, and the Medieval Trade in Walrus Rostra," *Quatenary Science Reviews* 229 (2020).

91. The 1978 Universal Declaration of Animal Rights also drew attention to the vulnerable state of the walrus. The Convention on International Trade in Endangered Species of Wild Fauna and Flora (CITES), Appendix III (November 2023), controls the global trade of walrus ivory.

92. Arnaktauyok and Oh, *My Name Is Arnaktauyok*, 54; Igloliorte, "Forever Hooked on Primitive Peoples," 79, 83. Hessel distinguishes the different generations, those born on the land, those in settled communities, in *Inuit Modern: The Samuel and Esther Sarick Collection*, co-curated by Gerald McMaster and Ingo Hessel (D & M Publishers, 2010), 188; Ruth B. Phillips, *Trading Identities: The Souvenir in Native North American Art from the Northeast, 1700–1900* (McGill-Queen's University Press, 1998).

93. Adam Alorut, "Additions to the City of Ottawa Art Collection," Karsh-Masson Gallery, Ottawa, 2019; Aron Kleist, artwork at Nuuk Museum of Art.

94. Sheila Watt-Cloutier, *The Right to Be Cold: One Woman's Story of Protecting Her Culture, the Arctic, and the Whole Planet* (Allen Lane, 2015); George W. Wenzel, "Canadian Inuit Subsistence and Ecological Instability: If the Climate Changes, Must the Inuit?" *Polar Research* 28 (2009): 89–99; Igor Krupnik and Dyanna Joly, *The Earth Is Faster Now: Indigenous Observations of Arctic Environment Change* (Arctic Research Consortium of the US, 2002).

95. Matthew Betts, "Burning Libraries: The Race to Save Canada's Coastal Archaeological Sites before They're Washed Away," *Canadian Geographic*, November 6, 2023; June 27, 2019.

Closing Entry: Compost

1. *Le Dictionnaire du moyen français (1330–1500)* or *DMF* (CNRS and Université de Lorraine, 2016–23), nos. 21–24. Also transcribed as *comput* in *Tobler-Lommatzsch Altfranzösisches Wörterbuch*, vol. 2, col. 637; *Dictionnaire Littré*, vol. 2, p. 710.

2. "Ca se traie qui veut aprendre dou compost coment il doit prendre des festes qui ne sont mie dites en nule kalendier ne escrites." Paris, BnF, f. fr. 412, fol. 1. This *Compost*, dated around 1285, confirms their widespread presence across languages. Faith Wallis, "What a Medieval Diagram Shows: A Case Study of the 'Computus,'" *Journal in Iconography* 36 (2015): 4.

3. London, BL Cotton Nero A. V., fols. 1–6; Philippe de Thaon, *Comput*, ed. Ian Short (Anglo-Norman Society, 1984); Vatican mss. Reg. lat. 1244, fols. 53–58v (the word "Compost" is added near the first line in a later hand, fol. 53). "E cumpot pur cunter e ben esgarder Les termes et les clés E les festes anvels" ["And 'cumpot' is for counting and looking well at the terms and keys for annual feasts"] (ed. Short, ll. 47–50, p. 5). Thomas O'Donnell, "The Gloss to Philippe de Thaon's *Comput* and the French of England's Beginnings," in *The French of Medieval England: Essays in Honor of Jocelyn Wogan-Browne*, ed. Thelma Fenster and Carolyn P. Collette (D. S. Brewer, 2017), 15, 29.

4. Dennis Tenen, *Plain Text: The Poetics of Computation* (Stanford University Press, 2017); N. K. Hayles, on the computational universe, in *My Mother Was a Computer: Digital Subjects and Literary Texts* (University of Chicago Press, 2005), 3–4.

5. Communities in the north and east of today's France, and in England, were especially involved in this *computus* tradition; the treatise *De computo* of Abbo of Fleury, c. 1000, played a major role: Munich, Bayerische Staatsbibliothek, ms. Clm. 10270, fols. 11–21v; ed. Albert Lohr, *Abbonis Floriacensis Miscellanea de computo* (Brepols, 2019). *Computus and Its Cultural Context in the Latin West, 300–1200*, ed. Immo Warntjes and Dáibhi Ó Cróinin (Brepols, 2010).

6. Linguists describe the strange affinities between words to help explain how the term *comput* was drawn to and taken for *compost*, via *compoz*, and the verb to compose. This affinity makes particular sense for writers such as Thaon writing in Romance languages. See "*comput*" in the *Tresor de la langue française*, "*computus*" in the *Französisches Etymologisches Wörterbuch*, "compost" in the *OED*. See also *Le comput en franceis*, another such treatise, from England (1267) and part of the collection of Notre-Dame de Paris: Paris, BnF, f. fr. 25408, fol. 67v (fols. 67v–70), and a third work from England, in French, English, and Latin (c. 1310–50), *Art du Kalender*, "*en romance*," identified by the Latin explicit, "de computu secundum Radulfum de Lynham," Cambridge University Library, ms. Gg. 1.1, fols. 8–16v. Two editions: Östen Södergard, *Art de Kalender* (Almqvist, 1989); Tony Hunt, *Kalender* (Rauf de Linham) (Anglo-Norman Text Society, 1983).

7. "Scavoir le compost du souleil et de la lune de partir des ans et trouver les bisextes et leurs conjunctions des lunes pour ordonner," in *Art de Dictier*, Paris, BnF, f. fr 840, fol. 394v; ed. Dauphant, 588. Simon de Phares, *DMF*, nos. 21–24; Paris, BnF, f. fr. 25408, fol. 67v. See also Clothilde Dauphant, "Compter selon Deschamps," in *Eustache Deschamps. Facettes d'un poète au XIVe siècle*, ed. Fleur Vigneron, *Acta Litt & Art* 17 (2023), Université de Grenoble-Alpes.

8. John Grand-Carteret, *Les Almanachs français, bibliographie, iconographie, 1600–*

1895 (J. Alisie, 1896), xviiii–xxii; *Le Calendrier et Compost des Bergers* (Nicolas Bonfons, 1600) figures as the second one in the repertory (1).

9. *Almanach chantant pour l'an second de la République* (Paris, 1793–94), Paris, Bibliothèque Estienne.

10. Midden, an Old Norse, Scandinavian word, enters English through Scotland and northern England, c. 1425, *OED*, 1789. The archaeological term, coming from Denmark, is established in the mid-nineteenth century. For a related meditation on debris, see Vincent Bruyère, *Environmental Humanities on the Brink: The Vanitas Hypothesis* (Stanford University Press, 2023), 43–59.

11. Laurent Olivier and Mireille Séguy, *Le passé est un événement. Correspondances de l'archaéologie et de la littérature* (Éditions Macula, 2023).

12. Entry "compost," in *Tobler-Lommatzsch* and *Tresor de la langue française*; Édouard Bonnaffé, *Dictionnaire étymologique et historique des anglicismes* (Delagrave, 1920), 34.

13. Oresme, *Le Livre du ciel et du monde*, "compost'; *DMF*, nos. 4–18; Christine de Pizan, "homme qui est le plus compost," *Le Livre de l'advision Cristine; DMF*, no. 1.

14. Graham P. Chapman and Thackwray S. Driver, "Time, Mankind, and the Earth," in *Time-Scales and Environmental Change*, ed. G. P. Chapman and T. S. Driver (Routledge, 1996), 4.

15. Judith Schlanger has much the same view, *Présences des œuvres perdues*, 10.

16. Christine de Pizan, Charles d'Orléans, "composer," *DMF*, nos. 1, 10. Sarah Delale, *Diamant obscur. Interpréter les manuscrits de Christine de Pizan* (Droz, 2021), 73, 79, especially part 2, "Composition et Disposition," 182. Christine's commentary in *Le Livre des fais et de bonnes meurs de sage roy Charles V*, book 2; Julia Simms Holderness, "Compilation, Commentary and Conversation in Christine de Pizan," *Essays in Medieval Studies* 20 (2003): 47–55.

17. This compositional technique is apparent across cultures c. 800–1400. For the major Persian-Muslim example, Bilal Orfali, *The Anthologist's Art: Abū Mansūr al'Tha' ālibī and his Yatīmat al-dahr* (Brill, 2016), 10–33. For the central importance of this practice in England, Scotland, Wales, Ireland, and on the European continent, debated over a generation of historians and literary critics: Alistair Minnis, "*Nolens auctor, sed compilator reputari*: The Late Medieval Discourse of Compilation," in *La méthode critique au Moyen Âge*, ed. M. Chazan et G. Dahan (Brepols, 2006), 47–64; and Bernard Guénée, "L'Historien et la compilation au XIIIe siècle," *Journal des savants* (1985): 119–35.

18. On the implications of the heterogeneous character of such manuscript books, Anna Dorofeeva, "Introduction," in *Art of Compilation: Manuscripts and Networks in the Early Medieval Latin West*, ed. Anna Dorofeeva and Michael. J. Kelly (Punctum Books, 2025), 31–34.

19. Paris, BnF, ms. f. fr. 24366; Stockholm, KB, Vu 22.

20. Jean Froissart, "It is said and is true that . . . all sizable rivers are made and come together from various places, and several sources; knowledge or science is also made, compiled, and extracted from several clerics, and what one does not know, another does." "On dit et voirs est, que . . . toutes grosses rivieres sont faites et rassemblees de divers lieux et de pluseurs sourses, aussi les sciences sont faites et compilees et extraittes de pluseurs clercs, et ce que l'un ne scet, l'autre scet." Besançon, Bibl. mun. 864, fol. 1v. Prologue, in *Chroniques*, ed. Peter Ainsworth and Godfried Croenen, available online:

The Online Froissart, version 1.5 (Sheffield: HRIOnline, 2013), http://www.dhi.ac.uk/onlinefroissart.

21. Anne F. Garréta, *La Décomposition* (Grasset, 1999).

22. Gérard Genette, *Palimpsests: Literature in the Second Degree*, trans. Channa Newman and Claude Doubinsky (University of Nebraska, 1997) [*Palimpsestes*, 1982].

23. *Dictionnaire historique de la langue française*, 3243. Gilles Deleuze and Félix Guattari, *Rhizome*, Introduction (Éditions de Minuit, 1976). Cerquiglini-Toulet introduces this figure for Villon, and mentions the 1493 almanach. *Villon*, xxxix.

24. Brunetto Latini, *Le Tresor*, book 1, part 3, chap civ–cvii; BnF, f. fr. 566, ed. Spurgeon Baldwin and Paul Barrette (Arizona Center of Medieval and Renaissance Studies, 2003), 66–74.

25. Édouard Glissant, *La Terre*. The exhibition, *Arts du Tout-Monde*, at the Montréal Musée des Beaux Arts transforms this in visual arts; beginning with a stone sphere, from Costa Rica, the Chiriquí period, c. 300 BCE–1500.

26. Caroline Ford, *Natural Interests: The Contest over Environment in Modern France* (Harvard University Press, 2016), 6; Ford, "Nature's Fortunes: New Directions in the Writing of European Environmental History," *Journal of Modern History* 79, no. 1 (2007), 114. E. C. Spary, *Utopia's Garden: French Natural History from Old Regime to Revolution* (University of Chicago Press, 2000), 151.

27. "un cite de grant fantosme qui fu jadis faite pour l'omme"; Paris, BnF, f. fr. 146, fol. 16; *Le Roman de Fauvel*, ed. Armand Strubel (Paris: Lettres gothiques, 2012).

28. Chapman and Driver, "Time, Mankind, and the Earth," 3.

29. Augustin Berque, *Poetics of the Earth: Natural History and Human History*, trans. Anne-Maroe Feenberg-Dibon (Routledge, 2019), viii [*Poétique de la terre*, 2014]; Berque, *Écoumène. Introduction à l'étude des milieux humains* (Bélin, 2009), 9–17. Ecocritics are investigating this through works from around 1500: Pauline Goul and John Philip Ussher's collection, *Early Modern Ecologies: Beyond English Ecocriticism* (University of Amsterdam Press, 2020); also in that volume, Sara Miglietti, "Between Nature and Culture: Integrated Ecology of the Renaissance," 137–60. See also Louisa Makenzie, "It's a Queer Thing: Early Modern French Ecocriticism," *French Literature Series* 39 (2012): 15–42.

30. As I write this, lines of a Nikky Finney poem ring out: "Drink the ephemerides. Lay with the almanacs. Become the lunations . . . Keep yourself rooted in the sun, rain, and darkly camphored air. Grow until you die . . ." "Instruction, Final: To Brown Poets from Black Girl with Silver Leica," in *Head Off & Split* (Northwestern University Press, 2011), 97.

31. Alain Chartier, *Quadrilogue Invectif*, BnF, f. fr. 126, fol. 191v; ed. Bouchet, 4.

32. "The artificial . . . that is the art of calculating the movements of the sun and the moon to determine the years and foresee the extra day in a leap year . . . the other music is called natural because no one can learn it without applying their own propensity for it naturally." [L'artificielle . . . c'est l'art de calculer les mouvements du Soleil et de la Lune pour déterminer les années et prévoir les jours bissextiles . . . La autre musique est appellée naturele pour ce qu'elle ne puet estre aprinse à nul se son propre couraige naturelment ne s'i applique.] *Art de Dictier*, Paris, BnF, f. fr 840, fol. 395; ed. Dauphant, 589–90. Music follows the section on astronomy.

33. Also known as Louis de Langle and, in his Latin work, Ludovicus de Angulo. Luis de Angulo, *De Figura seu de imagine mundi*, ed. Étienne Hustache (École des Chartes, 1980). This figure details further an image in Gossuin de Metz, *Image du monde*, Rennes, Bibl. mun., ms. 593, fol. 63v, in the same handbook where "almenack" appears first; BnF, f. fr. 2174, fols. 41, 64v.

34. NASA scientists released their first findings in summer 2022: Webb Space Telescope, the Space Telescope Science Institute. Chanda Prescod-Weinstein reminds us of the value of thinking in this time-scale: *The Disordered Cosmos* (Bold Type Books, 2021).

Index

This index is alphabetized in word-by-word order. Italicized page numbers indicate reproductions in the text including photographs, miniatures, and diagrams.

Printed and bound by CPI Group (UK) Ltd, Croydon, CR0 4YY
15/10/2026
14983224-0001